From El Dorado to Lost Horizons

THE SUNY SERIES

HORIZONS OF CINEMA

MURRAY POMERANCE | EDITOR

From El Dorado to Lost Horizons

Traditionalist Films in the Hollywood Renaissance, 1967–1972

∽

Ken Windrum

Cover image: *El Dorado* (Howard Hawks). Paramount Home Video/Photofest © Paramount Home, 1966.

Published by State University of New York Press, Albany

© 2019 State University of New York

All rights reserved

No part of this book may be used or reproduced in any manner whatsoever without written permission. No part of this book may be stored in a retrieval system or transmitted in any form or by any means including electronic, electrostatic, magnetic tape, mechanical, photocopying, recording, or otherwise without the prior permission in writing of the publisher.

For information, contact State University of New York Press, Albany, NY
www.sunypress.edu

Library of Congress Cataloging-in-Publication Data

Names: Windrum, Ken, 1962– author.
Title: From El Dorado to Lost Horizons : traditionalist films in the
  Hollywood renaissance, 1967–1972 / Ken Windrum.
Description: Albany : State University of New York Press, [2019] | Series:
  SUNY series, horizons of cinema | Includes bibliographical references and
  index.
Identifiers: LCCN 2018021846 | ISBN 9781438473970 (hardcover : alk. paper) |
  ISBN 9781438473963 (pbk. : alk. paper) | ISBN 9781438473987 (ebook)
Subjects: LCSH: Motion pictures—United States—History—20th century. |
  Motion pictures—Social aspects—United States—History—20th century.
Classification: LCC PN1993.5.U6 W56 2019 | DDC 791.430973—dc23
LC record available at https://lccn.loc.gov/2018021846

10 9 8 7 6 5 4 3 2 1

Contents

List of Illustrations	vii
Acknowledgments	xi
Foreword	xiii
Introduction: 1967: Searching for El Dorado	1
1 Big-Budget Musicals	11
2 War Spectacles	51
3 Naughty Sex Comedies	73
4 The Last Roundup	125
Conclusion: 1972: Lost Horizons	165
Works Cited	173
Index of Films	181
Index	185

Illustrations

Figure 0.1	The $375,000.00 Harmonia Gardens set from *Hello, Dolly!* (Gene Kelly, 1969).	xvii
Figure I.1	The aftermath of Bonnie Parker's (Faye Dunaway) shockingly gory death in *Bonnie and Clyde* (Arthur Penn, 1967).	5
Figure I.2	Extreme wide-angle cinematography by James Wong Howe along with nonrealist set design in *Seconds* (John Frankenheimer, 1966).	7
Figure 1.1	Tevye (Topol) bends tradition in *Fiddler on the Roof* (Norman Jewison, 1971).	17
Figure 1.2	Fanny Brice (Barbra Streisand) in narcissistic splendor in *Funny Girl* (William Wyler, 1968).	24
Figure 1.3	Faron's (Petula Clark) racially integrated flower-power wedding against a burned-out church in *Finian's Rainbow* (Francis Coppola, 1968).	28
Figure 1.4	The entire town of "No Name City" collapses around Ben Rumson (Lee Marvin) as a result of greed in *Paint Your Wagon* (Joshua Logan, 1969).	33
Figure 1.5	Telephoto composition of an unlikely musical performer—Clint Eastwood in *Paint Your Wagon* (Joshua Logan, 1969).	42
Figure 2.1	General Patton (George C. Scott) addresses a utopian audience in *Patton* (Franklin J. Schaffner, 1970).	55

Figure 2.2	Weary and disillusioned, Dick Ennis (Robert Mitchum) talks to General Leslie in *Anzio* (Edward Dmytryk, 1968).	58
Figure 2.3	The granite sneer of future action star Clint Eastwood blows us away in *Where Eagles Dare* (Brian G. Hutton, 1969).	66
Figure 2.4	Captain Ferraday (Rock Hudson, bottom far right, crouching) and the treacherous Vaslov (Ernest Borgnine, to Ferraday's right) amid Styrofoam ice and against rear projection in *Ice Station Zebra* (John Sturges, 1968).	70
Figure 3.1	Flat lighting, the ubiquitous and artificial-looking dark-walled office set of late 1960s Universal films, and broad acting from Edmond O'Brien and Maureen Arthur in *The Love God?* (Nat Hiken, 1969).	79
Figure 3.2	Wendell Armbruster, Jr. (Jack Lemmon), and Pamela Piggott (Juliet Mills) enjoy therapeutic adultery in *Avanti!* (Billy Wilder, 1972). Naughtiness only exists once nakedness is concealed.	99
Figure 3.3	Frank Benson (Bob Hope) and Oliver Poe (Jackie Gleason) literally trapped by middle-class chicanery in *How to Commit Marriage* (Norman Panama, 1969).	105
Figure 3.4	Abner Peacock (Don Knotts), a would-be Hugh Hefner in *The Love God?* (Nat Hiken, 1969). Note the period-specific superimpositions and costumes.	114
Figure 3.5	A zoom-in focuses on Doris (Barbra Streisand) in classic fetishizing/voyeurizing fashion in *The Owl and the Pussycat* (Herb Ross, 1970).	119
Figure 4.1	Infirmity and camaraderie between Cole Thorton (John Wayne) and J. P. Harrah (Robert Mitchum) in the autumnal *El Dorado* (Howard Hawks, 1967).	130
Figure 4.2	Michael McCandles's (Chris Mitchum) new mode of transportation lies in wreckage behind him after his father has twice knocked him to the ground in *Big Jake* (George Sherman, 1971).	134

Figure 4.3	Age and youth: "Rooster" Cogburn (John Wayne) and Mattie Ross (Kim Darby) as he discusses serving a "writ for a rat" in mockery of the legal system in *True Grit* (Henry Hathaway, 1969).	141
Figure 4.4	James Stewart in frayed hysteric mode as Johnny Cobb desperately crawling for his gun at the climax of *Firecreek* (Vincent V. McEveety, 1968).	145
Figure 4.5	Nightlinger (Roscoe Lee Browne), a black Renaissance man out west in a racially charged image of lynching, along with psychopath supreme Bruce Dern, in *The Cowboys* (Mark Rydell, 1972).	154
Figure C.1	New and old stars: Marlon Brando and Al Pacino in *The Godfather* (Francis Coppola, 1972).	167

Acknowledgments

I want to thank those who have helped out over this project's very long gestation.

The late Bob Sklar first suggested a version of this idea in the 1990s by highlighting the significance of the late 1960s and early 1970s in American film history and encouraging my work on the period.

My dissertation committee at UCLA—Nick Browne (chair), Steve Mamber, Peter Wollen, and Jan Reiff—gave me advice and support over my years in the PhD program.

Fellow students and now professional colleagues, Vincent Brook and Jerry Mosher encouraged me to move this from dissertation to published work. Both gave constructive feedback when I was proposing this as a manuscript to SUNY Press.

At the press, my editor Murray Pomerance has been patient and helpful; he's given many good suggestions and much advice over various iterations of this work. Also at the press, James Peltz has been encouraging and given much thoughtful advice. Rafael Chaiken has fielded many of my inquiries there. I also wish to thank the two anonymous readers, who did much to improve this work.

Once in production, Ryan Morris helped guided me through copyediting. Aimee Harrison made a key suggestion about the table of contents and Daniel Otis did some very thorough overall copyedits that improved the book's quality.

My colleagues at Pierce College—Jeff, Jill, Tracie, Matt, Rob, and Sean—have been wonderful to work with and have shown interest in this seemingly endless project. Yes, "the book" is finally arriving.

Various people in my personal life have been extraordinarily helpful. My late father George and my mother Gloria constantly encouraged and supported me, as did my sister Gayle and her family. Several others—Kathleen, Frank, Elizabeth, Jay, Susan, Beth, Christeen, Susanne, Cindy, and Brandon—have provided emotional support, practical advice, good ideas, and encouragement. In particular, Kathleen read over my introduction in the very final stages and helped out immensely.

I thank everyone.

Foreword

A canon of groundbreaking motion pictures made between the mid-1960s and late 1970s continues to fascinate cinephiles. Film historians favor these productions so much that the entire period is typically called "the Hollywood Renaissance." They have created an ironically stable characterization of an unstable, tumultuous era that focuses on innovative filmmakers challenging classical Hollywood's norms with iconoclastic, "maverick" movies per Drew Casper's phrase (Casper xv–xvii). Meanwhile, a larger group of more conventional-seeming films is either ignored or marginalized by historians as bad, clueless objects against which more favored productions can shine, even though many were financially successful and well-reviewed. Discussing these "traditionalist" movies provides an alternative account of the period.

∽

The era is usually described by historians as a result of the major studios' economic woes after both the sale of their theater chains and the overall box-office decline caused by television. Simultaneously, young filmmakers influenced by European art cinema began to produce innovative works with more overt sociopolitical content, greater frankness in representing violence, sex, and use of profanity, and an antiestablishment, often left-wing perspective. The financial success of *The Graduate* (Mike Nichols, 1967), *Bonnie and Clyde* (Arthur Penn, 1967), and *2001: A Space Odyssey* (Stanley Kubrick, 1968), and especially the surprise profits of the low-budget *Easy Rider*, are credited with spawning a wave of similar titles over the next several years. Drew Casper discusses how these have become a critical canon of maverick films with "radical formal experimentation . . . and uncompromised liberalist critique" (xvi–xvii).

A few choice quotes typify the dominant historical construction of the period as groundbreaking and revolutionary. For instance, Peter Biskind's popular *Easy Riders, Raging Bulls* describes how in 1967 *Bonnie and Clyde* and *The Graduate* "sent tremors" through the culture and ushered in a true golden age of films "that defied traditional narrative conventions, that challenged the tyranny of technical correctness, that broke the taboos of language and behavior, that dared to end unhappily" (Biskind 15–16). From a more academic perspective, Robert Sklar's *Movie-Made America* (1994 edition) created a framework for understanding the period. He discusses how *M*A*S*H* (Robert Altman, 1970), *2001: A Space Odyssey*, and *Little Big Man* (Arthur Penn, 1971), while "overturning movie conventions both aesthetically and ideologically, found such wide popular approbation" as their baby-boomer audience "was primed for artistic rebellion as few audiences before or since" (Sklar 325). Finally, a more focused work, Glenn Man's *Radical Visions: American Film Renaissance 1967–1976*, exhaustively typifies this dominant approach as he gives fifteen paradigmatically maverick auteur texts close, insightful readings. Like many accounts, including Biskind's, he privileges *Bonnie and Clyde*, which "opened the way for a new American cinema" when its "new wave characteristics and its shocking, honest treatment of sexual and violent themes paved the way for other filmmakers to punctuate the American scene with bold, unsettling achievements" (Man 31). There only a few exceptions to this focus on the maverick, such as Drew Casper's *Hollywood Film 1963–1976*, whose nature as a textbook unfortunately precludes detailed analysis (Casper, passim). Similarly, Leslie H. Abramson's chapter on 1968 in Rutgers's *Screen Decades* series includes traditionalist films (Abramson in Grant 206–10, 212–13).

I am not disputing these authors' basic thesis that particular circumstances allowed for the success of iconoclastic films. It certainly provides a coherent characterization of the period for a broadly conceived book such as Sklar's or Mast and Kawin's *A Short History of the Movies*. This framework of progress and innovation also informs standard historical accounts outside of cinema studies. For example, Todd Gitlin's seminal *The Sixties: Years of Hope, Days of Rage* describes alternative lifestyles and sexual attitudes, environmentalism, and an increase in direct political action and protest as the era's legacy (Gitlin xv–xxii). Furthermore, then-contemporary cultural commentators were aware of and encouraging toward social, aesthetic, and political change.

Similarly, this work is not intended to dethrone the maverick classics or impugn their aesthetic merits. These films have refreshingly frank representations of violence and sexuality, and take a more overt political stand. Their directors experimented with elliptical, ambiguous, and slice-of-life narrative structures and stylistic innovations such as zoom lensing, discontinuous editing, psychedelic visuals, and a general bravura self-consciousness. *Bonnie and Clyde* and *The Graduate* are emotionally engaging, thrilling, and still fresh in many ways. And in my opinion, *2001: A Space Odyssey* perhaps defines the specific expressive power of cinema better than any other movie.

Nevertheless, although a certain patch of ground has been trampled, much remains to be understood about the American cinema from 1967 to 1972. I hope to provide a more nuanced, complete depiction of these years by focusing on a group of neglected titles. Since these are less familiar, I want to provide a basic definition of the traditionalist corpus and discuss the particular films mentioned.

∼

The unhip movie—how even to define such films besides noting that any educated viewer knew the difference between *Bonnie and Clyde* and *How to Save a Marriage (and Ruin Your Life)* (Fielder Cook, 1968)? Similarly, *The Graduate* and *Easy Rider* were and are somehow "cool," while *Camelot* (Joshua Logan, 1967) and *True Grit* (Henry Hathaway, 1969) were square. This dichotomy still lurks behind many discussions of films and canons, whether in academic or more casual settings. To this point, John Belton remarks that "For moviegoers, there were at least two 1960s." One was for "the younger, more liberal, middle- and lower-class audience . . . gradually drawn away from their parents' movies" to the maverick classics. The other was "for the conservative, middle-aged, middle-class mainstream who went to big-budget historical spectacles, lavish musicals, Doris Day and Rock Hudson sex comedies, Disney family pictures, and cartoon-like, gadget-filled James Bond spy thrillers" (Belton 344). This evokes aspects of the traditionalist movie and begs the question, "If there were two sixties, why has only one been accounted for by film historians?" A more specific definition of these neglected films is required which shows that they are both easily ignorable through their uncool accouterments while their complex formal and ideological dimensions problematize the more typical understanding of the period which focuses on "maverick" films and neglects or maligns the "traditionalist" movie.

First, I would add to Belton's description that traditionalist productions are also overtly distinguished from maverick movies by featuring venerable male actors (John Wayne, James Stewart, Glenn Ford, Dean Martin), who typically have short hair and dress conservatively. Younger, noncountercultural performers include Walter Matthau, Barbra Streisand, and Julie Andrews. Beyond such obvious markers, how to define the traditionalist film?

Second, these movies are seen by contemporary critics and current academic accounts as old-fashioned, anachronistic, or simply conventional if discussed at all. This calls to mind one of Bill Nichols's tentative definitions of a documentary: a production is a documentary when an institution such as a distributor or television network calls it a documentary (Nichols 17). Therefore, the discourse surrounding traditionalist motion pictures by then-contemporary critics and more recent historians separates them from the era's maverick productions.

Third, these films typically contain "least-objectionable" generic content seemingly divorced from overt sociopolitical commentary. They avoid the graphic representation of sex and violence and the use of profanity that the new ratings-based system allowed. Therefore, they are almost always rated G or M (later GP and PG) by the Classification and Ratings Administration (CARA) of the Motion Picture Association of America (MPAA).

Finally, traditionalist films do not overtly, noisily break with the status quo the way maverick films do. They seemingly hew to classical Hollywood practices of content, narrative structure, and style, and fall within established genres. The line becomes blurry, though, when the specific form and politics of these films is analyzed and a more complex reality is revealed.

Traditionalist motion pictures often follow the expected plotlines of established genres. Similarly, they mostly exemplify principles of narrative clarity and easy accessibility for viewers, with stories generally resolving definitely. Furthermore, traditionalist narrative structure typically eschews the episodic, character-centered or slice-of-life narratives more typical of maverick productions. Style is also generally "invisible" and nonreflexive, although musicals are more likely to break these rules. The viewer should ideally ignore formal qualities that could obscure the narrative, such as an inaudible soundtrack, low or natural lighting, jump-cutting, out-of-focus frames, or objects placed between characters and the camera. Nevertheless, the many exceptions to these principles make the traditionalist movies a more intriguing, ambivalent canon than might be expected.

These film's complexity extends to their ideology. Status-quo attitudes are sometimes clearly maintained, but often directly opposed or expressed incoherently. For instance, these movies seemingly support the interests of the dominant class, sex, and race, portray American history positively, support Cold War policy, and refrain from challenging family, monogamy, or heterosexuality. And yes, such conservative positions are expressed within the corpus. But interestingly, such ideologies are also countered by many traditionalist movies that directly revise their genre's typical worldview and appear forward-thinking. Some use allegory to convey progressive attitudes, unlike blatantly topical maverick classics such as *The Graduate* or *Easy Rider*. This problematizes standard historical accounts and allows for a more nuanced understanding of the era in which these unlikely texts express progressive beliefs.

This is a crucial reason why traditionalist films are worth studying. They surprisingly and consistently reflect the era's progressive dimensions through form and content. Their analysis serves as a shadow history to the familiar discussion of maverick titles' reflection of the period's innovations. To my knowledge, this point has not been raised before by film historians.

~

In terms of the actual movies discussed here, four genres or subgenres organize this study into individual chapters.

The traditionalist musical is unfairly treated by many as a mere poster child for the reactionary forces being countered in the Hollywood Renaissance. A slew of bloated super-musicals attempted to replicate the box-office bonanza of *The Sound of Music*, but despite occasional financial success, they often failed with viewers and critics. In fact, these musicals pushed the major studios to near-insolvency during the late 1960s. For instance, the twenty-five-million-dollar *Hello, Dolly!* is blamed for

Figure 0.1. The $375,000.00 Harmonia Gardens set from *Hello, Dolly!* (Gene Kelly, 1969).

nearly sinking Twentieth Century Fox. Its excessive costs (mostly due to immense back-lot-filling sets) were not matched by the box-office returns, which were disappointing (Dunne 168–70, 227; "Big Rental Films of 1970").

These musicals also prove highly traditional because they follow long-established generic paradigms and rely on popular performers to garner box-office success. They seem particularly old-fashioned today especially through their elaborate, nostalgic creation of an idealized past.

Nevertheless, these films are products of their time and do negotiate sociocultural and political upheavals, albeit metaphorically, and they employ innovative style and narrative structure. For instance, many musicals challenge matrimony, portray women seeking gainful employment who financially outstrip male characters, employ feminist discourse, and represent the sexual revolution. In fact, they tackle these issues more consistently than the era's often male-centered or even sexist (Robert Altman) maverick creators. In this "Age of Aquarius," these films question the representation of racial diversity and ask what might make for an ideal society. Furthermore, a period-specific psychedelic aesthetic and self-conscious, over-the-top and nonclassical style are prominent in these films. This may be partly due to the musical genre's penchant for excess, but is also typical of the "cinema of sensation" noted by Paul Monaco (which mostly uses maverick texts as examples) as characteristic of the 1960s (Monaco 188–97).

The war film, particularly World War II narratives, shares common features with the super-musical. These productions also marshal all-star casts, and use spectacular set pieces for impressive visual appeal beyond the powers of television. Such movies are, on the surface, patriotic and politically conservative. However, they find ways to also allegorically criticize American involvement in Vietnam, question the U.S. Army's chain of command or authority in general, consider war's purpose, and even display a nihilistic view of combat's futility. These qualities are hardly typical of earlier military spectacles.

The "naughty" sex comedy is a subgenre that engages openly with the sexual revolution of the 1960s. These films originate with the double-entendre-ridden satires of Billy Wilder (*The Seven Year Itch*, 1955; *The Apartment*, 1960; *Kiss Me Stupid*, 1964) and Frank Tashlin (*The Girl Can't Help It*, 1956; *Will Success Spoil Rock Hunter?*, 1957). The 1959 Doris Day–Rock Hudson vehicle *Pillow Talk* (Michael Gordon) is the subgenre's ur-text. These produced a new style of bedroom farce that combines a *Playboy* magazine swinger aesthetic, sexy actresses, and a smooth light-comedy star such as Tony Curtis or Dean Martin. By the late 1960s these "naughty" films dealt with increasing sexual permissiveness, a rising divorce rate, and the era's famed generation gap. They vainly tried to synthesize modern and old-fashioned attitudes toward promiscuity, matrimony, and the mores of parents and children. Interestingly, despite their lurid trappings, these may be the most ideologically and formally coherent films discussed here. Rather than use a traditional mode for potentially progressive purposes, naughty comedies often reinforce the status quo. They present a defense of marriage and family. Previously, these movies had been mostly forgotten, whereas I attempt to define an overall aesthetic for this category as an actual subgenre.

The era's traditionalist Westerns mix conservative and progressive notions and betray structural and stylistic similarities when compared to the more celebrated iconoclastic titles of Peckinpah, Leone, and others. An elegiac, autumnal tone, again reminiscent of more overtly groundbreaking productions, also defines these Westerns. The genre was winding down, and many great cowboy stars were dead or aging. These Westerns reflect an increasingly liberal and self-critical attitude toward the classic sheriff or cowboy hero, the portrayal of Native Americans, and celebration of white "civilization." They metaphorically critique colonialism and U.S. foreign policy, particularly military involvement in Vietnam. Mortality and senescence, technology that alters the frontier lifestyle, and threats posed to the traditional hero by youth, women, and ethnic minorities are constantly represented in the period's Westerns.

∽

These films' complex engagement with both sociopolitical and aesthetic developments provides a key reason for their discussion, but they also raise other historiographic and theoretical issues.

One could argue that uncovering every strand or dimension of film history is inherently valuable, but why else should these neglected movies be discussed? Others have discussed *Easy Rider* (Dennis Hopper, 1969), so why analyze another film featuring Hopper from the same year, such as *True Grit* (Henry Hathaway, 1969)? The very lack of information is in itself significant, because other periods in American film history are not covered in such a limited fashion. For instance, Biskind's *Seeing Is Believing* tackles the 1950s through discussing both rebellious and conformist movies, unlike the limited take on the Hollywood Renaissance era in *Easy Riders, Raging Bulls* (*Seeing Is Believing, Easy Riders* passim). Interestingly, perusing *Daily Variety* shows that traditionalist films were often prominent at the box-office ("Big Rental Films of 1966"; "Big Rental Films of 1969"; "Big Rental Films of 1972"). Similarly, their prevalence in first-run and neighborhood theaters is revealed by visiting the archive of a major city newspaper, The *Los Angeles Times* (Display ads, "Movies Continuing." 1/1/67, 1/1/70, 1/1/73). Still, they are rarely discussed. Understandably, historians broadly characterize a period and give it a tangible identity. I often do this when discussing Hollywood in the 1960s and 1970s in my motion picture history survey course. But if film history is to avoid oversimplification, how can it ignore such a significant and profitable portion of the era's actual movies?

The traditionalist film's engagement with cultural and artistic innovation also allows a richer and deeper understanding of the Hollywood Renaissance era. This study's approach, rather than simply focusing on a few key films, provides a more complex model for how movies relate to contemporary ideologies and artistic trends. Similarly, the simplistic causality of many previous accounts requires revision. Some historians create a billiard-ball-like pattern, in which the economic reality of postclassical Hollywood is met with innovation, which results in young filmmakers creating a new breed of maverick movie. However, if you look deeper you can see how traditionalist films reveal that seemingly conventional and conservative productions also reflect the new.

Nevertheless, most historians look at this time period as exemplified by a limited cinematic canon. The previous, classical era is only invoked for its economic, ideological, and formal failings, which the maverick film transcends and rebukes. By doing so, film historians end up favoring the idea of the Hollywood Renaissance as a radical break from the past and describe it synchronically as part of an iconoclastic time. The more conventional aspects of these movies are usually neglected. A more-complete characterization of the period discussing an entirely different set of movies suggests that this zeitgeist analysis only provides half the picture. Traditionalist films *can* also be viewed as part of the era's progressivism *and also* as part of an historical continuum, since these productions also reveal the many vestiges of studio-era form and content. They may challenge sexist or racist attitudes, particularly in the musical and Western, while also defending the institutions of marriage and monogamy in the naughty sex comedy. Many hew to principles of continuity editing, transparent style, and causal, logical narrative structure, while others foreground outrageous, self-reflexive camerawork and new-wave-inspired montage within often unusual plot constructions tending toward the episodic or inconclusive.

Ultimately, taking traditionalist movies seriously counters the typical understanding of the Hollywood Renaissance, in which they are simply viewed as throwbacks, if discussed at all, and only maverick productions are deemed expressions of their sociohistorical background, albeit just its more progressive dimensions. Instead, this method foregrounds a significant group of traditionalist productions as they engage with the period's innovations while also showing the persistence of classical practice.

Before analyzing this corpus, describing the American film industry in 1967 and defining this year's significance is required for context. Previous accounts have so favored this temporal marker as a "threshold" that it needs discussion—if only to provide the foundation for a reconfigured account of the Hollywood Renaissance in which a larger group of films is discussed.

Introduction

1967: Searching for El Dorado

Howard Hawks's autumnal Western *El Dorado* debuted in 1967 and provides an apt metaphor for the American cinema of this period. The film's narrative recycles story elements and dialogue from other films by Hawks—in particular his previous Western, *Rio Bravo* (1959)—yet adds new elements such as a focus on aging and infirmity, and helped introduce a new actor, James Caan, who would become a major star at the end of the period in Coppola's maverick classic *The Godfather*. The coexistence of remnants of earlier times and synchronically relevant contemporary qualities is noticeable and a hallmark of traditionalist productions (and perhaps the "dirty secret" of the maverick canon). The search for El Dorado undertaken by Hawks and the Hollywood of 1967 was hardly the mystical quest of Edgar Allan Poe's famous poem, but simply involved hewing to the principles of the industry's golden age while incorporating current elements in hopes of box-office treasure. *El Dorado* performed well and was the year's twelfth-highest-grossing film (McCarthy 625). Hollywood would be less fortunate during the next five years.

Setting the Scene

In 1967, the Hollywood studios were still searching for El Dorado via the industrial and aesthetic practices of the classical era and by copying costly super-productions (and less expensive generic fare). In contrast, younger audiences were courted through increasingly relevant content and formal innovations.

Historical accounts typically invoke a series of disastrous events culminating with the motion picture companies' near-bankruptcy in the late 1960s (Schatz, *Boom or Bust*; Lev, Monaco, passim). Concomitant with the 1948 *United States v. Paramount* decision, which forced the five largest studios (RKO, MGM, 20th Century Fox, Warner Brothers, and Paramount) to sell their profitable theater chains, movies began a steady decline in popularity. This increased industrial frugality, resulting in eliminating the notorious long-term contracts for creative personnel, and selling off property that occupied valuable real estate. Simultaneously, Hollywood was beleaguered by competing leisure industries. The postwar era was marked by the baby boom and relocation of families to newly developed suburbs. The standard argument states that moviegoers were increasingly diverted by the amenities of suburban living, which seemed preferable to attending deteriorating picture palaces in declining inner-city neighborhoods. Better yet, one could stay home and watch television, which, after the initial high purchase cost, was essentially free.

Scholars then stress how studios responded by using their technological superiority to differentiate their product from television by making films in widescreen, color, and (occasionally) 3D. Similarly, content shifted as spectacles were released involving large crowd scenes and huge sets that the other medium could hardly approximate, such as *The Ten Commandments* (Cecil B. DeMille, 1956) and *Ben-Hur* (William Wyler, 1959). Simultaneously, increasingly risqué films such as *The Man with the Golden Arm* (1955) and other Otto Preminger productions, Elia Kazan and Tennessee Williams's infamous *Baby Doll* (1956), and Stanley Kubrick's adaptation of Vladimir Nabokov's scandalous novel *Lolita* (1962) distinguished motion pictures from the networks' offerings. Furthermore, as it was easier to join than fight, the studios began making television programs and, beginning with RKO in 1956, selling their film libraries to broadcasters. Both strategies proved lucrative (Lev 135–39).

By the mid-1960s, political, cultural, and aesthetic developments began to noticeably influence filmmakers and result in surprisingly popular, zeitgeist-capturing movies. To use Peter Biskind's subhead, "The Sex-Drugs-and-Rock 'n' Roll Generation Saved Hollywood." In contrast, old-fashioned, often costly productions failed at the box-office. Per the dominant conceptualization, the studios groaned into 1967 ready to take a chance on new talent.

Periodizing 1967–1972

On the one hand, I am choosing to demarcate 1967 to 1972 as a historical period in line with standard characterizations of this interval. Put briefly, the studios neared bankruptcy and began to make more socially relevant films by younger talent, movies that manifested a newfound representational freedom. These five years also culminated with Hollywood retrenching and profitably releasing a new form of the blockbuster that synthesized the industry's innovative and traditional valences. On the other hand, this period is also unique as a moment of fraught coexistence, not radical transition, an epoch marked by newer, innovative developments yet also one where traditionalist films incorporated progressive content and aesthetic qualities into seemingly conservative, generic formulas.

Nineteen sixty-seven, seen as the "watershed" year by Paul Monaco, serves as a nexus for varied industrial and aesthetic developments and marks this period's beginning (Monaco 182). I am aware that privileging this year and using this phrase may seem to fall into the trap of other accounts that see it as a threshold that dramatically broke with the past. Again, this description is not wrong so much as incomplete because it only focuses on innovation. This results in only discussing maverick films and, at best, painting traditionalist movies as irrelevant and uninteresting rather than themselves responsive to the era's upheavals.

First, 1967 saw the release of *Bonnie and Clyde*, a maverick film in many respects, certainly in terms of critical views of its various innovative qualities and expression of new aesthetic trends. Originally marketed by Warner Brothers—as an undistinguished, exploitative gangster movie—and panned by many critics, *Bonnie and Clyde* struck a chord with youthful audiences and was subsequently re-reviewed, and praised as innovative and relevant. Charles Marowitz in the *Village Voice* summarized the general discourse by stating "It has transcended art to become a 'psychic convenience.'" A time of unrest had seemingly found its cinematic representation as, per Marowitz, "audiences related to the rootless alienation of the film's milieu" (Monaco 184–86). Alexander Walker called it "a film from which we shall date reputations and innovation in the American cinema" (Halliwell 103). Ultimately, *Bonnie and Clyde* received multiple Academy Award nominations—including Best Picture, Best Actor (Warren Beatty), Best Actress (Faye Dunaway), and Best Original Screenplay (Robert Benton and David Newman)—and won Oscars for Best Cinematography (Burnett Guffey) and Best Supporting Actress (Estelle Parsons) (Monaco 184–86).

Bonnie and Clyde exemplified the newfound, almost instantaneous representational freedom subsequent to the Production Code's demise. Furthermore, the film revealed the growing influence of both the American exploitation movie and European art cinema paradigms, and featured newer actors and performance styles. Each of these factors requires individual consideration as influences coalescing during 1967 and in *Bonnie and Clyde*. Again, noting the film's innovations does not reify the maverick work of Penn and others, but reflects the critical consensus that has helped periodize the Hollywood Renaissance.

By 1967, films were basically free of the long-standing Production Code enforced by the Motion Picture Association of America (MPAA). These self-censoring strictures had certainly been relaxed in their last decade of enforcement from the universally applied moral philosophy of the 1930s and 1940s. Nevertheless, profanity, all nudity, and graphic violence were still proscribed for Hollywood filmmakers. Movies instead resorted to double-entendre, suggestion, and euphemism. Beginning, in 1962, though, selected titles circumvented the code by forbidding admission to children below a minimum age. This practice began with Stanley Kubrick's less-than-explicit *Lolita*. Furthermore, English and European productions such as the United Artists–released James Bond films (*Dr. No*, Terence Young, 1962), *From Russia with Love* (Young, 1963), *Goldfinger* (Guy Hamilton, 1964), or Fellini's *La Dolce Vita* (1960) were relatively frank about sexuality and achieved some of their American success based on their alleged prurience. The real watershed in removing the Code was *Who's Afraid of Virginia Woolf?* (Mike Nichols), which broke new ground in 1966 through strong language and frank discussion of sexuality. Andy Klein writes "Edward Albee's play had a powerful literary pedigree; and there was no way the material could be substantially softened without turning it into an embarrassing travesty . . . *Virginia Woolf* was released with the caution: 'No One Under 18 Admitted Without Parents.' What had been blatant censorship had become an impromptu advisory ratings system" (Klein 13).

The Production Code did not officially die in 1966, but this was the last year serious modification of content influenced American films, whereas European productions, including Antonioni's *Blow-Up* with its infamous glimpse of female pubic hair, were already being released uncensored without code seals through the major studios' distribution subsidiaries (Monaco 61–62; Harris 265). A new, more-lenient code lasted from 1966 to 1968 and considered a film's overall context or quality. The classification "Suggested for Mature Audiences" was formally introduced (Harris 235–36). The current ratings system began in 1968 and jettisoned any vestiges of the Production Code. This arrangement categorized films as G (General audiences, i.e., family fare); M (Mature audiences; slightly objectionable, soon GP—General Patronage and then PG—Parental Guidance); R (Restricted to those over sixteen unless accompanied by a guardian; films with profanity, nudity, or graphic violence); and X (forbidden to those under seventeen; ultimately synonymous with pornography) (Leff and Simmons 271–73). Jack Valenti, a political associate of President Lyndon Johnson, was hired to enforce the new ratings.

In other words, movies were no longer de facto censored, and *Bonnie and Clyde* itself sailed by the interim Production Code (Monaco 62). Filmmakers could "realistically" represent the formerly forbidden. Blood could spatter, naked bodies appear, and characters use profane expressions familiar to many viewers. The graphic representation of violence in *Bonnie and Clyde*, complete with blood squibs and visible entrance wounds, was unprecedented in American motion pictures. Similarly, the film portrays an unmarried couple who live together (probably the least of their sins) and overtly represents the pair's unsatisfactory sex life. In fact, Clyde's impotence is dealt with fairly directly ("I ain't much of a lover boy") while Bonnie is, to Murray Pomerance, "perhaps the blatantly sexually hungry female in American film" (Pomerance 180).

The focus on youthful characters, criminality, violence, and sexuality in *Bonnie and Clyde* was reminiscent of drive-in movies. Arthur Penn's background was in theater and major Hollywood productions, but exploitation films (and producer Roger Corman) allowed young talent such as Coppola, Scorsese, and Bogdanovich to learn their trade and, more

Figure I.1. The aftermath of Bonnie Parker's (Faye Dunaway) shockingly gory death in *Bonnie and Clyde* (Arthur Penn, 1967).

relevantly, create formally innovative, even arty, yet still low-budget films marketed toward younger viewers by highlighting sex and violence.

By 1967, European art cinema had already influenced Hollywood. Sidney Lumet's *The Pawnbroker* (1965) borrowed from Alain Resnais's *Hiroshima, Mon Amour* (1959), while Arthur Penn's *Mickey One* (1965) was indebted to Fellini's *8 1/2* (1963). Simultaneously, a new generation of moviegoers and directors appeared who attended "art" and "repertory" cinemas or had studied film in college. Successful and sexually frank European movies such as Claude Lelouch's *Un Homme et Une Femme* (1966) and *Blow-Up* were released in America around this time to critical and box-office acclaim. Therefore, it seems fitting that Francois Truffaut and Jean-Luc Godard were considered as directors for *Bonnie and Clyde*. Penn self-consciously employs formal innovations typical of European art cinema (which violate the feigned invisibility of classical Hollywood practice) such as low and distorted camera angles, gauze over the lens, fast editing, slow motion, conspicuous pulling of rack focus, and even quotes from the Odessa steps sequence in Eisenstein's The *Battleship Potemkin* (1925) when one of Clyde's victims is shot in the face.

Finally, the "method" acting pioneered at the New York Actors Studio and exemplified by Marlon Brando, James Dean, and Montgomery Clift was influencing a new generation of earthier, rawer, less obviously manufactured performers such as Warren Beatty himself, Robert Redford, Dustin Hoffman, and Jack Nicholson. Similarly, Barbra Streisand, who would at best have been an anomaly in the classical era, became a huge box-office draw despite her unconventional looks and strong ethnic identity. The mostly method-trained cast of *Bonnie and Clyde* were unknown to audiences except the relative veteran Warren Beatty. Only he and Faye Dunaway, albeit in the largest roles, are attractive in a classical movie-star manner.

Second, beyond the presence of *Bonnie and Clyde*, 1967 is the first year in which a significant corpus exists of films considered to be maverick titles and thus used by previous accounts to periodize the Hollywood Renaissance era. In 1965, three such domestic movies appeared—*Mickey One* (Arthur Penn), *The Pawnbroker*, and *The Loved One* (Tony Richardson). The first of these is a New Wave–inspired American art film that employs a kitchen sink of disorienting stylistic and narrative tricks, such as jagged cutting that breaks rules of continuity editing and fragments time and space, an impulsively moving camera that uses the new zoom lens technology, and surrealist, Felliniesque imagery. *The Pawnbroker*, as noted above, contains temporal jumps and rapid cutting inspired by Resnais and also had a groundbreaking moment (for a Hollywood production) of female nudity—a topless prostitute—yet still received a

Code seal. *The Loved One* is adapted from an English novel by Evelyn Waugh, and directed by British New Wave figure Tony Richardson, but is a literal condemnation of American culture and Hollywood itself—it was even shot in Metro-Goldwyn-Mayer's front offices. The Production Code–challenging *Who's Afraid of Virginia Woolf* and *Seconds* (John Frankenheimer) debuted in 1966 and *Blow-Up* opened domestically that December and played successfully throughout the United States the following year despite lacking a seal. *Seconds* initially contained full frontal female nudity (excised for its initial release but available on the Criterion DVD) and is marked by the extreme wide-angle lenses and other camera tricks employed by veteran cinematographer James Wong Howe. The film's portrait of American bourgeois society is unsparingly grim.

American films of 1967 generally considered maverick were more numerous and included, most notably, *Bonnie and Clyde* and *The Graduate*. *Cool Hand Luke* (Stuart Rosenberg), with its famous line about "failure to communicate," features an antisocial antihero martyred by a brutal penal system and captured the rebellious mood of some viewers. *In Cold Blood* (Richard Brooks) featured highly subjective fantasies and flashbacks and overtly flashy cinematography, and makes a pointed critique of capital punishment, an institution viewed uncritically in almost every classical-era Western. *Point Blank* (John Boorman) continues the art-cinema-inflected trend with highly stylized mise-en-scène evoking Antonioni's

Figure I.2. Extreme wide-angle cinematography by James Wong Howe along with nonrealist set design in *Seconds* (John Frankenheimer, 1966).

use of architecture to visualize alienation, time-fragmenting editing, and ambiguous narrative events. It could be read as an extended dream or reverie on the moment of the protagonist's death. *The President's Analyst* (Theodore J. Flicker) is a treasure-trove of hipster and druggie comedy, Pynchonesque paranoia, highly flamboyant cinematography by William Fraker, and an almost nonsensical and absurd series of narrative events. *Reflections in a Golden Eye* (John Huston) is well summarized by Murray Pomerance as "a symphony of perversity, vituperation, retaliation, nude horseback riding at night through the woods, effeminacy, adultery, nipple-slashing and more." The film used an experimental desaturated color processing in line with what Pomerance describes as a general aesthetic trend in 1967 toward stylistic rebellion partly through "innovative excesses of cinematography" (Pomerance 172–73). Finally, Sergio Leone's influential "Dollars" trilogy—*A Fistful of Dollars* (1964), *For a Few Dollars More* (1965), and *The Good, The Bad, and The Ugly* (1966)—was released in America and shocked many through their cynical, often amoral presentation of violence in a West no longer viewed as the site for Christian or American values to tame the wilderness. Instead, savagery seemed victorious in Leone's idiosyncratic vision.

In contrast, 1967 began a five-year financial (not production) drought for the blockbuster traditionalist film. Thomas Schatz's essay "The New Hollywood" describes 1965 to 1975 as a unified period characterized by the industry's failed attempts to recapture the success of *The Sound of Music* and *Dr. Zhivago*. He sees *Jaws* (Steven Spielberg), not *The Godfather*, as christening a new, lucrative blockbuster era (Schatz, "The New Hollywood," 13–25). My conceptualization recognizes that *The Sound of Music* (released in March 1965 and still returning money through early 1967) made some money (about $10 million) and *Dr. Zhivago* (which opened on December 31, 1965) made most of its revenue in 1966 ("Big Rental Pictures of 1965," "Big Rental Pictures of 1966," "All-Time Boxoffice Champs"). From 1967 until very late in 1972, no epic films succeeded on this level. Instead, Schatz notes "relatively inexpensive offbeat films" such as *Butch Cassidy and the Sundance Kid* and *M*A*S*H* performed well, as did low-budget efforts like *Easy Rider* (Schatz, "The New Hollywood," 14–15). From the last box-office tricklings of *The Sound of Music* to the first flow of money from *The Godfather*, 1967 to 1972 are unique in postwar American film history for their dearth of blockbuster hits and the prevalence of costly flops.

Third, significant sociopolitical changes were occurring in the United States. The year 1967 famously signifies the American counterculture's plateau when "be-ins" occurred in San Francisco's Golden Gate Park during the "Summer of Love," while The Beatles released *Sgt.*

Pepper's Lonely Hearts Club Band—the quintessential musical document of the burgeoning youth movement. In terms of the political, Hollywood may have only started to release progressive films, but the civil rights struggle, which defined the decade's minority empowerment efforts, had already climaxed, while other movements, such as feminism, Chicano activism, and gay rights, were coalescing. Roughly, 1967 was also the dividing line between peaceful civil disobedience and increasingly violent and radical action. The civil rights and anti–Vietnam War movements were poised between protest and revolt. The following year would be marked by political assassination and bloody demonstrations.

Therefore, 1967 can certainly be constructed as a nexus point of converging factors that changed American culture *and* influenced Hollywood. Noting one exact year as the precise beginning of a period is something of a parlor game. More important is providing understanding of how an era is fundamentally distinguished while in constant relationship with prior and subsequent periods.

In Hollywood itself, two related economic developments—sinking profits and corporate takeovers—indicate a new phase in the industry's history. Meanwhile, black-and-white cinematography, an aesthetic choice, became obsolete when television converted to a full-color roster in 1967.

Box-office revenues shrank from $1.692 billion in 1946 to $1.298 billion in 1956 and $1.082 billion in 1967, despite rising ticket prices (Balio 401; Conant 539). Yearly attendance dropped from 3.352 billion in 1948 to 1.011 billion in 1958 and 553 million in 1967 (Conant 539). Ninety million people a week attended films in 1946, forty million in 1960, and twenty million in 1970 (Monaco 40). By 1968, only Disney and Universal were showing a profit while others were losing between $15 million and $145 million annually, Fox and Columbia were close to receivership, and MGM abandoned distribution and reduced production (Balio 438).

Second, by the late 1960s many studios were no longer independently owned. Universal had been the first to fall when purchased by Lew Wasserman's MCA in 1959 (Monaco 32). In 1966, Gulf Western bought Paramount, in 1967 United Artists was folded into Transamerica Insurance, in 1969 Warner Brothers became part of Kinney Leisure, and Las Vegas developer Kirk Kerkorian acquired MGM (Balio 439). Only Disney, Fox, and Columbia remained "independent" companies.

The television industry's purchase of films was an economic godsend during the postwar economic slump. In 1967, ABC paid Fox $20 million—and $5 million just for *Cleopatra* (Joseph L. Mankiewicz, 1963)—while CBS paid $52 million to MGM for forty-five titles (Champlin 11). Concurrently, the networks were completely converting to color programming after 1965 (Balio 427). Paul Monaco, discussing the decade's cinematography, notes how "Hollywood had to take the television market for feature films seriously" (Monaco 69). John Frankenheimer more directly stated that "television sales being much higher in color than in black and white" influenced the shift (Pratley 203). Meanwhile, Charles Champlin wrote, "One truth which Zanuck holds to be self-evident is that no studio can any longer afford to make a black-and-white film, since the networks want color, color, color" (Champlin 12–13).

In 1967, the Academy Award for Best Cinematography abandoned the separation into black-and-white and color categories, since the latter had achieved, per Monaco, "unchallenged dominance" (Monaco 67). The only major studio monochrome releases from 1967 were Richard Brooks's maverick *In Cold Blood* and the subway highjacking melodrama *The Incident*. No big-budget black-and-white films were attempted in Hollywood until 1971 when *The Last Picture Show* was seen as unique for using black-and-white (Monaco 67).

Furthermore, many significant figures that helped define classical Hollywood cinema were nearing the end of the road by 1967. John Ford directed his last film in 1966, Howard Hawks in 1970, and William Wyler in 1970. Biskind tells the story of nearly blind Norman Taurog, who made his first feature film in 1928, still directing musicals at MGM in 1966 despite needing a driver to ferry him around the back lot (Biskind 18–19). In terms of studio bosses, Jack Warner retired, Barney Balaban (Paramount) was replaced in 1966, Darryl Zanuck was deposed in 1969, and the other companies were no longer run by men associated with the classical era (Balio 443–46; Gustafson 576). In 1967 alone actors who died included Spencer Tracy, Vivien Leigh, Claude Rains, Nelson Eddy, Basil Rathbone, Jayne Mansfield, Ann Sheridan, Jane Darwell, Charles Bickford, Bert Lahr (the cowardly lion from *The Wizard of Oz*), and Paul Muni (Pomerance 173). Other performers' careers were winding down, including those of James Stewart, Robert Taylor, Katharine Hepburn, Bette Davis, Joan Crawford, and Boris Karloff.

Hollywood would spend the next five years catching up with and reacting against the period's aesthetic, economic, sociopolitical, and cultural upheavals. The studios vacillated between jumping on the bandwagon and producing traditionalist genre films that both reflected and countered the era's tumult.

1

Big-Budget Musicals

EXTRAVAGANT, COSTLY MUSICALS typify the complex and unique blend of classical and more innovative factors in ideology, form, and genre that characterize Hollywood's supposedly traditionalist productions of the late 1960s and early 1970s. These films also function as synecdoches for historians, and even did so for contemporary reviewers, whose accounts play a major part in constructing certain titles as traditionalist in discussions of the industry's most anachronistic and unsuccessful tendencies during this period. These qualities are contrasted with the maverick texts favored by such accounts. The standard, and hardly false, argument notes that the phenomenal success of *The Sound of Music* led to suicidally expensive offerings from almost every major studio. Large casts, elaborate sets or location shooting, and special effects reflect the pains Hollywood took to repeat past formulas.

∽

The musical, by the late 1960s, was a long-established Hollywood genre dating back to *The Jazz Singer* (Alan Crosland, 1927) and the dawn of the "talking" picture. The mode developed through classic phases such as the Warner Brothers' Depression-era backstage cycle (*42nd Street*, *Footlight Parade*, both Lloyd Bacon, 1933), the RKO Astaire-Rogers films (*Top Hat*, Mark Sandrich, 1935; *Swing Time*, George Stevens, 1936; and *Shall We Dance*, Sandrich, 1937) and MGM's postwar "integrated" Freed-unit spectacles (*The Pirate*, Vincente Minnelli, 1948; *An American in Paris*, Minnelli, 1951; *Singin' in the Rain*, Stanley Donen and Gene Kelly, 1952; *The Bandwagon*, Minnelli, 1953; and *It's Always Fair Weather*, Donen and Kelly, 1955).

These films were conceived directly for the screen, but starting with the first widely released 70mm production, *Oklahoma* (Fred Zinnemann, 1955), a trend began of lavishly adapting Broadway hits and releasing them in "road show" engagements with reserved seating, an intermission, and a souvenir booklet. This often resulted in profits and prestige. *West Side Story* (Robert Wise, Jerome Robbins) and *My Fair Lady* (George Cukor) were big hits and won Best Picture Oscars, respectively, in 1961 and 1964 ("Big Rental Pictures of 1962," "Big Rental Pictures of 1964"). The trend's financial apotheosis was *The Sound of Music*, which exceeded all box-office records set by *Gone with the Wind* (Victor Fleming, 1939), and single-handedly rescued Twentieth Century Fox from near-bankruptcy following the ruinous super-production *Cleopatra* (Harris 75, Monaco 35–37). This initial windfall from *The Sound of Music* led Fox to produce other extravagant musicals, which lost money. Meanwhile other studios jumped on the bandwagon, and a profusion of expensive Broadway adaptations, plus a few screen originals (notably *Thoroughly Modern Millie*, George Roy Hill, 1967; *Star!*, Robert Wise, 1968; and *Darling Lili*, Blake Edwards, 1970) were released between 1967 and 1972. A few were successful such as Columbia's *Funny Girl* (returning $16.5 million in 1969) and United Artists' *Fiddler on the Roof* (making $38 million on a $9 million investment), but many were colossal box-office failures. For instance, Paramount's *Paint Your Wagon* lost $14 million dollars, while *Darling Lili* returned only $3.3 million of its $22 million cost to become the biggest box-office failure of the 1970s. Fox's *Doctor Dolittle* (Richard Fleischer, 1967) and *Star!* effectively killed the road-show engagement ("Big Rental Films of 1969"; Cook 25, 209; Monaco 51). Most notoriously, *Hello, Dolly!*, as noted above, recreated New York's 14th Street, literally filled the Fox lot with its huge sets (some of which stand today, perhaps as a cautionary reminder), and almost bankrupted the studio (Dunne 168–70, 227).

The trend could be seen as the culmination of attempts to coax filmgoers away from their televisions through superior technological prowess (70mm, CinemaScope, color) and spectacle. It seems ill-fated in retrospect, especially considering newer industrial strategies that proved successful. For instance, David Cook notes how lower-budget, youth-oriented movies, typified by *Easy Rider*, often made more money even if they held little interest for many (read: older or more conservative) viewers. Similarly, *The Graduate* was the greatest financial success of the 1960s (Cook 71–72). Even in 1969, this distinction was apparent, as when Stephen Farber in *Film Quarterly* compares "traditional" and "giant-budget" titles such as *Star!*, *Paint Your Wagon*, *Darling Lili*, and *Sweet Charity* (Bob Fosse, 1969) and films "made on low budgets, with complete independence, away from the studios," such as *Alice's Restau-*

rant, Easy Rider, and *Medium Cool* (Farber 3). The latter type would become increasingly dominant after 1968 (and with the replacement of the Production Code by a ratings system), while epic productions would increasingly be associated with family entertainment and would diminish in number.

A few musicals would innovate to such an extent that they could be considered within this development noted by Cook and Farber. The key film between 1967 and 1972 in this respect is Bob Fosse's *Cabaret*. No previous movie musical had such a grim, ominous tone, despite its seemingly cheerful music-hall setting, in which the horrors of incipient Nazism seem to be the result of a decadent society as personified by Joel Grey's seedy emcee. Mild sexual kinkiness, promiscuity, bisexuality, and a graphic beating also were unusual given the genre, although tame in presentation compared to other canonized groundbreakers. The film also eschews integrated musical numbers and instead is structured around the Brechtian use of songs as direct commentary on the narrative and its historical background. Stylistically, Fosse uses reflexive techniques such as direct address to the camera (already a generic staple) and associational editing reminiscent of Eisenstein to convey ideas or provide ironic contrast. Maximalist style, present in the era's maverick and traditionalist films, entails much use of the wide-angle and telephoto lenses, hand-held camera, and dramatic camera angles. Looked at more carefully, many of the innovations can be viewed as having generic precedents, and ultimately Fosse is more coy and allegorical than politically pointed, but *Cabaret* is certainly a different animal than musicals such as *The Great Waltz* or *1776*, which were released the same year.

This chapter discusses how such seriousness of subject matter would evolve in the traditionalist musicals of the subsequent years to include more relevant contemporary matters such as the relations among monogamy, matrimony, the sexual revolution, and feminism and women's rights. Furthermore, issues of race and even discussion of how to govern a society composed of varied interest groups are crucial to the genre's narratives. Many of these films either progressively question, or reveal the incoherencies within, the male, heterosexual, white, bourgeois values promulgated by many (but not all) classical Hollywood movies. Others are more reactionary, but discussing them allows for a more complete presentation of both the period's musicals and the overall range of offerings, to avoid the monolithic construction offered in previous accounts. Furthermore, the presence of conservative ideologies in the era deserves notice; it is often minimized by the focus on sociopolitical progressivism. These productions also employ narrative structure and style more adventurously, yet many retain traces of classical form.

Narrative Content: A Strained Romance

Romantic love, needless to say, is a mainstay of most classical Hollywood films and often viewed by ideologically oriented critics as the ultimate example of a status-quo institution (especially when resulting in matrimony) receiving support from the motion picture industry. The musical focuses obsessively on courtship, especially when it ends at the altar. The traditionalist musical's innovative story elements, though, notably influence the genre's long-lived and generally conservative narrative presentation of love, matrimony, and conflicts between the professional and domestic lives of musical performers. How did these films deal not only with this story element but synchronically reflect and inflect changed societal mores?

Increasingly liberal attitudes about love, premarital sex, promiscuity, marriage, and divorce culminated in the "sexual revolution" of the 1960s and 1970s. For instance, premarital sexual activity and the number of sexual partners per "single" woman increased (Greenwood and Guner 1–2). Concomitantly, the Production Code's replacement by a ratings system and the allowance of nudity and overt sexual content encouraged frank representation of these developments. Since most traditionalist musicals, though, were aimed at family audiences, and hewed to earlier generic and industrial paradigms for acceptable content, they addressed these issues indirectly, but they often advanced more "liberated" positions than their general tone might imply.

Nevertheless, the allegedly joyous, obligation-free, premarital sex espoused by the counterculture rarely figures narratively. Instead, of the nineteen films surveyed here, eleven have actual wedding scenes representing either the period directly preceding the nuptials, the ceremony itself, or the matrimonial spectacle's aftermath. In three, the wedding scene is narratively crucial. The remaining eight still include romantic plot elements, and none eschew the subject. Even the children's movie *Doctor Dolittle* boasts a flirtation between the titular bachelor doctor (Rex Harrison) and the protofeminist Emma (Samantha Eggar), whose presence on his adventurous sea voyage ostensibly reflects her modern, daring spirit, but she was more likely inserted to facilitate a brief love interest in even this most family-oriented production.

In terms of actual representations of marriage, some traditionalist musicals unambiguously valorize the institution as the desired, highly pursued telos to the lives of young heterosexuals. *Thoroughly Modern Millie* deals with the old-fashioned trope of young New York City career girls who have marriage on their minds despite paying lip service to feminism. Millie (Julie Andrews) may sing about being "thoroughly modern" and entertain professionally (as a wedding singer, which suggests that marriage is never far from her thoughts), yet ultimately marries the boss (John Gavin) at the film's end. Millie speaks of gender equality, but only wants to work, and in the traditionally feminine role of stenographer, until her profitable nuptials. Other films portraying female characters as marriage-minded include *Finian's Rainbow*, *Goodbye, Mr. Chips*, and *Hello, Dolly!*

The last-mentioned is interesting for directly, almost reflexively foregrounding the patriarchal, reactionary male attitude toward the institution in Horace Vandergelder's (Walter Matthau) horrifying recitation "It Takes a Woman." This litany details how a "dainty" female can perform a plethora of household chores, such as "washing and bluing and cleaning the mare" and stables. These tasks sound particularly onerous and abject considering current domestic technologies yet seems historically accurate ("Housework in Late 19th Century America"). He states that women are fragile yet notes they will "work until infinity." These contradictory statements undercut his position. Furthermore, Horace's attitude is doubtlessly presented for amusement, to disavow the cruelty and dominance of his position, and ultimately softens once the aggressive, opinionated Dolly (Barbra Streisand) has become Mrs. Vandergelder. What remains reactionary is this idea's expression by a character not marked as villainous but at worst irritable, stubborn, and frugal, characteristic of what Barthes calls "Operation Margarine" where a seeming institutional critique "becomes a paradoxical but incontrovertible means of exalting it" (Barthes 41).

More astonishingly, several films—*Sweet Charity*, *Fiddler on the Roof*, *Camelot*, and *Paint Your Wagon*—occasionally show the vicissitudes of matrimony and reveal fault lines in the institution in a manner reflective of the period's reevaluation of traditional institutions. Few classical predecessors had ever performed such a critique. Astaire and Rogers spar, romantic couples often battle, but always over minor difference of personality and temperament or because of farcical misunderstandings. Once obstacles are removed, tranquil, loving marriage will presumably follow. A hybrid such as *Love Me or Leave Me* (Charles Vidor, 1955) synthesizes melodrama and musical to depict Ruth Etting (Doris Day) and her psychotic, jealous gangster husband (James Cagney) yet culminates with his death and her consequent freedom. Few maverick classics thoroughly or negatively portray the reality of matrimony (albeit secondary characters such as the Robinsons in *The Graduate* are clearly miserable). Two notable exceptions are Paul Mazursky's *Bob & Carol & Ted & Alice* (1969) and Mike Nichols's *Carnal Knowledge* (1971).

Sweet Charity and *Fiddler on the Roof*, both adapted from Broadway hits, show societal impediments to marriage, similar to the melodrama, but refrain from comment on the institution. The former is complicated by having two endings. The American version follows the Broadway play and has Charity (Shirley MacLaine) jilted by her fiancée but living "hopefully ever after," whereas the European cut has them reunited. Fosse shot the more cheerful version fearing Universal would demand an upbeat finale, but producer Robert Arthur, who replaced the more conservative Ross Hunter after he clashed with the director, supported the original, bittersweet denouement (McQueen). Ironically, the era's tendency for films to reflect social reality was strong enough that a major studio and producer chose to honor a less-than-happy ending rather than impose the typical Hollywood resolution. Nevertheless, after an unsuccessful roadshow engagement, a remnant of once-successful exhibition practices, Universal cut fifteen minutes and substituted the happier ending. Interestingly, current release prints and DVDs feature the "canonical" downbeat denouement (Gottfried 197–98; Grubb 136).

In this version, Charity is condemned to spinsterhood, if not chastity, since the neurotic and respectable Oscar Lindquist (John McMartin) retracts his marriage offer after exposure to the seedy Times Square dance hall where she works. On the other hand, the European version shows him transcending his prudishness, and they reunite. In either case, *Sweet Charity* operates within a venerable narrative tradition of dark secrets that scotch imminent nuptials. In the American version, the conventional mores, which typically would be unchallenged, seem unnecessarily cruel considering the immense kindness and warmth of Charity (abundantly communicated through Shirley MacLaine's performance) and Lindquist's milquetoast sensibility. In the European version, social impediments are actually transcended. The question remains whether the downbeat ending more realistically reflects a society rent by class division or reinforces this schism between rich and poor. Similarly, does the happy ending show a progressive transcendence of economic boundaries or simply replicate the cheery, monogamy-and-marriage-valorizing ending of a typical Hollywood musical? The divided nature of many supposedly traditionalist films between progressive and conservative interpretations, classical-era residuum and synchronic influences, is readily apparent.

Fiddler on the Roof links the replacement of tradition by modernity and the dissolution of the quaint, idyllic turn-of-the-century Russo-Jewish shtetl Anatevka with generational conflict reflective of the 1960s and 1970s discourses of youthful revolt against parental mores and authority. This patriarchal community declines within a film that was a late exemplar of the more hierarchical, rule-based, and certainly Jewish, studio system and its "traditions." This mirroring links *Fiddler on the Roof* to another marital saga—*Camelot*. In particular, the film presents changed attitudes through the device of debating the matchmaker-arranged marriage, an institution that in itself few would champion by the 1970s. First Tevye (Topol) *allows* his oldest daughter to marry for love, then his second child simply *asks* for the patriarch's blessing while insisting that she and her fiancée, a proto-communist student (who may remind viewers of the period's campus radicals), will wed regardless of his response. The third daughter marries outside the faith (to a Christian) and then tells Tevye, who rejects the act and states that one can only bend so far without breaking.

Each of these confrontations contains a strange visual effect where a shocking cut jumps from a shot of Tevye, the daughter in question, and her suitor to reveal the patriarch alone a hundred or so feet away with the other two characters shown out of focus in the background. This device isolates him so that he may dialectically ponder his decision by repeating the phrase "on the other hand" while stating reasons for choosing to bless or condemn the engagement. Style becomes so overt and breaks classical paradigms exactly when patriarchal authority itself is challenged. Needless to say, these scenes altogether merely bend stylistic patterns, just as the genre itself or familial power structures are only altered, not destroyed, and once Tevye gives his approval (except for the final daughter), a cut occurs and the parameters of classical montage and mise-en-scène are reestablished.

Of course, Tevye, genre, and classicism are not infinitely malleable, which is why he disavows his third daughter's interreligious marriage. Suddenly, the hysterical rigidity of all paradigms is evinced when he tautologically, defiantly sings the word "Tradition," a phrase used in an explanatory and justificatory manner at many other key narrative

Figure 1.1. Tevye (Topol) bends tradition in *Fiddler on the Roof* (Norman Jewison, 1971).

moments, within a traditionalist musical. A rich ambiguity arises. The customs he validates are represented as valuable anchors in a stormy world where one is as precarious as "a fiddler on a roof." Similarly, as a sympathetic protagonist, his decision to disown her, which stays in place even after the family splits apart and leaves their community (under the Tsar's orders), is presumably endorsed. In fact, the parallels between his increasing permissiveness and the demise of Anatevka are obvious and could prove a cautionary tale to then-contemporary parents or even studio executives trying to be "with it" to remain relevant. As mentioned above, this discourse is ironically fitting in a film itself exemplary of an older mode of production.

In contrast, the daughters all wish to marry for love, a notion so firmly embedded in American society it functions as a tradition. In fact, academic surveys of college students in 1967 showed little active acceptance of marriage based solely on pragmatic reasons, yet 71.7 percent of women were undecided on the issue (possibly for security as an economically vulnerable group), while 64.6 percent of men were negatively predisposed. By 1976, love had seemingly conquered all, since both sexes were closely aligned with over 80 percent disapproving of nonromantic matrimony (Simpson, Campbell, and Berscheid 363–66). Since the daughter's desires in *Fiddler on the Roof* would seem reasonable to most viewers and were gaining acceptance among younger spectators, the movie supported their generational rebellion against earlier traditional values. After all, each is engaged to a sympathetic character and ends up in a seemingly fruitful union. The first (and least radical) marriage proves particularly "successful," since it results in a male heir *and* a nice dowry, which includes a sewing machine. Furthermore, the matchmaker Yenta appears a bit hysterical in her late-in-the-day attempt to keep the institution alive by proposing two boys, each about twelve, as matches for Tevye's remaining daughters, who are also barely pubescent. She mixes up the young suitor's identities, which adds a comic dimension to a last-ditch effort to resuscitate the corpse of a tradition, a metaphor not lost on those who made and consumed the period's old-guard musicals.

Another portrait of a lost utopia, *Camelot*, based on Lerner and Loewe's stage hit, goes further and speculates on the problematic reality of marriage itself, detailing Queen Guinevere's (Vanessa Redgrave) adulterous relationship with Sir Lancelot (Franco Nero), and King Arthur's (Richard Harris) reaction to the affair. Their actions, and particularly her role as Eve/destroyer, cause the decline and fall of an Edenic state where, per the title song, perfect weather is ordained by royal proclamation.

As the last major production of soon-to-retire Warner Brothers founder and studio boss Jack Warner, the film also seems like a last hurrah for a classical, hierarchical golden age. Similar to Arthur's failed regime, the hope was for rejuvenation, but *Camelot* and other costly musicals ended up leading to ruin, just as the king's bad decisions hasten his utopia's demise (Harris 191). Instead, the film can only sadly portray the old order fading away because of its rigidity while a newer attitude looms into view.

Do these occurrences present a critique of matrimony? Guinevere and Arthur's nuptials are prearranged, as are Tevye and Golde's in *Fiddler on the Roof*, and despite genuinely mutual affection, one can discern some disparagement of the matchmaker concept as guaranteeing lasting bliss. The marriage only proves successful until Lancelot arrives to woo the Queen and create jealousy, although the King initially remains calm since he recognizes their unchanged loyalty to the Round Table. Ultimately, this obedience and her continued love for Arthur, and by implication marriage as an institution, are impotent against passionate, amorous adultery. This proves quite relevant to American cinema and culture circa 1967. The causal nature of sexual pleasure (despite only implicit, metaphoric representations of erotic bliss) vis-à-vis her relation with Lancelot (emotion presumably also factoring into the equation) suggests a maturity unfamiliar to earlier musicals, which usually view love as a happy feeling, not a sexual sensation (unless one counts the inevitable "seeing stars" or butterflies in the stomach) or a cause of significant grief. Furthermore, the actors use their bodies to "perform sexuality" through dance, suggestive movements, facial expressions, and other signifiers of eros, which, according to Megan Woller, indicate sensuality "at odds with the implications of the original stage production" and also indicate increased sexual representation under the faltering Production Code (Woller 3).

Once their adultery topples Arthur's reason, social breakdown occurs in this most Aquarian society (note the earlier orgiastic, bucolic "Lusty Month of May" number) similar to the community's dissolution in *Fiddler on the Roof*. *Camelot* then reaches an impasse as the text can scarcely valorize a repressive, punitive marital doctrine advocating punishment of adultery, because this would contradict the Round Table's liberal tone. Nor can the film endorse therapeutic infidelity in the manner of a more progressive text such as Billy Wilder's *Kiss Me, Stupid*. Therefore, their chastisement is gloomily grafted onto societal breakdown, thus avoiding direct, puritanical condemnation and merely implying that their permissiveness will bend a tolerant culture to its breaking point. The film ends with imminent battle between Arthur and Lancelot. The narrative's punitive zeal is exhausted before actually representing either figure's violent defeat, because resolution is still difficult considering the discursive backdrop of an American society itself barely beginning to consider issues of adultery and marriage. Therefore, the plot retreats into the past with Arthur reminding a youth, obviously symbolic of both his earlier, triumphant self and of future generations' potential, of the irretrievable glories of *Camelot*. The youthful spectator represented in this scene was unlikely to find a sympathetic avatar in the film's actual viewers, most of whom were far more likely to see another Warner Brothers release, *Bonnie and Clyde*, which Warner felt barely transcended B-picture status (Biskind, Easy Riders 30). Instead, *Camelot* resembles crepuscular Westerns of the period in briefly showing the contagion of modern societal trends, while mourning and exemplifying status-quo ideologies within time-honored genres.

Paint Your Wagon, also adapted from a Lerner and Loewe Broadway musical, was also dismissed by critics. "*Paint Your Wagon* doesn't inspire a review. It doesn't even inspire a put-down. It just lies there in my mind—a big heavy lump" began Roger Ebert's review, which goes on to comment on the film's huge budget (Ebert, "*Paint Your Wagon*"). *Paint Your Wagon* also proposes a more radical solution to problems of marital fidelity through suggesting a marriage-à-trois in keeping with the sexual revolution, an element missing from the 1951 Broadway production, which according to James Robert Parrish focused on a "drunken old prospector . . . and his romance-hungry daughter, who finds love with a Mexican outcast." Fearing a possible flop, having seen the writing on the wall with the underperformance of the first post–*Sound of Music* roadshow musicals, Paramount production head Bob Evans brought in acclaimed screenwriter Paddy Chayefsky to make the story more relevant by adding French whores, making the mining town a "Sodom and Gomorrah," and hoping that a "risqué ménage-a-trois would make *Paint Your Wagon* more relevant to 1969 moviegoers" (Parrish 65–67). Generic remnants and synchronic tendencies (as both a member of the corpus of roadshow musical and as a sexually progressive text) run throughout the film like a fault line, suggesting the eventual collapse of the story's mining community. Because of such provocative content, the film, chaste by modern standards, received the M rating (similar to a PG-13 currently), which hurt box-office performance (Parrish 77), while *Sweet Charity* (equally explicit) received a "G" (Casper 121). Either the MPAA was simply behaving whimsically or the idea of thinly veiled prostitution—especially since it was punished in the downbeat narrative championed by Fosse—seemed less transgressive than polyamory. Ebert feels the latter denied it the subgenre's "customary" G and also notes the words "hell" and "damn" (Ebert, "*Paint Your Wagon*"). These would probably have passed unnoticed but for the film's somewhat radical sexual politics, which are noteworthy when considering that a bisexual three-way relationship between Bonnie, Clyde, and C. W. Moss was nixed by producer Warren Beatty (Harris 207–9), albeit in *Paint Your Wagon* there is no suggestion of group sex or relations between male characters.

Cantankerous prospector Ben Rumson (Lee Marvin), his eponymously named "Pardner" (Clint Eastwood), and one-time Mormon bride (i.e., a practiced bigamist) Elizabeth (Jean Seberg) form this unholy trinity. She had been initially auctioned off to Ben, but he okays their union by stating that out west "We make things up as we go along," echoing communal and alternative living practices of the era (Rubin 718–20). A threesome soon evolves as the pens of Lerner and Loewe again provide a countercultural, Aquarian view of history. Furthermore, and somewhat surprising in Hollywood, Elizabeth presumably loves and desires both men.

More remarkably, the situation only disintegrates when the presence of a religious family amid this untraditional household encourages latent conformist, hypocritical tendencies in Pardner and Elizabeth, who request that Ben stay at the hotel, pour out his whiskey, and begin saying grace at the previously profane dinner table. Resolution of this conflict is avoided, though, since the town collapses (literally) and Rumson, a Daniel Boone–style pioneer who stays ahead of civilization, heads for the next frontier. Pardner and Elizabeth will putatively attempt traditional matrimony, although divorcing Ben is not mentioned.

~

A more significant threat to matrimony began in the United States during World War II when women increasingly joined the labor force, often in "masculine" jobs in factories ("Statistics on Women in the World War II Era"). Between 1940 and 1980, the percentage of women employed doubled (Toosi 22). Since musicals traditionally feature actresses portraying performers, conflicts between the gender roles of wife and star—a position that has allowed female agency—require attention.

The most traditional response to this challenge involves the woman sacrificing career for matrimony. *Goodbye, Mr. Chips*, a musical remake of the 1939 Oscar-winning MGM classic, has Bridges (Petula Clark) gleefully renounce her stage career to marry the titular hero (Peter O'Toole). Since he teaches at a strict, "respectable" boarding school, her West End brassiness presents a few embarrassments, as when she sings loudly at an assembly, but the marriage remains happy and his career successful. She does perform in a school play and for charity during World War II. This last performance of hers is ambiguously rendered, because despite the narrative's seeming approval of patriotic efforts, she is killed by a German bomb. A cautionary tale about staying at home could be discerned or, more likely, her death could allow her to be enshrined among the ranks of British martyrs.

The subgenre that most directly addressed these issues of marriage vs. career is the backstage musical biography, especially when representing a female stage legend's attempt to balance love and career. *Star!* and *Funny Girl* attempt to resolve this contradiction. Interestingly, the latter is more pessimistic, yet it was the box-office success. The well-publicized debut of Streisand, already a Broadway and recording star, in her Tony-winning role as Fanny Brice may have provoked greater interest than Julie Andrews playing against type as Gertrude Lawrence.

Star! responds obliquely to the marriage–career contradiction for more than half of its running time. Near the film's beginning, Lawrence (Andrews), who has lived on stage earnings since her teens, does marry a parasitic alcoholic who she financially supports, but she is clearly, unambiguously justified in solving this dilemma by divorce. Their marriage, though, has produced a daughter, keeping the duty-vs.-employment question alive. She absently parents the daughter until attempting to spend a vacation with her in the south of France. This interval ends as the daughter states that she prefers her mother's absence, allowing Gertrude to resume acting without guilt. In keeping with traditional morality that may have been shared by viewers surprised and discomforted by this weak parent–child bond, this action commences a period of decline, which contrasts with the film's triumphant first half, in which Lawrence's nonconformity is judged (literally) and questioned. She continues to date a variety of men and remain famous, but actually and metaphorically is deemed bankrupt by the courts, as an economic and moral rebuke to her spendthrift, decadent lifestyle, which is deemed frivolous during a worldwide depression.

She is rehabilitated and pays her "debt" through charitable work and by acting in a "serious," even theist, play, *Susan and God*. Gertrude's ultimate "redemption," though, comes predictably from romance in the form of Aldrich (Richard Crenna), a Wall Street banker and signifier of male dominance and propriety, who attempts to tame this headstrong, charming shrew. For instance, when she storms off stage during rehearsals, Aldrich, as both the play's producer and all-knowing analyst, forces her to admit that fear of spinsterhood causes her erratic behavior. He then suggests they dine together, which adds romantic entanglement to his arsenal of patriarchal control. Needless to say, they marry and drive away sparring, but now in the sexualized manner of another Lawrence stage hit: Nöel Coward's *Private Lives*. She does admit a need for understanding, indicating Aldrich's partial, therapeutic victory, but in contrast to his previously volunteered sympathy, she forcefully demands compassion. Gertrude ceases storming off stage and has married, but the film concludes with her ranting about needing complete sincerity "all the bloody time." This last line, indicating the persistence of her Cockney outspokenness, segues into the ironically celebratory title song, which mocks and valorizes her celestial persona. Their marriage promises sex, love, bickering, and an uneasy synthesis, as her professional career will continue, in accord with the genre's wife/performer dialectic.

Funny Girl is the sadder and wiser of the two films in respect to this dilemma. At first, Fanny Brice's (Streisand) stardom with the Ziegfeld Follies completely sequesters her from Nicky Arnstein (Omar Sharif), whose career involves gambling on cruise ships. At the end of the film's first act, though, she abandons a show in Baltimore, races to New York, commandeers a tugboat to overtake his ocean liner while singing the signature Streisand number "Don't Rain on My Parade." Here a dramatic point is made of a woman's not working. Once Fanny, or women in general, are shown as capable of careers, rebellion involves ditching employment for love. She and Nicky wed and are initially happy, but inevitably trouble arrives when gambling prevents his attending the Ziegfeld Follies opening night. More seriously, he begins losing at cards, but of course refuses to accept her financial support. Fanny then surreptitiously attempts to buy Nicky partnership in a casino, but he sees through this ruse and, in a moment of wounded pride, desperately enters a crooked bond deal to shore up his sagging finances. When caught by the police, he pleads guilty, preferring jail to admitting to being duped into the scheme; the former option indicates agency while the latter invokes his wife's attempt to be the silent partner in his casino management.

At this point, the film's narrative returns to the opening scene of Fanny's solitary, melancholic arrival at the Follies, which led into an extended flashback that concludes when Nicky enters her dressing room and pitiably asks "What have I ever done for you?" Fanny responds to his question by stating he made her feel beautiful. This scene occurs eighteen months after his incarceration, yet due to a lack of fades, dissolves, or other classical temporal markers, I initially felt surprised that the "present" had been regained and the flashback concluded, a temporal uncertainty unusual in a classical film (Bordwell, *Narration in the Fiction Film* 163). Nicky leaves, and multiple images of her are reflected in the dressing room's mirrors, which also suggest criticisms of narcissism often leveled at Streisand. Fanny is now self-contained, multiplied in an infinite *mise en abyme*, and trapped in her persona. She resolves the love/career dialectic by becoming a traditional, glamorous, visually objectified woman, but for pay not via marriage or romance. This could

Figure 1.2. Fanny Brice (Barbra Streisand) in narcissistic splendor in *Funny Girl* (William Wyler, 1968).

be considered a progressive outcome. Granted, she is still there "to-be-looked-at" (Mulvey 203), yet at least she has economic power via her lucrative (and presumably creatively satisfying) employment. Of course, one could also see her as a victim forced into celibacy by a system that will not allow her to keep her sexy, worthless man the way a mistress could be discreetly squired without societal condemnation. She then takes the stage and sings "My Man (I Love Him So)." This number acknowledges the need for love, but at this point Fanny/Streisand seems sufficiently satisfied with simply performing her emotions.

Neither film has recourse to any clear solution and certainly not to the classical-era musicals' denouement where the woman either joyfully, unquestioningly renounces her career or the couple unite but continue to perform together. The latter option is precluded since neither Crenna nor Sharif are singer–dancers in the Astaire/Kelly mold. Sharif was cast in a musical, as were such well-paid actors as Lee Marvin and Rock Hudson, for box-office appeal as part of the roadshow spectacles' overall production strategy of amplification and expense. The residuum of earlier ideologies within a time-tested genre is present in both films since either star could choose to renounce fame, but they are placed within a period of feminism and challenges to social institutions that makes such an easy solution impossible. Similarly, an established genre continues to function while establishing a new paradigm of bloated excess (by following in the footsteps of predecessors such as *The Sound of Music*) readable as expressing a then-prevalent, failed industrial strategy. Furthermore, the genre tries to progressively negotiate current social issues.

Only *Paint Your Wagon* suggests that traditional matrimony is not the preferred condition, and even this film must eventually retreat from this position. These other movies, though, are significant in revealing contemporary fault lines suggesting that marriage rarely achieves this sort of utopia.

Race Mattered

Another significant discourse of the 1960s, which mirrors the concomitant "liberation" of women, involves the civil rights movement and African American response to white hegemony. Most films, whether considered maverick or traditionalist, elided these issues, but there were exceptions such as *Guess Who's Coming to Dinner* (Stanley Kramer, 1967) about interracial marriage, and *In the Heat of the Night*, which portrays a redneck southern sheriff (Rod Steiger) and black northern detective (Sidney Poitier) teaming up to solve a murder. The blaxploitation cycle of the 1970s provided a sustained cinematic discourse on race in films lacking official culture's approval.

Surprisingly, some elaborate traditionalist musicals, albeit covertly, addressed these issues through the time-worn means of allegory. For instance, in *Doctor Doolittle*, the titular medic's pleas for kinder treatment of animals could be imagined to reflect a benign and supportive attitude that would probably extend to less-privileged human groups. Not only does the doctor sound countercultural when described as "one of the beautiful people" but he makes statements such as "We create their wretched status and then we use it to malign them," which invokes the title of Frantz Fanon's classic anticolonialist work *The Wretched of the Earth*. This concern puts a positive spin on passages from Fanon such as "the terms the settler uses when he mentions the native are zoological terms. He speaks of the yellow man's reptilian motions, of the stink of the native quarter, of breeding swarms, of foulness, of spawn, of gesticulations. When the settler seeks to describe the native fully in exact terms he constantly refers to the bestiary" (Fanon 42). Furthermore, he asks why we cannot love a creature with a different face which again pleads for tolerance of the "other." The colonizer animalizes his subject while Dolittle humanizes his patients. Unfortunately, when the film enters Africa the portrait of indigenous peoples hits levels of cartoonish cliché, invalidating previously progressive dimensions. Oddly enough, Sidney Poitier was considered for the role of a college-educated tribal chief (Harris 130, 158) until the producers decided to dramatically reduce the part to save the costs of hiring another star. His presence in this film,

In the Heat of the Night, and *Guess Who's Coming to Dinner* in the same year is provocatively reflective of traditionalist, moderately maverick, and seemingly liberal films in potential dialogue.

Francis Ford Coppola's *Finian's Rainbow* is particularly surprising in directly detailing issues of racial persecution and tension in the American South, a subject mostly elided by maverick texts. The film's narrative, which also spoofs the American-dream ideology, deals with Finian McGonnigle (Fred Astaire), who travels to the United States with a pot o' gold (stolen from a leprechaun) so his treasure may grow osmotically through being planted near the federal gold depository at Fort Knox, Kentucky. This plot device comically literalizes metaphors about "the land where the streets are paved with gold" and shows the ridiculousness of believing such notions. Needless to say, no magic transformation occurs, although other supernatural events related to issues of race play an important narrative role.

Finian's Rainbow is heavily inflected by the civil rights discourse of the 1960s in portraying an America dominated by white property owners and their police lackeys, who attempt to drive a racially mixed sharecropper collective off their land. Senator Rawkus (Keenan Wynn), a character whose slogan is "Forward to Yesterday" (almost the motto of certain traditionalist musicals as critically constructed) and who spouts states-rights tirades against federal bureaucracy, resembles demagogues such as Governors Wallace and Faubus, who similarly defied authority. The film primarily presents racism's idiocy and relieves tensions via the magical solution of Finian's daughter Faron (Petula Clark) casting a spell rendering the senator black, which causes his formerly trusty dog to immediately bark at him. This references how canines traditionally aided law enforcement in the South to suppress civil rights protests. The film conveys the arbitrariness of color and hence the senselessness of bigotry, since he remains the same unpleasant, hate-filled individual. The film posits that character, not pigment, significantly determines one's worth.

The ideological sands shift, though, when a leprechaun (Tommy Steele) then alters Rawkus's personality, rendering him arbitrary and mutable and causing him to join an itinerant black gospel quartet. Three varied messages can be gleaned from this situation. The first implies that since every known quality could be instantly reversed, hysterical vigor in the fight against change and in defense of tradition is particularly necessary in an uncertain world. Second, perhaps all values are relative, illusory, and open to interpretation. Finally, the narrative could simply champion kindness over cruelty. Of course, the senator regains his whiteness in the end, defusing the issue and stifling a truly radical textual solution in which he remains black. Instead he merely transforms into a kinder, gentler southerner. A tolerant message emerges, but the reliance on magic speaks despairing volumes about actual pragmatic action to solve such problems in the cinematic universe, as the civil rights movement was successfully doing in real life. This echoes Frederic Jameson's notions of utopian solutions often providing answers that realist narratives are precluded from offering (Jameson 104–5).

This fictive/fantastic outcome is ironic since the film also directly addresses demeaning racial stereotyping *within* the culture's own fictions. For instance, a black scientist oddly working as the senator's butler is instructed by another servant to walk slowly, shuck and jive in a Stepin Fetchit–like manner, and behave like black performers in "some of the *new* movies like *Birth of a Nation* and *Gone with the Wind*." *Finian's Rainbow* may magically, and therefore unsatisfactorily, heal racial wounds, in the whimsical manner of Hollywood or other palliative pop culture texts, but it simultaneously shows the permanent role of cultural representation in promoting stereotypes. This relatively traditional film critiques both *Birth of a Nation*, the production that helped establish the classical model Coppola often follows, and *Gone with the Wind*, generally considered the studio era's apex and key release of the annus mirabilis 1939. This scene also shows that, at least for the misinformed or willfully ignorant, these movies are still regarded as current and instructive. This reflexivity, and Coppola's maverick directorial style, distinguish the film from classical cinema but within the context of a Broadway adaptation starring Fred Astaire, the quintessential Hollywood musical performer, and featuring a singing leprechaun. Again, the so-called traditionalist genre's movies host both innovative and conventional aspects, which here are further complicated by Coppola's authorial presence.

The Road to Utopia

Musicals concerned with specific problems involving racial and gender equality also consider, on a macro level, issues of how society traditionally or ideally functions. The contemporaneous questioning of governmental legitimacy by Vietnam War and civil rights protesters provides a background to the often utopian or progressive strain in these productions, their solutions to problems, and their proposed methods of governance.

Beginning with texts that seemingly advocate the status quo, *Fiddler on the Roof* portrays a society where the word *tradition* governs with hysterical rigidity and is invoked tautologically since it is beyond logic. This inflexibility, though, is preferable to societal dissolution, since persecution by the Tsar and a concomitant diaspora commence once the village, symbolized by Tevye, accepts a marriage based on love, not arrangement. A pogrom literally occurs directly after the first such nuptials.

At the end, the town's Jews are literally pushed off their land. The matchmaker, Yenta (Molly Picon), moves to Jerusalem, another perilously held territory. Fear of such dispossession haunts both Israelis and Palestinians and furthers religious animosity. Adamantine traditionalism, including a shunning of interreligious marriage, also characterizes factions on both sides of that conflict. The decline of Anatevka, read one way, could serve as a cautionary tale for modern Jews (or Palestinians even) about the disastrous effects of liberalism, modernity, and tolerance.

Finian's Rainbow unambiguously champions the status quo but via its figuration as an at-risk interracial commune of poor black and white sharecroppers threatened by white, Capraesque land-owning villains who want to foreclose on their property. In case their "progressive" nature is unclear, their charismatic leader is a guitar-playing folksinger named Woody, first viewed on a train, who invokes the persona and lyrics of communist, populist balladeer Woody Guthrie. A violent southern law-enforcement presence, at the time inherently associated with violent reaction against Civil Rights protesters, incites a mob who attempt to burn Woody and Faron alive in a barn, reminiscent of the violent climax to Arthur Penn's "hate letter" to Texas, *The Chase* (1966), in which a junkyard of used cars is burned and exploded by a jeering, drunken citizenry to flush out an escaped convict. Coppola's film is less corrosive since the crowd members change their minds and help quench the fire by communally passing around water buckets. The film ends with the two wedded, in Aquarian fashion, in the flower-bestrewn, charred remnants of a burned-out church. Unlike the sad denouement of *Fiddler on the Roof*, in *Finian's Rainbow*, a progressive community remains functional,

Figure 1.3. Faron's (Petula Clark) racially integrated flower-power wedding against a burned-out church in *Finian's Rainbow* (Francis Coppola, 1968).

reactionary forces are corrected, and a traditional religious wedding with period-specific overtones furthers the synthesis of conservative and liberal tendencies.

The countercultural nature of this scene might also invoke the pastoral, experimental communes founded by young people desiring a more fluid, egalitarian, spiritually satisfying, and "natural" existence built on shared tasks and rewards, and removed from technology, stress, and urban malaise. The most-noted progressive text to represent these is Hopper's *Easy Rider*, in which Captain America (Peter Fonda) blesses a commune by saying "they're gonna make it" after Billy (Hopper) expresses doubts. Interestingly enough, traditionalist musicals such as *Camelot*, *Finian's Rainbow*, and *Paint Your Wagon* often showed more positive, less ambiguous portrayals of alternative living than the period's "innovative" films.

1776 details the founding of America and Thomas Jefferson's (Ken Howard) writing of the Declaration of Independence. It does not show the formation of a youth-culture utopia, but the film's narrative delineates the practical means of creating a better society through portraying the dialectical resolution of opposing opinions held by participants in the First Continental Congress. The South, for instance, wanted each state to function as a sovereign nation, a discourse reminiscent of their later "states rights" arguments against federal imposition of civil rights laws, whereas the northern faction advocated a more centralized government.

The film's narrative first demonstrates consensual decision-making when Jefferson, who as a Virginian is geographically poised between North and South, is appointed to represent the land-owning classes and write the Declaration with aid from a Massachusetts lawyer, John Adams (William Daniels), and Pennsylvania sage Benjamin Franklin (Howard DaSilva). This trio, each representing a different region and profession, will supposedly balance various interests just as modern presidential candidates often pick a running mate to appeal to other constituencies. The plot's key compromise concerns an antislavery clause in the document. This is favored by the North and opposed by the South (clearly connecting their states-rights views with legitimized racism). In an argument unlikely to convince many spectators in 1972, southern delegates note that New Englanders are also involved in the slave trade. Nevertheless, the practice's injustice itself is not debated, because contemporary audiences would presumably lack sympathy for characters vocally advocating ownership of human beings. Instead, the film valorizes compromise (which also reflects actual historical reality) with the South, thus achieving a moderate position ostensibly acceptable to any viewer's ideology.

America's founding usually is described as achieving a new, superior form of government in the "real world" via actual, practical matters of drafting a Declaration of Independence and defeating the British army. In contrast, *Camelot*, as previously noted, and *Lost Horizon* (Charles Jarrott, 1973) both portray utopian, "unreal" societies and thus bookend the period in question. Richard Dyer claims that the musical as entertainment does not "present models of utopian worlds . . . the utopianism is contained in the feelings it embodies. It presents . . . what utopia would feel like rather than how it would be organized" (Dyer 177). Nevertheless, this highly unrealistic genre is certainly hospitable to such narratives.

Lost Horizon is a musical remake of Frank Capra's 1937 version of James Hilton's (*Goodbye, Mr. Chips*) novel about Shangri-La: a mythical, completely peaceful, valley paradise with a perfect climate high in the Himalayas. Into this Eden arrive a cross-section of refugees from an unnamed war in some vaguely Mongolian nation. This group includes a U.N. official and pacifist dreamer, Richard Conway (Peter Finch), and his pragmatist brother George (Michael York), a wealthy mining engineer (George Kennedy), a *Newsweek* reporter (Sally Kellerman), and a washed-up comedian (Bobby Van).

Predictably, these interlopers adapt differently to this paradise, suggesting that this lifestyle, like its "real world" analogues, may not enchant every visitor—especially the worldly, linear-minded George, who fails to understand Shangri-La's highly relativist, paradoxical, one could even say "inscrutable" and Orientalist discourse. Expressions describing a child's seeming largeness compared to other life forms and axioms about how perspective depends "on where you are in the circle that is spinning round," since "half of the time we are upside down" fall on deaf, empiricist ears. George represents the Westernized establishment figure unable to "dig" the Easternness of this metaphor or certain tenets of 1960s youth culture.

Lost Horizon, though, is not an exclusivist text. Shangri-La can possibly appeal to anyone willing to remain open-minded. Sam, the engineer, for instance, initially notes the omnipresence of gold (because it is nonutilitarian, the metal is considered worthless) and schemes to remove these riches and leave. Soon, though, he regains the youthful idealism he put aside for worldly success, and is convinced to use his engineering abilities to improve the Shangri-La irrigation system. Meanwhile, the comedian warbles parable-like ditties such as "Question Me an Answer, Answer Me a Question" and frolics with local infants as their new school-teacher. Seemingly anyone can drop out into this utopia.

In contrast, one resident, Maria (Olivia Hussey), falls in love with George and wishes to return with him to "civilization." This situation reveals the community's secret identity as an island of timelessness. She is actually one hundred, but appears twenty, and is played by the actress best known as Zefirelli's teenage heroine in the youth-culture-targeted *Romeo and Juliet* (1968). The idea of elders acting young was mocked by the counterculture but here proves successful as they actually attain eternal agelessness. Furthermore, this literalization of the fountain-of-youth idea relates to the era's often idealized (or pandering) view of a "younger generation" who might themselves feel positively toward the ecologically benign, communal existence based on Eastern relativist philosophy the film presents. This fantasy, appealing to all ages (who would become, in fact, indistinguishable in a world like Shangri-La), is perhaps "too good to be true" and, therefore, to be imaginable.

Capitalism also at times places restrictions on or destroys any narratively envisioned utopias. Thus, a stern tone intended to suggest the requisite sacrifice of the paradise dweller soon prevails as Maria rapidly ages on departing Shangri-La; this society accepts all refugees but is inherently accessible to few and is pitilessly punitive toward those who leave. On the other hand, perhaps the film's ideology attempts to both show the bitter reality of this communal ideal yet still reflect a counterculture fantasy of eternal youth, realizable only via removal from, not revolutionary transformation of, a poisonous civilization. One can commemorate this society archivally (the Lama's grand dream involves creating a Himalayan Alexandrian library preserving the world's culture after imminent apocalypse), but not rejoin. Such sobering notions of utopia as possible only through renouncing the "real world" may reflect the sense allegedly felt in the early 1970s by many in the counterculture after Nixon's triumphant reelection. Certainly, popular discourse concerning the death of the 1960s stresses this event as a last nail in the counterculture's coffin. The final discursive vestiges of Camelot or the Aquarian ideal of its "The Lusty Month of May" musical number and its real-world analogue in 1967's "Summer of Love" had seemingly been jettisoned from the culture and remained as merely a lost horizon of possibility. In this respect, allegedly traditionalist musicals are just as synchronically relevant as maverick films that also suggest alternatives yet end tragically (*Bonnie and Clyde, Easy Rider*), ambiguously (*The Graduate*), or wistfully (*Alice's Restaurant*).

Interestingly enough, *Lost Horizon*, perhaps more concerned with allegory, focuses scant narrative attention on pondering how such a society is actually managed, just as the maverick film could rarely provide a workable alternative. *Fiddler on the Roof* showed tradition as social glue, *Camelot* posited a regent as effective for cohesion, while *1776* discussed the need for political compromise and legislative action. *Lost Horizon* portrays the ultimate fantasy of a perfect utopia since, beyond Shangri-La's hermetically sealed and basically inaccessible reality, few internal problems exist; only desire for the external world creates tension. The citizens seem to automatically understand their roles and implicitly follow the Lama's seemingly benevolent ideology without an obvious repressive state apparatus proving necessary (Althusser 144–47). This is the dreamiest variant on utopia—little labor is required to maintain this geographically sequestered paradise's governance, which is why spectators probably simultaneously disbelieve in Shangri-La's reality while understanding its necessary isolation from their own society and the need to punish those who leave its fragile, removed, perfectly functioning confines. The communal dwellers in *Easy Rider* at least are shown attempting to plant a crop, although the verdict is split between Captain America (Peter Fonda), the optimist, and the more cynical Billy (Dennis Hopper) over whether the kids will "make it."

Paint Your Wagon comes closest to providing a potentially workable utopia. In its boom-town paradise, a noisy, fractious society inundated with booze, whores (whom they have kidnapped), and gold potentially metaphorizes both the underlying hedonism of hippiedom and a proto-Vegas swinging resort community. The boisterous town meetings hearken back to the Continental Congress and rowdy Students for a Democratic Society (SDS) conventions and function as truly participatory electoral democracy. This is a society where, as Rumson explains, "rules are made up as we go along," which could exemplify the pioneer spirit, a countercultural ethos, or the aesthetic of spontaneity espoused by many avant-garde postwar artists, musicians, and writers (Belgrad 1–12).

The variant of desire and dissatisfaction that causes the community's literal collapse in *Paint Your Wagon* is not adultery, as in *Camelot*, but simply greed. The scene of the town literally sinking into the ground provides an unwitting summary of the underlying nature of the costly musical's timely demise. Rumson organizes a party to tunnel under the saloon and collect gold dust that has fallen through the floorboard, which causes the entire town to literally collapse into the mud in a truly spectacular scene. This calamitous spectacle not only delivers a standard lesson about greed, but has literal and metaphorical significance. This event suggests the financial collapse visited on the studios who built these types of elaborate sets for such expensive movies.

The film's production designer, John Truscott, had just worked with Logan on the costly, financially unsuccessful *Camelot*, and, using John Gregory Dunne's phrase, managed to "fail upward" (Dunne 98), successfully demanded access to "the truth of nature" through shooting on location. This resulted in filming forty-seven miles from the nearest town; the crew to need two hours a day to get to the set and Paramount had to pay $10,000 a day for road repair. The giant set itself cost $2.4

Figure 1.4. The entire town of "No Name City" collapses around Ben Rumson (Lee Marvin) as a result of greed in *Paint Your Wagon* (Joshua Logan, 1969).

million (Parrish 71–73). On the allegorical level, these often-bloated musicals' creators, like the miners, tried to recapture the surplus gold of earlier filmmakers whose search for El Dorado had produced financial gain. Instead, both the town and the genre collapsed. Not coincidentally, and as noted previously, *Paint Your Wagon* was panned by critics (Kael, *Deeper into Movies* 32–38; Ebert, "*Paint Your Wagon*") and disappointed at the box-office.

Ideologies of Form: Narrative Structure

Turning to narrative structure allows for analysis concerning adherence to classical principles in light of the indispensable work of Bordwell, Staiger, and Thompson. Many seemingly traditionalist musicals challenge ideologies of patriarchal monogamy, but follow the genre's canonical plot structure of detailing love, courtship, and potential roadblocks to romantic happiness. In contrast, causality, closure, and linearity often are problematized during this period while the signature musical numbers often proceed aberrantly. Once again, both the remnants of previous practice and alignment with innovation should be noted.

Causality, an obsessive hallmark of the classical paradigm, demands that one event logically lead to the next, motivated by the characters' attempts to reach specific goals (Bordwell, *Narration in the Fiction Film*, 157). Most traditionalist musicals follow this pattern. For instance, Fanny Brice's desire for stardom in *Funny Girl* results in a series of successes but creates discord in her relationship with Nicky. Of greater interest are films where plotting via ellipses replaces direct presentation of story information, or in which the film stops short of full narrative closure in the manner of maverick texts.

Camelot, for instance, is coherently told and the characters' behavior is clearly motivated but elides directly representing the period of Arthur and Guinevere's initial marital bliss, her adultery with Lancelot, and lessened love for the king. Instead, these events are discussed afterward by the characters. This sort of "focused gap" fulfills the classical cinema's demand for clarity by soliciting "exclusive and homogenous hypotheses" unlike the "diffused" gaps that never settle key enigmas of canonical art cinema, such as *L'Avventura* (Michelangelo Antonioni, 1960) (Bordwell, *Narration in the Fiction Film* 55, 193, 207). Nevertheless, this strategy may frustrate spectators demanding more obvious presentation of narrative events and, also contradicts the observation by Bordwell, Staiger, and Thompson that "narration shows the important events and skips the intervals between them" (Bordwell, Staiger, Thompson 44). Here dramatic and crucial story elements are not presented visually. Similarly, in *Funny Girl* the eighteen-month gap including Nicky's incarceration is ambiguously elided, but we can quickly guess that she has been working and he floundering. Linking the scenes by a montage or even a simple dissolve or fade to indicate time passing would follow typical classical narrational rules (Bordwell, Staiger, and Thompson 44).

In *Camelot*, despite Arthur and Lancelot inevitably becoming enemies, the specific act that leads to their mutual declaration of war is again not represented. The film ends immediately before military engagement, so the result of their battle is unknown, and neither side is obviously positioned as a likely victor in the way that Jefferson Smith presumably will be vindicated in Capra's *Mr. Smith Goes to Washington*. This sort of "permanent causal gap" is a hallmark of art cinema narration (Bordwell, *Narration in the Fiction Film*, 206). Camelot will dissolve and is already nostalgically mourned, but little else is certain. Granted, *The Sound of Music* has a similarly "open" ending where we only assume the Trapp family successfully escape Nazi-occupied Austria, but in *Camelot* the results of the battle are truly unknown. The only definite information given is that no matter who "wins," the great society is over. *The Sound of Music* also ends hopefully on a note of resolve and inspiration with the singing of "Climb Every Mountain," more in keeping with the generic paradigms of cheery resolution than the crepuscular denouement of *Camelot*, which resembles the period's traditionalist and maverick Westerns.

Fiddler on the Roof is similarly open-ended, although change has trumped tradition. The Jews leave Anatevka, but will their future be better? Many immigrants prospered in America, where Tevye and Lazar Wolf are headed. "On the other hand," to use Tevye's dialectical expression, their customs are lost, families are torn apart, and the twin specters of communist oppression and the Holocaust implicitly await.

Sweet Charity, like *Camelot*, ends inconclusively in its American version, with the title card "And she lived hopefully ever after" on the screen following Charity's morning greeting by hippies (including maverick icon Bud Cort), who literally give her flowers, flash the peace sign, and say "Love." The mood is upbeat but she is clearly traumatized and unsure. The indeterminacy is furthered as its European cut ends with Oscar and Charity reuniting. Therefore, causality is ambiguous, because his discovery of her past may or may not upset their wedding plans.

These putatively traditionalist musicals partake of less obvious presentation of story events that are still located within classical narrational paradigms described by Bordwell, yet they are more willing to have permanent causal gaps via open endings. Generic demands intersect with the traces of golden-era storytelling within an era where art cinema narrational strategies increasingly inflect film practice.

In contrast, causality is relentlessly, almost reflexively, mechanistic in the Broadway adaptation *How to Succeed in Business Without Really Trying* (David Swift, 1967), which gently spoofs the corporate world. Herein the titular book is followed rigorously by J. Pierpont Finch (Robert Morse) and explains exactly how to climb the ladder, and even presents contingency-based instructions such as for eliminating potential enemies. The tome's discourse is literalized through voice-overs issuing statements such as "By now you should have a job in the mail room!" Making narrative progression a literal series of precisely ordered, predictable steps may satirize classical plot structure's generic nature. In terms of classicism, though, this sort of self-consciousness is rarely used outside of the opening scenes as "narration becomes less self-conscious" (Bordwell, Staiger, and Thompson 27). Furthermore, unlike many texts that naturalize their story through foregrounding a particular, individually characterized protagonist's progress, this film reveals how any reader can "succeed in business without really trying." The climb is further simplified as the company Finch chooses seemingly produces nothing but a nonsensical product called "wickets" and is staffed by blasé employees who are either beneficiaries of nepotism and incompetent or spend the day ogling secretaries and taking coffee breaks.

Flashbacks are the classical system's only permissible nonlinear device, but are still fairly rare between 1917 and 1960, only present in fewer than 10 percent of the works in Bordwell, Staiger, and Thompson's statistical survey of the era (42–43). Few major Astaire–Rogers, Warner Brothers, or Freed-unit productions used this method. In contrast, *Doctor Doolittle*, *Camelot*, *Star!*, *Funny Girl*, and *On a Clear Day, You Can*

See Forever (Vincente Minnelli, 1970) all employ narratively significant flashbacks, but stick to the classical rule of confining them to expressions of a character's memory (Bordwell, Staiger, and Thompson) while scarcely using the sort of modular, alinear rescrambling of time prevalent in today's cinema after Tarantino's *Pulp Fiction* (1994) (Cameron 1). *Doctor Dolittle*'s narration uses flashbacks to convey back story when the doctor's friend (Anthony Newley) explains how Dolittle realized that his true vocation was caring for animals rather than humans. This analepsis is smoothly deployed, but unusual in a children's musical.

More notably, *Camelot*, *Star!*, and *Funny Girl* are basically told through extended flashbacks, which are not generally used to structure musicals because the device often produces a melancholic, nostalgic tone or deterministic foreboding as in film noir. In *Camelot*, for instance, Arthur glumly muses on his already lost kingdom, while in *Funny Girl* a sad, husbandless Fanny Brice recalls her triumphant rise and heartbreaking romance with Nicky. Melancholia and the inevitability of failure permeate both films. A great distance has been traversed from *Shall We Dance* or *On the Town*.

Star! uses temporality even more ambitiously through a framing device showing a fortyish Gertrude Lawrence watching and commenting on a cheery newsreel/docudrama about her career. Robert Wise, the editor of *Citizen Kane*, again uses nonlinear narration to reveal a famous person's life but sticks to one character's point of view. Periodically this screening halts for her ironic, uneuphemized comments concerning this prettified biography, which could either casts aspersions on the truthfulness of *Star!* itself or present Wise's film as a corrective to the newsreel.

These biographical recreations' distracting nature is amplified by their being shot in 1.33:1, black and white that jars reflexively against a widescreen and color visual register. Furthermore, the spectator might wonder whether these scenes consist of actual archival newsreel footage or are staged by Wise's crew. These questions hardly encourage engulfment in a realist narrative. The segments of the newsreel set in the 1910s and 1920s, before sound film, plausibly include intertitles and the actual Fox Movie Tone News logo and contain "documentary" visual tropes. The presence of Julie Andrews in the black-and-white footage is acceptable since she is the actress playing the older Lawrence, yet indicates that this too is a fictional recreation. Similarly, devices more reminiscent of Hollywood style than documentary form are included during the section depicting young Gertrude's childhood in working-class Clapham. For instance, a point-of-view shot from her perspective is included, yet it inherently represents the cameraman's vision in a nonfictional newsreel's mise-en-scène and not function as a classical Hollywood stylistic technique conveying a character's visual experiences, which is how Wise employs this device. Similarly, the improbability of a documentarian photographing an anonymous lower-class child's environment points out the scene as seemingly fictive even within the diegesis. Ultimately, each flashback is "seamlessly" transposed into the bulk of the film *Star!*, in which Andrews and other actors recreate Gertrude Lawrence's life. Nevertheless, this highly unclassical foregrounding of narrative structure and film style is unusual, especially in a supposedly reactionary and bloated musical. The film actually has a more "adventurous" narrative structure than more linear "progressive" texts such as *Bonnie and Clyde* or *Five Easy Pieces*.

Finally, a significant auteur, Vincente Minnelli, produced a text radically ambitious in using flashbacks to convey a dialectic between past and present. *On a Clear Day, You Can See Forever* stars Barbra Streisand as Daisy Gamble, a neurotic big-mouth (i.e., a caricature of her star persona) who asks the well-known psychiatrist Dr. Chabot (Yves Montand) to cure her cigarette addiction. When put under hypnosis, though, she regresses to a past life in Georgian England as Melinda Wayne-Tentries, a scandalous adulterer, accused spy, and high-society sexpot. During one scene, almost avant-garde in its radical time fragmentation—reminiscent of the Resnais/Duras linkage between past trauma and present memory in *Hiroshima, Mon Amour*—the narrative jolts back and forth between Melinda's two separate court trails and Daisy in Chabot's office. As the sequence builds, the shot length becomes about a quarter-second until step-printed superimpositions create multiple images of Streisand within each temporality. These, combined with the rapid cutting, literally blur past and present into a giddy frenzy. These two levels are distinguishable since Streisand alternates between a glamorous Cecil Beaton–begowned lady and vaguely modish frump. The film relentlessly employs this juxtaposition to raise questions concerning reincarnation and the nature of individuality and personality more typical of art cinema than Hollywood musicals. The film expresses the dialectic between a director attuned to formal experimentation, itself inflected by art cinema, and the genre's classical narration.

The most interesting and radical example of the genre's breakdown in classical practice, though, involves the failure or aberrance of its most characteristic element: the musical number. Certainly many of these productions feature recognizable set pieces with synchronized singing and dancing. For instance, Fosse's lively choreography in *Sweet Charity* or the athletic dance numbers by Michael Kidd in *Hello, Dolly!* are paradigmatic.

In contrast, many films discussed here are strangely eccentric. Beyond the dubious vocal stylings of performers such as Richard Harris and Vanessa Redgrave in *Camelot*, Clint Eastwood and Lee Marvin in *Paint Your Wagon*, or Peter O'Toole in both *Goodbye, Mr. Chips* and *Man of La Mancha*, something is genuinely awry with these movies' actual musical numbers. These nonsingers and nondancers were cast for their supposed box-office clout. Dubbed performers such as Natalie Wood in *West Side Story* or Audrey Hepburn in *My Fair Lady*, or actors with highly limited singing such as Rex Harrison in the latter, had been featured in financially successful Oscar winners. The making of *Paint Your Wagon* is instructive, because the producers not only saw Lee Marvin's popularity as valuable but hoped his "antiestablishment reputation would appear to the era's growing number of authority-hating younger moviegoers." Similarly, they courted rapidly rising star Clint Eastwood (who became dubious about his singing yet honored his commitment) by claiming numbers would be worked around his musical range (Parrish 69–70). Once again synchronic factors inevitably influence a production also viewed as reactionary by many.

Period reviews often attacked such deficiencies and helped create the genre's current low reputation. Among numerous negative reactions, a few examples from major critics will suffice. Pauline Kael refers to the musical numbers in *Star!* (one of the more competent and fluid entries here and actually featuring a musically gifted star) as "poorly staged and performed" and "anachronistically . . . in late-forties movie musical style" (Kael, *Going Steady*, 197). Vincent Canby's review of *Man of La Mancha* complains that the plot is "interrupted" by musical numbers (perhaps the harshest imaginable criticism considering the genre) and notes "There is something decidedly off-putting about an operetta without real singers in the leading roles." He also complains of shaky camera, which, "produces jiggly images that, on the huge movie screen, are almost seasick-making" while noting "tight close-ups" that make it "impossible to tell who is doing what to whom" (Canby, movie review, "*Man of La Mancha* Comes to Screen"). Finally, Roger Ebert's savaging of *Paint Your Wagon*, which he calls an "ordeal," states boldly that "Eastwood and Jean Seberg can't sing, and neither can Marvin" while commenting on the deafening, diegetically inappropriate "booming" and "enormous" male chorus accompanying Eastwood: "There's no feeling that this might be a guy in the forest, singing a song" (Ebert, "*Paint Your Wagon*"). Even when giving *Goodbye, Mr. Chips* one of its few basically positive reviews, Ebert comments approvingly that director Herb Ross "hasn't let the songs intrude . . ." as "there's not a really first-rate song in the show" (Ebert, *Goodbye, Mr. Chips*). These accounts barely scratch the surface of a highly dismissive discourse.

In terms of briefly cataloging such aberrance, many musical numbers within this corpus do not feature directly synchronized lip movements but function as interior monologues, as when Mr. Chips muses affectionately about his students or, during a montage of scenic Pompeian ruins in long shot, Bridges (Petula Clark) sings in voice-over while they stroll. These scenes lack dancing or any direct revelation that the stars actually recorded their vocal parts. In *The Great Waltz* a singing narrator voices the character's emotions and also furthers the story by briefly summarizing narrative developments. *Sweet Charity*, despite two competent singers, also includes interior soliloquies. Are such instances even musical numbers, or are they musicalized monologue and montage sequences? *Paint Your Wagon* and *Song of Norway* (Andrew L. Stone, 1970) include scenes where a group supposedly sings, but since they include both long shots and close-ups that avoid showing faces, the sound, not clearly synchronized with lip movements, makes it clear that a professional chorus was used, as noted by Ebert ("*Paint Your Wagon*").

Prior musicals' inherent fakery was partially canceled out by knowledge that the stars were genuinely talented singers and dancers. In contrast, the title song to *Paint Your Wagon* about wandering and prospecting is "sung" by a group of wagon-riding prospectors in a long shot. During a later scene, at a muddy celebration dance after striking gold, the camera is far enough away to render invisible the synchronization of lips and singing. In fact, this scene is so quickly edited, breaking the general rule of using long takes in medium or long shot (to show the performer's entire body) and filled with foot fetishizing close-ups that it falls scandalously short of being a fluid, competently realized musical number. Similarly, James Parrish comments that "Many songs are performed in voice-over during visual montages or with the singer in long shots. (During close-ups it is very obvious that the vocals were recorded separately on a sound stage or dubbed in as with Seberg's numbers" (Parrish 78). Considering the ludic bliss of hearing a great singer who the viewer "knows" is actually singing or witnessing a jubilant dancer's trained, expressive body, these numbers seem bizarre. Furthermore, the genre's true utopian dimensions, per Dyer, reside in the feelings it "embodies" (Dyer 177), this word itself implying a physicality scandalously lacking in many of the period's super-musicals. These numbers' staging also points to a necessary discussion of stylistic concerns.

Narrative structure in these traditionalist musicals synchronically yet often mildly echoes art-cinema paradigms in terms of closure. The mode's use of flashbacks, though, suggests the sort of "intensified continuity" discussed by David Bordwell as partly developed during the 1960s, in which a classical device is amplified yet still abets narrative coherence and relates to big-budget movie practices of the golden age (Bordwell, *The Way Hollywood Tells It*, 121–38, 141–47). The musical numbers are of poor quality, which led critics to judge them harshly. The lack of singing ability relates to the industrial pressure to deliver big stars as part of the intrageneric trend of producing super-musicals in the wake of *The Sound of Music*.

Ideologies of Form: Style

The movies of the Hollywood Renaissance era often employed a veritable Pandora's box of new formal devices. Some of these devices involved technological innovation, others simply revived neglected practices. These methods included use of zoom and telephoto lenses, freeze frames, slow motion, time-lapse photography, split-screen processes, and a variety of fast, disruptive, nontransparent editing techniques. Many of these methods broke with the classical Hollywood paradigm of stylistic invisibility, and many are covered within Bordwell's category of "intensified continuity" (Bordwell, *The Way Hollywood Tells It* 119–21). The supposedly traditionalist musical, already in a genre given to formal excess, gleefully adopted these devices. The psychedelic aesthetic of "abstraction and distortion," elegantly characterized by Jonathan Harris as "flattening and stretching the image of things, an attenuated sinuosity of pattern and ornament, a chromatic overkill of acute contrasts and overexposures," is particularly appropriate for locating these films in the alleged Aquarian era (Grunenberg and Harris 15). Beyond their mere presence, what possible meaning or metaphorical value vis-à-vis American society (a question partially addressed by invoking psychedelia) and its discourses during this period can be construed from these techniques' employment? In other words, using Jameson's term, what could be their "ideology of form?" (Jameson 76–77). This question will serve to avoid simply cataloging the traditionalist musical's usage of the period's characteristic, often formally innovative, stylistic devices.

The zoom lens currently functions as the Hollywood Renaissance's quintessential stylistic signifier; it is rarely used in fiction films unless to satirize the period's style. Zooms shift quickly from long shot to close-up (or vice versa) without moving the camera (or changing depth and perspective). The lens's use eliminates the time and effort required to set up tracks and thus can simply function as a form of "intensified continuity" if overused (Bordwell, *The Way Hollywood Tells It* 144), and may also facilitate an improvisational style via an unobtrusive, distant recording presence. Employed subtly, the device has merits but the jarring speed and constant use of zooms soon became excessive, defying the industry's preference for unobtrusive style.

Turning to the traditionalist musical, many examples of this device are noticeable. In *Sweet Charity*, when the Star (Ricardo Montalban) and Charity enter a swinging disco, zooms are fluidly synchronized to music and narrativized as simulations of the shocked, curious looks of various patrons wondering about her identity. Similarly, such a shot conveys Oscar Lindquist's surprise at their bridal shower when he first sees Charity's tattoo and then watches the club's seedy male manager casually slap her ass. The techniques show this sheltered man's violent surprise about the carnal and vulgar. Fosse, though, is not content with such relatively classical usages and also attempts bravura effects. In a number where Charity roams New York, he uses zooms and rack focus pulling, and while the image is unfocused, cuts to the next shot, creating an effect like a dissolve. This exemplifies a highly noticeable style and conveys both energy (through camera movement) and disorientation (through blurring). The effect is hazy and yet mobile, fluid but energetic, and quite effectively conveys a specific 1960s zeitgeist of druggy giddiness.

Most of these shots end on Charity's body, which is predictable in classical Hollywood, the zoom's voyeuristic/fetishistic potential being used to sexualize women. In *Thoroughly Modern Millie*, *Hello, Dolly!*, and *On a Clear Day, You Can See Forever* the device also highlights the lead actress's anatomy. The last-mentioned film is interesting because zooming is combined with shot-reverse shot patterning, in one of Daisy's repressed memories, to show Melinda and Robert's mutual gazes as the camera moves in simultaneously on both characters. Minnelli's montage grants each a point-of-view shot, and thus presumed subjective equality, which is unusual in an often-patriarchal visual economy, but Melinda is still the more objectified, eroticized figure; she is shown placing a champagne glass suggestively against her bosom. The scene's classicism also holds as the moment is narrativized since each is actually intently watching the other in a public flirtation, which justifies the excessive point-of-view editing and camera movement.

The telephoto lens also was used consistently during the Hollywood Renaissance. The device flattens out space and creates a limited depth of field. It produces a sharp, clear image of narratively crucial objects or persons, but surroundings are rendered fuzzy and unfocused. This haziness is typical of the "flattening" and "distorting" of the psychedelic aesthetic described by Jonathan Harris (Grunenberg and Harris, 15). The opening of *Finian's Rainbow* provides a beautiful example, furthermore, of how telephoto composition can be allied to and evince both traditionalist and maverick qualities. First, Petula Clark (herself a pop and rock hybrid with cross-generational appeal) is heard singing "Look to the Rainbow" (a Broadway-derived song) and shown with Fred Astaire (ostensibly a hero of the older viewer) walking (almost literally) across American landmarks such as Monument Valley and the Golden Gate Bridge. The scene's initial shot, though, is of flowers and bees in sharp, telephoto focus against a hazy background. The potential reference to the period's flower-power aesthetic, the multiculturalist connotations of rainbows, and the libidinal associations of the insect's mating rituals bestows a certain Aquariana on such a seemingly patriotic scene within a traditional genre.

Other films employ the device more conventionally. For instance, *Goodbye, Mr. Chips* uses telephoto lenses to keep Chips in focus while only suggesting the visual background of Roman ruins, whereas using a wide-angle lens would deny him narratively demanded compositional centrality. Similarly, some directors avoid crowding and distracting actors during close-ups or long takes. For instance, Joshua Logan employs a telephoto on Clint Eastwood singing "I Still See Elisa" in *Paint Your Wagon*.

If the above-mentioned lenses created a mobile and vivid, enlarged visuality, other devices froze and stopped time to allow for its analysis. Freeze framings and slow motion have existed since silent cinema but were used sparingly until the late 1960s. As an ebullient, countercultural expression, what better than to expand vision and simultaneously freeze, capture, and endlessly ogle such hallucinogenic imagery? In contrast, the period's more reactionary productions could employ these devices to literally stop progress or time itself, which recalls Senator Rawkus's slogan in *Finian's Rainbow* of "forward to the past." A dialectic again exists between these two possibilities.

Figure 1.5. Telephoto composition of an unlikely musical performer—Clint Eastwood in *Paint Your Wagon* (Joshua Logan, 1969).

The credit sequences of two Barbra Streisand vehicles exhibit mixed conservative and progressive valences. During the titles of *Funny Girl,* a series of nostalgic shots depicting old New York's ethnic, lower East Side crowded with immigrants is projected and then frozen into a stylized version tinted with bright, Day-Glo psychedelic colors. Freezing and thus commemorating images of the past is archetypically conservative and nostalgic. These are not images of small-town USA, though, or similar to the still photograph of a suburban street that comes to life at the start of *Meet Me in St. Louis* (Vincente Minnelli, 1944). Instead the credits depict the impoverished dwellings of the ethnic "others" perennially demonized by reactionary politicians. Furthermore, the image's use of Day-Glo pinks, greens, and oranges suggests the flower-power and psychedelic aesthetic.

Hello, Dolly! presents a slightly earlier, turn-of-the-century New York and also features a Jewish main character. In contradistinction to *Funny Girl,* the images become increasingly "realistic," progressing from black-and-white stills to color-tinted slides and then changing into standard moving frames. This evolution almost parallels the Bazinian and teleological account of motion pictures technology's ascension to greater realism (Bazin 23–40). Despite this movement, the image's frozen quality allows delectation of a quaint, presumably harmless past where, in the film's narrative, transgression involves eating in a restaurant without enough money to pay the check, not robbing banks or blowing up ROTC buildings.

Psychedelic colors, used as both freeze frames and over moving images, are strangely employed in *The Great Waltz* during a montage sequence representing the happy marriage of Johann Strauss, Jr. (Horst Bucholtz), and his wife (Mary Costa). Gaudy tints and negative-image effects are produced by the use of different color filters in the process of making dupe negatives, similar to the pioneering special effects of the Stargate sequence from Kubrick's *2001: A Space Odyssey* (Agel 150). These images are predominantly a vibrant yellow-green with bright red as a secondary shade. Other colors, particularly any blue or purple tinges, are removed, producing an almost monochromatic look. The film's titular waltz is the "Beautiful Blue Danube" used famously by Kubrick for the same studio four years earlier. A highly classical and anachronistic box-office disaster (returns of only $1.65 million) mostly issuing from the old-fashioned school of composer biopics, it manages to employ the same psychedelic effect as the most maverick of visionary science fiction productions ("Big Rental Films of 1973").

Once again, Bob Fosse's *Sweet Charity* takes stylistic innovation to an extreme. This film, like *Funny Girl,* begins with pink-and-blue-tinted freeze frames under the credits, albeit of contemporary New York. Later, three scenes function innovatively as a synthesis of photography or slide shows with the moving picture. The first presents Charity pensively strolling around town, the second her date with Oscar at the Museum of Modern Art, and the third, which also involves black-and-white imagery, their "bridal party" at the Dime-a-Dance hall. These are related intertextually with photography, particularly the glossy, narrativized spreads of fashion magazines such as *Vogue* or even the seedier monochrome exposures of grotesquery associated with Diane Arbus. These images commemorate the fashionable/sleazy present of a teeming Manhattan, not a halcyonic past as with the Streisand vehicles. Furthermore, by the sequences invoking art photography, and with one occurring in a museum, cinema is linked to a "higher" cultural tradition. This speaks to maverick filmmakers' desire to bestow aesthetic legitimacy on a popular medium.

Slow motion also highlights images or moments yet retains movement and hence is specifically "cinematic." Siegfried Kracauer described how this device (as well as fast motion) could show "movements of so transitory a nature that they would be imperceptible were it not for[these] cinematic techniques" (Kracauer 308). Fosse's *Sweet Charity* employs this technique in perhaps the era's most easily satirizable type of scene: the lyrical romantic montage showing an amorous couple behaving playfully. Charity and Oscar canter gaily, albeit through a parking garage, holding hands and skipping. While using traditionally sentimental representation, the scene celebrates love between a borderline whore and a square john in a contemporary urban world, not the squeaky-clean couplings of virginal naïfs in *Hello, Dolly!* or *The Song of Norway* amid a Disneyesque kitsch utopia.

In *Fiddler on the Roof* this technique is employed ambiguously, in a scene where Tevye imagines his daughter Hara and her gentile lover Fiyetko dancing in slow motion. He sees not an actual nostalgized moment, but a fantasy in which he accepts their marriage. This reverie ends abruptly with his refusal to sanction their nuptials, which already have occurred. He may try to synthesize change into his vision of paternal authority and Jewish purity, but realizes this dialectic is impossible (hence the fantastic nature of slow motion).

Camelot also employs slow motion to valorize a possible Aquarian-age utopia during the "Lusty Month of May" number and particularly in flashbacks to Guinevere and Lancelot's adultery where they are shown swimming or when she is lit softly, hair gently wind-swept, as he enters her chamber. Sentimentalized nostalgia (a conservative tendency) blends with celebration of the adultery (scarcely a traditional position) that ruins a countercultural paradise. Therefore, a retrospective yearning for a lost utopia mixes with commemorating (and romanticizing) the actual event that caused its destruction. The inherent ideological confusion of such texts is clearly visible in this example of narrative incoherence that celebrates adultery, a tendency also germane to the naughty-sex comedy, while decrying the destructive possibilities of such permissiveness.

In contrast to the aforementioned techniques, time-lapse photography speeds the image dramatically but without the comic effect of normal fast-motion. Again, floral imagery is favored. The precredit sequence of *On a Clear Day, You Can See Forever* shows flowers sprouting rapidly without any clear reason for this miracle. Eventually the cause is revealed—Daisy (her name is significant) uses telepathy to speed up their growth. The rapid images again suggest an enhanced, irrealist visuality characteristic of the period's psychedelic aesthetic.

Both superimpositions and the infrequently used split-screen device fall somewhere between camera techniques and the editing each inherently eschews. These effects date back to the silent era, but were deployed sparingly until the 1960s. In fact, the wide-screen processes of the 1950s stressed a large and wide but whole image, fostering realism through grandiose size and by filling up the spectator's peripheral vision, not encouraging image fragmentation. Nevertheless, some musicals (per the genre's reflexivity), such as *It's Always Fair Weather* (Gene Kelly and Stanley Donen, 1955), broke the rule. Two films from 1968—*The Thomas Crown Affair* (Norman Jewison) and *The Boston Strangler* (Richard Fleischer)—creatively and influentially used split screens. The device's apotheosis in theatrical movie production occurs in the multipanel compositions in *Woodstock* (Michael Wadleigh, 1970).

Superimpositions suggest plenitude as two images are present simultaneously. *On a Clear Day, You Can See Forever* ends with Streisand singing the title song, which describes the clarity of ESP, while superimposed against a cloud-laden orange sunset as she stretches out her arms and sustains its last words, "ever more." Daisy has already been associated with the Eastern belief in reincarnation, mirroring the popularity of non-Western thought in the counterculture. This linkage is furthered by a scene where students, dressed in hippie garb, protest disciplinary action against Professor Chabot for believing and announcing her stories of prior existence, thus validating a "fringe" position in the eyes of the conservative administration. Daisy also admits to being an addict, invoking fear of youth and drug abuse despite her addiction being to nicotine. She is unemployed (but attends college classes), grows flowers, has psychic powers, and consorts with a sitar-wielding brother-in-law, Thad (Jack Nicholson, his mere presence suggesting the maverick tradition). Her attempt to conform, by marrying the quintessential Organization Man, Warren (Larry Blyden), fails dramatically. Daisy Gamble is a constellation of countercultural character traits and ultimately ascends from frump to sky-piloting psychic in the final, hallucinatory image. Is love necessary with the ability to both regress to a past life and hold the cosmos in one's palms?

Fiddler on the Roof uses superimpositions more conservatively. During the Sabbath sequence, Tevye's image literally dominates the entire village. This scene celebrates religious tradition, but could also represent his primacy over the town as its narrator and representative, or simply inscribes the character in its status-quo culture. Either way, the film's hero/protagonist represents convention just as the song "Tradition" functions throughout as his musical leitmotif.

The more outré split-screen process was used less frequently because it creates a significant degree of reflexivity in a genre already known for artifice. As this device is potentially radical, it requires narrativization as in *How to Succeed in Business Without Really Trying*, when Mr. Bigley (Rudy Vallee) is shown talking on the phone and then the frame slides over simply to reveal his wife on the other end of the line. The method is only mentioned as a marker of the period's stylistic eccentricities, which generally invaded the musical's oft-experimental or artificial formal paradigms.

The Hollywood Renaissance period witnessed a variety of obtrusive and radical editing techniques, often imitative of European art cinema. They were used in both allegedly maverick and traditionalist films. The late 1960s were known for a decrease in the average shot length, while very briskly cut individual sequences began to flourish (Salt 345). Two key "progressive" films—*Bonnie and Clyde* and *The Wild Bunch*—used fast cuts to graphically, jarringly enhance gory bloodshed. The musical spectacle, perhaps an unexpected locus for this technique, also witnessed the manifestation and employment of rapid montage.

Sweet Charity, as perhaps expected, indulges in some quick-cut sequences such as the flashy discotheque scene mentioned above. As with the use of the zoom lens, these could be narratively justified as simulating the surprised reactions of patrons to a lowly dime-a-dance girl accompanying a big star, plus they are smoothed over by synchronization to music. In contrast, the scene discussed earlier with focus pulled to create a blurry image and edits occurring during these moments is more aberrant as not character-focalized, yet still fits within the period's psychedelic, fuzzy, flattened aesthetic. Nevertheless, Fosse himself later commented that "I guess I had too many cinematic tricks in it. I was trying to be kind of flashy" (Gottfried 197). In fact, when preparing for *Cabaret*, Fosse's desire to reteam with cinematographer Robert Surtees, who had just been credited as bringing a "new" look to Nichols's *The*

Graduate, was deemed inadvisable by his new producers. They felt that he would "symbolize everything that had gone wrong with *Sweet Charity*—the zooming, the freeze frames, the overshooting, the overspending" (Gottfried 206).

More jarring are quick cuts within "period" films, especially Logan's *Camelot*, where an idyllic tone, not a jarring mood, is expected. For instance, a rapid transition to Arthur combined with a track-in on him occurs as he sits under a tree musing on the knight's using "might for right," not assuming that "might is right," an ideologically vague statement that even a cold warrior might find acceptable. Following this, a quick edit reveals him in a stable proposing this idea. Granted that a fevered formal exuberance may appropriately convey his thoughts and ideas, such a violent montage sits uneasily during scenes ostensibly promoting pacifism. Similarly, the Dionysian "Lusty Month of May" number contains fast cuts transitioning from general dancing to a medium shot of Guinevere surrounded by revelers to a close-up of her, and then to a montage of various lovers carousing and kissing. The abruptness of these shots, combined with their awkward deployment, obtrusively dampens the amorous mood.

Many other musicals of the period function similarly because their self-conscious cutting seems narratively inappropriate. One apt example involves an oddly realized scene from *1776* showing Richard Henry Lee of Virginia being dispatched by horse to secure his state's approval of the Declaration of Independence. Nine separate, briefly held shots convey nothing more than his mounting a horse and riding away. One take simply shows his foot entering the stirrup before cutting to a medium shot of him halfway up the animal's side. The presence of a horse plus the fragmented fetishism of these shots' presentation of a simple action is more reminiscent of Muybridge than classical editing's efficient conveyance of narrative information.

The most aberrant use of fast cutting in this genre, though, is when it destroys the rhythm of musical numbers, as in *Paint Your Wagon* during the awkward staging of the miners' celebratory dance. Conventionally, a stylistic plan of long shots and long takes would be employed and the entire sequence could be easily completed with fewer than five cuts (while Blake Edwards or Minnelli might avoid editing completely). In contrast, this scene is rapidly cut, yet without rhythm, and the dancers' grace or physical presence are not communicated. Instead, a fragmented series, containing many almost fetishistic close-ups of feet, is cut to non-synchronized singing.

Disorienting results are also produced when films break actual editing "rules." Coppola's direction in *Finian's Rainbow* provides a textbook case of subverting classical montage paradigms that, as a film-school graduate and Roger Corman protégé, he obviously knew and would employ appropriately later in his career. For instance, during the "Old Devil Moon" number where Faron and Woody cavort through the woods and sing of their mutual enchantment, the camera constantly crosses the 180-degree line. This could be narratively motivated as representing their amorous disorientation and as an enhancement of the forest's mystical qualities, or dismissed as attention-getting in disrupting classical principles.

The film's strangest editing effect, though, occurs during the song "Woody's Coming," in which the titular town hero's train journey is depicted by three sped-up forward tracks through a passenger car, which are edited together to suggest one very long moving shot. Woody is in different positions in each—first on the left aisle with guitar, then on the right asleep, and then at the compartment's back door—hence viewers only realize that separate temporalities are being conveyed if they are attentively focused on Woody amid this fast-motion camera movement with its blurred, shaky image, and also if they note the sequence's three almost invisible cuts. This device could enhance the train's momentum while depicting different stages of his journey, but such a shot is usually subjectivized as character vision, whereas this movement could only represent a supernatural entity's point of view, an unlikely possibility even in a narrative about leprechauns and magical pots o' gold under rainbows. This stylistically eccentric moment equals the formal radicalism of any film during this period.

Singularly aberrant editing choices also occur in *Fiddler on the Roof*, helmed by Norman Jewison, who used split screens excessively in *The Thomas Crown Affair* and later directed a rock musical—*Jesus Christ Superstar* (1973). I've discussed the unusual cutting revealing Tevye suddenly many feet away from his prior position while monologuing with himself over nuptial issues. Another scene dealing with the subject of matrimony also has a noticeably odd montage strategy, again involving freeze frames. This occurs when Tevye ponders whether to approve his oldest daughter, Tzeitel's, marriage to Lazar Wolf. At this point, a brief shot of about a second shows Lazar's eyes widening in anticipation, in close-up, until the image freezes for about another second. A pattern follows of cutting between Tevye in motion deliberating and still images of Lazar literally frozen in suspense. Finally, approval is granted and the circle closes as the freeze frame of Wolf is reanimated and his eyes pop open in a quick, one-second reaction. Again, a narrative event—expression of shock—motivates the cut, but the effect is strangely overt (like the surprised discotheque patrons in *Sweet Charity*) and unusual in a period film, where it overwhelms any narrative function like a cup of mushroom gravy garnishing an after-dinner mint. Even a conservative text within a moribund genre enjoys great stylistic freedom and evinces nonclassical form.

∼

The narrative structures and stylistic tendencies of these traditionalist musicals show the complex, uneasy mixture of classical and progressive dimensions, which problematizes a construction based on the dichotomy between these and maverick texts. Instead, these films mixed new and old within the confines of a genre, at the mercy of economic factors, and at times dependent on the whims of auteurs. Discussion of their content, as noted, revealed the use of allegory. After all, with a few exceptions, Hollywood Renaissance–era musicals seem obsessed with the past, whereas many classical-era musicals had contemporary settings. *Many* maverick films used history allegorically, as in *The Wild Bunch* or *Bonnie and Clyde*, while *almost all* traditionalist musicals, besides *Sweet Charity* and *On a Clear Day You Can See Forever*, are period pieces using their temporal setting as a metaphor for then-contemporary questions. Nevertheless, timely discourses and progressive positions involving marriage, women's rights, sexuality, minority struggles for empowerment, society, and government are easily spotted and raise issues that maverick films often ignore, particularly feminist and civil rights struggles. War films also rely on allegory to discuss pressing social, cultural, and political concerns while hewing much closer to classical precedent in terms of narrative structure and style than the spectacular musical.

2

War Spectacles

Discussing the period's other significant form of spectacular production, the World War II combat movie, requires a different method. Noting their stylistic qualities is less illuminating, with occasional exceptions, because this corpus proves less innovative and more obdurately classical. A few main themes conveyed via narrative or its structuring provide the most fruitful means of discussing these films. In particular, conflicting or ambivalent contemporary societal attitudes toward the value and ideals of armed conflict in general, and both past and present U.S. military efforts, are relevant to show how the genre relates both to the patriotic and conservative tone of earlier war films while reflecting then-current antimilitaristic attitudes. Richard Slotkin and others often describe the era's Westerns as metaphors for the Vietnam War, but films portraying World War II are also readable through this allegorical framework. Furthermore, a strong antiauthoritarian tendency, reflecting countercultural attitudes partially forged to express opposition to this so-called "police action," and to institutions such as the army, is present in many combat movies of the period. How did a typically patriotic genre respond to the hostility, alienation, fatigue, or, at best, ambivalence of many Americans toward war, the military, and authority?

Two key subgenres of the World War II combat film existed during this period. The first includes spectacular battle productions detailing an elaborate engagement or, as with *Patton* (Franklin J. Schaffner, 1970), a series of conflicts. The mold-casting forebear is *The Longest Day* (Ken Annakin, Andrew Marton, and Bernhard Wicki, 1962*)*. The second tendency presents a small combat unit, often composed of "misfits," who undertake an often underhanded, murderous, quasi-official guerrilla raid on the enemy. The undeniable prototype here is Robert Aldrich's hugely successful *The Dirty Dozen* (1967), which spawned imitators and allowed the director to purchase his own studio ("Big Rental Films of 1967"). Although the film itself is too much a maverick text for discussion, it influenced less clearly innovative productions. Furthermore, two significant war films fitting into neither subgenre—John Wayne and Ray Kellogg's *The Green Berets* (1968) and *Ice Station Zebra* (John Sturges, 1968)—and dealing with different historical periods require discussion.

Robert Altman's maverick classic *M*A*S*H* would provide a seeming foil to these productions, particularly through seeming more directly attuned to the current conflict in Vietnam than even *The Green Berets*. Yet it still functions within the realm of allegory as do most supposedly traditionalist war movies of the era. Certainly, the film's innovative revival of Hawksian overlapping dialogue combined with zoom lensing, constantly moving camera, and the often washed-out look created the director's signature style, which varies from classical paradigms. The narrative structure is also loose and episodic in art-cinema fashion with climactic moments occurring almost as afterthoughts. On the surface, it is a seemingly biting condemnation of military pomp and bureaucracy; however, Altman's misogyny and sexual objectification of women harkens back to the worst qualities of classical cinema now allowed direct, frank presentation.

The Big Picture

The battle spectacular is the more conventional subgenre and somewhat conforms to earlier World War II films' representation of significant military engagements such as Pearl Harbor (*Tora! Tora! Tora!*, Richard Fleischer, Toshio Masuda, and Kinji Fukasaku, 1970) and the battle at Remagen Bridge (*The Bridge at Remagen*, John Guillermin, 1969). Within this narrative framework these texts are either supportive, critical, or, most often, ambivalent toward the efficacy of both war and the American military.

A key distinction of these films is that many criticize the U.S. Army and avoid glorifying combat in the manner of earlier flag-wavers such as Alan Dwan's *Sands of Iwo Jima* (1949). Complicating the maverick-traditionalist dialectic, these generally conservative productions, working within a patriotic and ideologically complicit genre, are often synchronically attuned to the period's progressive discourses and attitudes.

Nevertheless, *Tora! Tora! Tora!* and *Patton* most resemble the typical pejorative depiction of an industry bestowing lavish budgets on old-fashioned material hewing to generic paradigms and require discussion partly to provide contrast with more innovative World War II narratives.

Both were released in 1970 by Twentieth Century Fox, which had produced *The Longest Day*, on the heels of *Doctor Dolittle*, *Star!*, and *Hello, Dolly!*. *Patton* was one of the last in the sixteen-year continuum of American films shot completely on 65mm film. *Tora! Tora! Tora!* was eventually only "blown up" to 70mm for theatrical projection, although initially intended as a true 70mm roadshow production (*Tora! Tora! Tora!*: For the Crew 1). A further indication of its massive budget comes from this folder given to crew members stating "For the first time to my knowledge we will have two separate first unit production companies functioning on the same film" (*Tora! Tora! Tora!* 3). This referred to a Japanese unit originally to be directed by Akira Kurosawa who was replaced by two other directors—Toshio Masuda and Kinji Fukasaku. These films were not flops, in fact both were on *Variety*'s annual Top 10 grossing films list with *Patton* placing higher, but like many super-musicals neither was hugely profitable since they were very costly (Cook 183).

Interestingly, both *Patton* and *Tora! Tora! Tora!* also possess an emotional distance. They represent the elite, perhaps old-guard, perspective on war with few obvious identificatory moments for direct spectatorial identification. This chilliness is potentially readable as an innovative (or perhaps just misguided) development in the genre, which could even, in a perverse application of Brecht, alienate viewers into more carefully attending to the films' ideological stakes since they were detached from emotional involvement. In contrast, these productions most likely represent an out-of-touch industry more comfortable focusing on history through the prism of authority and lacking the energy required to create complex, vivid, empathetic depictions of average soldiers as in classic World War II combat movies. Generic development is usually linked with ideological progressivism. One assumes that a mode becomes more liberal, enlightened, and relevant partly through mirroring societal changes. What about films that are innovative in terms of their genre yet out of touch with their contemporary historical background? War movies with a lofty perspective had existed previously (Abel Gance's *Napoleon*, 1927; *Command Decision*, Sam Wood, 1948), but the conventional Hollywood combat narrative usually eschewed this tendency. These films break the rules yet hardly in the manner of maverick war narratives such as *M*A*S*H* or *Catch-22* (Mike Nichols, 1970). The traditions they violate might actually have allowed these movies more resonance with the supposedly nonconformist motion picture audience of 1970.

Tora! Tora! Tora!, the most resolutely old-fashioned of these two films, mostly hews to the dominant critical line about Hollywood's obliviousness leading to irrelevance and the needed countermeasures of maverick filmmakers. This super-production includes a host of generic clichés.

For instance, it boasts an all-star cast (E. G. Marshall, Martin Balsam, James Whitmore), detailed battle scenes, and the macho, technicist discourse beloved of war buffs such as "The lower deck aft's flooded and we're listing eight degrees" and the response: "Well counterflood! Dammit! Counterflood!" Printed titles introduce major characters by name and rank to bolster the facticity enjoyed by armchair military historians seeking "realism" and "accuracy."

Despite these qualities, *Tora! Tora! Tora!* seems deviant compared to *The Longest Day*. The latter featured genuine stars (John Wayne, Henry Fonda, Robert Mitchum), humor, emotion, and character development rather than a procession of data and one-dimensional, interchangeable figures advancing toward the film's raison d'être: a costly, spectacular recreation of the Japanese surprise attack on Pearl Harbor using real battleships. Perhaps this lack of feeling mirrors many contemporary spectators' weariness with actual U.S. military engagements and their cinematic representation. Furthermore, while *The Longest Day* ends with triumph, how much energy can be summoned when a narrative's climax involves the slaughter of unprepared sailors? Devoting one-third of its running time to the Japanese perspective, though, positively distinguishes *Tora! Tora! Tora!* from the genre's paradigms and suggests a more even-handed, less jingoistic consciousness in keeping with the era's more enlightened attitudes toward nationalism and race. Ironically, this distancing framing also diffuses the admittedly racist, but emotionally engaged, spectatorial identification of Dwan's film or Howard Hawks's *Air Force* (1943), where a bomber crew jubilantly downs enemy planes and sinks battleships. The film does commence with a Japanese officer claiming a sleeping giant has been awakened, to remind viewers that the United States would ultimately strike back and triumph. Nevertheless, the film's narrative structure builds to the tragic loss of American troops, weaponry, ships, and planes.

Certain of the era's progressive discourses also inflect *Patton*, yet the film is uniquely old-fashioned in both presenting a series of unambiguous U.S. military victories and showing these as righteous actions. From the beginning, where Patton's exciting exhortations set a bellicose tone, through a series of successful battles, little doubt exists about the war's outcome or the moral superiority of Allied forces.

Nevertheless, as with *Tora! Tora! Tora!*, viewer identification is potentially weakened. The film's famous first scene with the general in front of a gigantic American flag occurs in an imaginary, utopian space where he addresses an unseen, unheard audience. His speech seems an idealized distillation, perhaps occurring on another plane of existence, a militarist utopia, of an accumulation of similar pep talks, not an actual address

Figure 2.1. General Patton (George C. Scott) addresses a utopian audience in *Patton* (Franklin J. Schaffner, 1970).

to a specific group of soldiers. This stylization renders his discourse as an example of jingoistic patriotic bellicosity, not as actual incitement of either inter- or extra-diegetic spectatorial fervor in the manner of other rallying moment's functioning in paradigmatic World War II films. In contrast, Patton does directly address the spectator by looking into the camera and saying things such as "When you look into a puddle of goo that was your best friend's face, you'll know what to do."

Furthermore, the movie frames victory by creating (limited) identification only with a specific character—General George S. Patton, Jr.—who disobeyed orders, made controversial public statements, and most notoriously, slapped a shell-shocked soldier whom he accused of malingering. In other words, only through the figure of a semirebel and poet who believes himself reincarnated from past military figures, not the modest figure of Omar Bradley (Karl Malden, an actor incapable of suggesting glamour or revolt) or via the representation of enlisted men, can the audience glory in America's victories. In one sense, his nonconformism resonates with characters such as Hawkeye and Trapper in *M*A*S*H*. On the other hand, a paradigmatic World War II narrative creates an ethnically and economically diverse platoon whose development as a cohesive fighting unit provides the viewer with a surrogate for vicarious identification. Patton is clearly an authority figure approached at a distance with respectful adoration.

The film concludes with Patton's commission revoked, which prompts his recollection of glory's fleeting nature, whereas the unspoken denouement of more paradigmatic war productions is to translate triumph into a domestic utopia when brave soldiers, similar to the viewer, return to America. Patton, in contrast, simply rides off into the mountains and in reality died only months later. The final image shows a windmill, which suggests the general's dreamy, anachronistic, quixotic nature. The audience can idolize but not empathize. The downbeat tone of the scene, as with the conclusion of *Tora! Tora! Tora!*, is again related to the bleak endings of many maverick productions.

General Patton is further removed from the average viewer since he is representative of the elite. The Germans note that he is the wealthiest American officer, while he prominently employs a faithful black servant (James Edwards). The film seemingly endorses his solitary, detached regency as the soldiers he commands are rarely shown unless interacting with him, except for one telling, seemingly populist-tinged, scene where an unidentified soldier, referring to the general's nickname, declares "Our blood, his guts." This concisely reveals that, unlike an infantryman, this eccentric rebel is relatively immune from dying in battle.

∽

Tora! Tora! Tora! and *Patton* may deviate from classical paradigms encouraging viewer identification, but each resides on the genre's conservative end via a detached, authoritarian perspective dissonant from the concerns of many then-contemporary spectators. In contrast, combat films focusing on lower-ranking officers and infantrymen are less positive, more questioning, in representing the American military, although more classical through allowing greater spectatorial empathy. Many of these productions even resemble antiwar texts through showing the hellish field-level reality of battle. *The Bridge at Remagen* is particularly innovative in terms of content. *Anzio* (Edward Dmytryk, 1968) and *Tobruk* (Arthur Hiller, 1967), although more conservative ideologically and stylistically, share relevant similarities to the genre's other significant subcorpus—combat movies that used the narrative template of Aldrich's *The Dirty Dozen* where a small group attempt an "impossible" mission.

Unlike that production, none of these films was profitable or made the box-office top thirty as calculated by *Daily Variety*. The most successful—*Tobruk*—only returned $2 million in rentals. ("Big Rental Films of 1967," "Big Rental Films of 1968," "Big Rental Films of 1969"). Quickly perusing the promotional campaign for *Anzio* reveals in miniature the type of hoopla unsuccessfully used to sell super-musicals such as *Doctor Dolittle* or *Camelot*. The press kit came in an over-the-shoulder army bag, while the film was also promoted with a hopeful hit song (by a very traditional singer, Jack Jones) and a contest, via American Express, whose prize was a trip to the actual beachhead in Italy ("Anzio"). Clearly, despite certain synchronically progressive tendencies noted below, these productions proved financially unsuccessful, on a quiet level, just as *Tora! Tora! Tora!* and the period's super-musicals noisily failed to interest mass audiences.

The Bridge at Remagen is resolutely classical stylistically (even the period's characteristic employment of telephoto and zoom lenses is narrativized through allowing the coverage of significant space in one take) and narratively follows a causal, goal-oriented deadline of, depending on allegiance, either destroying or saving a strategic bridge. The cast, though, is fairly au courant and features George Segal, about to get shaggy and become a major counterculture star; Robert Vaughn from the hip spy show *The Man from U.N.C.L.E.*; and Ben Gazzara, soon linked with the Indie cinema's pioneer John Cassavetes in films such as *Husbands* (1970) and *The Killing of a Chinese Bookie* (1976). Furthermore, the film's tone is similar to that of the liberal production and Academy favorite *The Bridge on the River Kwai* (David Lean, 1957) in detailing the futility of creating or destroying a strategic point. The bridge's significance is reduced to a metaphor for the high cost in human life for a seemingly minimal military victory. In fact, the film's ironic coda states that ten days after this slaughter, the bridge collapsed.

As this grim narrative progresses, a cavalcade of cruelty, sexual license, and barbarism further the film's antiwar stance and mirror relevant discourses concerning U.S. troop behavior in Vietnam. In the first scene, the ironically named Angel (Gazzara) is shown looting a German corpse, prompting Lt. Hoffman (Segal) to call him a pig (an epithet usually reserved for police officers within countercultural parlance). Later Angel kills a teenage German sniper and wagers over when the bridge will be destroyed.

Patriotic sentiments or justifications for the American war effort, which might balance out this disenchanted representation, are never uttered. The grim portrait of military cruelty extends to the Germans, who use Polish forced labor and readily execute "traitors," since a sympathetic portrait of Nazis is hardly possible. The World War II film is unable to reverse sympathy in the manner of the period's Westerns romanticizing of Native Americans. The narrative can provide more complexity, though, by presenting German Major Krueger (Vaughn) as humanely attempting to keep the bridge open, which allows civilians and soldiers a safe retreat. He is executed as a traitor, but his actions provide the sole idealistic narrative event in a story lacking even relief over the war's imminent end. A film set in March, 1945, could stress that this battle helped hasten Allied victory. In contrast, the lingering impression conveyed suggests a futile slaughter over a bridge. The John

Wayne–style flag-waver has ceased as an ideological template for even a so-called traditionalist film.

Anzio and *Tobruk* describe unambiguously victorious engagements, unlike *The Bridge at Remagen*, yet also contain progressive, revisionist dimensions.

Produced by Dino DeLaurentis, *Anzio* is technically an Italian movie yet features an American cast, screenwriter, and director. The film, made in English, also conveys the perspective of the U.S. Army. On the conventional side, a victorious, daytime engagement ends the film and without requiring the structure of a biopic as with *Patton*. *Anzio* is also lavishly filled with extras and highlights spectacular Italian locations, and stylistically classical, even including a relentlessly telegraphed score. Boldness proves superior to caution, per paradigms set by earlier war films, since General Leslie's (Arthur Kennedy) unwillingness to mobilize on landing at Anzio costs many American lives. This might echo hawkish attitudes concerning Vietnam, which encouraged the U.S. military to proceed aggressively. Nevertheless, revisionist elements are also prominent, such as reflexively contemplating the act and meaning of war, while the narrative's structure is oddly bifurcated as a traditional account of large-scale endeavor becomes a tale of small-group warfare behind enemy lines.

The film's philosophical tone, reminiscent of moments in Cornel Wilde's odd mixture of avant-garde editing and gore *Beach Red* (1967), begins when Dick Ennis, a war reporter (Robert Mitchum, carrying his intertextual weariness like a mantle), asks General Leslie how a normally peaceful man can kill and, befitting this officer's mild nature, is told that such events occur out of necessity. In contrast, Rabinoff (Peter Falk)

Figure 2.2. Weary and disillusioned, Dick Ennis (Robert Mitchum) talks to General Leslie in *Anzio* (Edward Dmytryk, 1968).

states men only fully exist in combat, where thoughts are sharpened and affect heightened. "I'm more," he states, "There's more to living than just breathing. War's part of you." The film's title song (Music: Riz Ortolani, Lyrics: Doc Pomus) equivocates between positions and questions how a dreamer can become a fighter. Beyond echoing Leslie and calling war "Necessary Hell," the lyrics describe the requisite cold-heartedness and fearful rage created by battle. Nevertheless, battle is ultimately described as transcendent since despite not providing answers and even destroying dreams, it grants soldiers omnipotence—as Jack Jones intones, "This world is yours, all you men, take the land, take the sea, it's yours." These lyrics are more unabashedly traditional and patriotic than the actual film, which makes sense considering how title songs often seem cooked up without direct consideration of the production they serve.

After these multiple perspectives, Ennis echoes Rabinoff's statements and puts in the last word on the matter, when he tells Leslie that after this war ends people will fight anew as they enjoying killing; despite nothing being solved, they live intensely while in battle. Leslie calls his philosophy a condemnation of mankind. This sort of abstract philosophical speculation is far more akin to art cinema such as Bergman's, which lets the facade of "story" reveal the "discourse" underneath (Metz 91), than a seamless, narrative-centered Hollywood-style combat movie. Actually, the war genre's survival may have even rested on such discursiveness, which dovetails with its inherent suitability for addressing the day's concerns about aggression and military adventurism. Contemporary critical accounts took little notice of this ambitiousness. *Los Angeles Times* critic Charles Champlin states that *Anzio* "doesn't waste any time being terrible" while viewing the film's dialectical ambiguity as a simple matter of having "it both ways: to be an angry statement about the futility or irony of war" yet showing battle scenes that are "tidied up: no putrefaction, no carnage; instant, pain-free, not very bloody death. Not much worse than a lively Saturday night in old Dodge City." Interestingly, Champlin did note the film's reference to Vietnam War general Mark Clark in "publicity conscious General Carson" (Champlin, "*Anzio* Opens Citywide Run"). Similarly, *Daily Variety*'s critic bemoans how Peter Falk and Robert Mitchum "discuss some basic philosophical points, one of several forced injections of 'meaning' . . . which depress it further into banality" ("Film Review: *Anzio*").

The evenly bifurcated narrative also takes a decidedly novel turn when two platoons advance toward Rome and are ambushed. Only seven soldiers, including Ennis and Rabinoff, escape the slaughter. The film shifts from spectacle to intimate portrait of a dangerous mission, a familiar generic storyline exemplified by *The Dirty Dozen*. This section does invoke classic humanist tropes, such as being sheltered and fed by a friendly Italian family, whom the soldiers teach an American pop song (rather than sharing the usual chewing gum or chocolate). More unusually, it occurs parallel to the German attack on the Anzio beachhead, which resulted in a significant loss of American forces, an event that is only described, not represented. Avoiding such an obviously spectacular sequence is more typical of the small-group narrative, yet not showing such a depressing slaughter, while making it abundantly clear that Leslie's caution is to blame, avoids producing too devastating an account of warfare (and reduces a film's budget!). In keeping with the dangerous-mission template, the group learns extremely valuable information, Leslie is relieved of his duty, and the triumphant final scene shows Rome liberated and the GIs greeted by ecstatic Italian civilians in quintessential images from the genre's imaginary.

Tobruk is set during the African campaign against Rommel. Short on traditional heroics or patriotism, the film suggests deceptive guerilla tactics, associated with the Nazis in *Anzio*, are required for victory while presenting a new variety of valorous warrior conversant with these methods: German Jewish soldiers identified with the embryonic nation of Israel.

The film's seeming "hero" is a selfish, reluctant Canadian, Major Donald Craig (Rock Hudson), who is literally impressed into joining a dangerous mission to sabotage the German fuel supply at Tobruk. This goal is explained through old-fashioned voice-of-God omniscient narration over a map that, along with Hudson's presence, suggests a traditional war narrative. Instead, the mission involves sneaky and deceptive acts. Camouflaged in German uniforms, the participants travel openly through enemy lines and even trick German and Italian troops into attacking each other. Their morally ambiguous acts seem fair enough within a war narrative, yet the fact that a British plane strafes the mission's convoy, killing eight members, and must then be shot down indicates that the groups' subterfuge both harms their own welfare and creates casualties among their comrades. Furthermore, they even dress like Germans and many speak the "enemy's" language perfectly, which creates a visual and aural equivalence between the group and their brutal, ruthless foe.

The unit successfully destroys Rommel's fuel supply and mercilessly slaughters German troops. Craig displays selfless bravery and the battle ends victoriously, but the film is hardly rousing. During a period of intense questioning of U.S. military policy and its enforcement of free-world "liberty," the film suggests that our strength, like that of the Viet Cong, lies not in straightforward combat but in guerilla actions.

The pragmatic suggestion of subterfuge as a successful tactic relates to the concomitant romantic portrait of Zionist German Jews, who will implicitly use such methods in subsequent years to reclaim ancestral lands. Their leader Bergman (George Peppard) states, "We're beginning to think and feel as a people. The days of the wandering Jew have come to an end. We're going home." Craig asks if this remark refers to "Palestine" and Bergman replies "Israel." Bergman may insensitively complain about burying the British plane's crew and proves willing to execute a Nazi spy's daughter, but does neither. He and his men, who as German citizens would face a concentration camp if captured, are undeniably the narrative's most admirable characters. Craig is merely self-interested while the British soldiers, portrayed as either comic relief or jailbirds impressed into military duty (per the paradigm of *The Dirty Dozen*), are led by a stereotypical martinet and anti-Semite, Colonel Harker (Nigel Green). Arabs are shown as Nazi sympathizers or, at best, unreasonable and argumentative.

The Jews possess both admirable ideals and the courage of martyrs. Harker, invoking typical racist tropes, claims their "sort" always consider "percentages," yet Craig states that Bergman's men were the heaviest casualties of the British plane's mistaken attack. The narrative avoids Zionist proselytizing, though, and also displays contradictory character traits more typical of artistic representation than straightforward propaganda. For instance, Harker also behaves heroically by sacrificing his life and shooting a Jewish soldier who is actually a Nazi spy. This revelation furthers a sophisticated, nonpropagandistic theme of consistently problematizing "true" identity, since the turncoat was seemingly another eloquent spokesman for Zionism, and shows an error in judgment among the super-heroic Jews, as this traitor was their trusted second-in-command,

The depiction of proto-Israeli characters also granted Tobruk contemporary relevance since American foreign policy under President Johnson was increasingly supportive of the new-found Zionist state ("The 1967 Arab-Israeli War"). Coincidentally, the film was released months before the Six-Day War when Israel achieved a decisive victory over Egypt and annexed significant territories. *Tobruk* presents a cinematic analogue of Jewish valor and commitment which furthers the era's tradition of pro-Israel Hollywood productions, such as Otto Preminger's *Exodus* (1960) and *Cast a Giant Shadow* (Melville Shavelson, 1966).

The self-sacrifice of Jewish martyrs provides a noble dimension to a story of deception and slaughter. Furthermore, the mission is also successful and, per viewer knowledge and the opening narration, would lead to an Allied victory over brutality and fascism. Nevertheless, American characters or their patriotic ideals are completely elided. The only surviving major character, the Canadian Craig, is potentially readable, via Hudson's star persona, as a proxy American. In a modest version of Rick Blaine's template-setting character arc in *Casablanca* (Michael Curtiz, 1942), he becomes relatively selfless but unlike his cinematic predecessor who represents an awakening and heroic American fighting spirit, Craig mainly serves as a spokesperson for Anglophone admiration of these plucky proto-tough Jews. When Bergman leaves on his final, suicide mission, Craig says "mazel tov" to a representative of the budding nation whose patriotic struggle is by proxy the truly heroic narrative element in a traditionalist war film, which typically should invoke the United States as the exemplar of idealism.

In 1971 Universal reused footage and the basic story from *Tobruk* in a low-budget production, *Raid on Rommel* (Henry Hathaway) starring Richard Burton. The former's most socially relevant narrative element—the Israeli characters—is omitted while the latter film's hero is deliberately captured and joins a group of prisoners rather than escaping from captivity. The overall goal is the same: destroying the German fuel supply at Tobruk. *Raid on Rommel* was given a perfunctory release without first-run engagements, playing in double features in neighborhood theaters, in early 1971 (Display ad, 3/19/71) and was shown on network television by November, an extremely brief window at a time when moderately successful films might play theatrically for six months ("Mondays TV Programs"). Competently and classically directed, *Raid on Rommel* is of little interest, although its recycled elements and B-film status suggest the genre's exhaustion. In fact, Hollywood produced very few World War II films during the rest of the 1970s.

The one intriguing narrative element is the accidental presence on the mission of Vivi (Danielle de Metz), a sexy, stereotypically "hysterical" Italian woman. The war genre usually avoids charges of misogyny by simply eliding female characters. In *Raid on Rommel*, Vivi is represented as a nuisance who the men silence with painkillers, allowing one soldier to rape her, and abandon her in Tobruk like an unwanted hitchhiker. During the final raid on Rommel's fuel dumps, almost completely compiled from existing footage, she is heard screaming, although not present at the scene, when a British soldier is gunned down in the slow-motion technique pioneered by Peckinpah. This moment's narrative incoherence renders her cries readable as nondiegetic commentary on the costs of war, a thematic element present in other combat films of the period. Later, in more footage from *Tobruk*, the entire city explodes and her screams return. Presumably, these cries represent Vivi's actual death, although her body is not shown. The genre goes down limping—even Burton is uncharacteristically subdued—but the female principle is still eliminated, albeit violently rather than via simple narrative omission.

Seemingly traditionalist World War II battle spectacles had clearly outlived their patriotic relevance and box-office rationale, except as nostalgia for a limited set of older male viewers, yet could not transcend their generic status, partially since they are usually directed by mediocre filmmakers, and become antiwar critiques. As with the big-budget musical, these films are near the end of a continuum and attempted relevance through expressing the more progressive, synchronically informed pacifist ideas of the day. Despite having "happy" endings, they show war as increasingly pointless and the character of American soldiers as increasingly dubious. A subset of the genre provided even more fertile ground for revisionist discourses.

Glorious Bastards

Robert Aldrich's extremely successful *The Dirty Dozen* created a new narrative template for the genre's traditionalist canon, in which a handful of misfits led by a rebellious superior officer undertake an almost impossible task, while reflecting the period's sociohistorical realities. Previous World War II combat movies had represented small groups on "suicide" missions. For instance, *The Guns of Navarone* (J. Lee Thompson, 1962) and *Tobruk*, which opened four months earlier in 1967, detail desperate sabotage efforts. A different corpus also exists of espionage narratives set during wartime, such as *Cloak and Dagger* (Fritz Lang, 1946) and *13 Rue Madeleine* (Henry Hathaway, 1946).

Nevertheless, most World War II combat films deal with "normal" out-in-the-open, above-ground fighting where one directly, "fairly" attacks the enemy. In contrast, Aldrich's film is about a ruthless guerilla attack on a luxurious resort, supplied with women, for Nazi officers. The mission in *The Dirty Dozen* is top secret—whereas typically battles are public events directly coordinated by constantly informed superior officers—and also performed by twelve criminals and psychopaths (many who have received death sentences) led by Lieutenant Reisman (Lee Marvin) from the military stockade. Beyond these narrative innovations, the members of this "dirty dozen" are also emblematic of their period, and its cinematic representations, both as nonconformist societal rebels and guerrillas reminiscent of the infamous Viet Cong. Their actions also, at points, are reminiscent of cold-blooded murderers and invoke Nazi genocide.

The great financial success of *The Dirty Dozen* is presumably linked to successfully combining these varied elements into films more readable as traditional, since they lack Aldrich's more visceral, overtly antiauthoritarian tone. A cycle of similar, although increasingly divergent and iconoclastic, narratives followed in the film's wake but proved less successful at the box-office and with critics. Aldrich himself contributed a revisionist entry, which further blurs the borders between these and more maverick war movies, in this subgeneric cycle.

The first, *The Devil's Brigade* (Andrew V. McLaglen, 1968), is almost a direct, tamed remake of *The Dirty Dozen* with William Holden (a more traditionally heroic actor than Marvin) playing Colonel Frederick, who whips a group of rebels into fighting strength for covert, dangerous missions. Like Reisman, he is viewed as argumentative by superiors and his appropriateness for the mission questioned. Unexplainably, Colonel Mountbatten views these traits as beneficial and Frederick is appointed without further difficulty. Correspondingly, the film's spirit is less iconoclastic, in keeping with the U.S. Army's direct cooperation with the production through supplying three hundred Utah National Guardsmen. ("*Devil's Brigade*' Gets Army Cooperation OK"). Half of the brigade are misfits, but aside from one rapist, they are disciplinary cases not felons. Drunkenness on duty and going AWOL are their principal "crimes." The rest of the unit are highly trained and obedient Canadian troops. At first, the two factions spar but soon bond in a bar brawl against civilians. Law-abiding and criminal, rebellious values are successfully synthesized to create a cohesive fighting group.

Similarly, there is less tension between the brigade and the "regular" army, partially because they are an "official" combat unit, not a top-secret group of guerrillas. At first the unit is dismantled, but once Frederick charms a few officers, they are sent to Italy. Later, though, he is chastised by General Hunter (Carroll O'Connor) for disobeying orders but simply claims he viewed them only as suggestions. The potential conflict is resolved and the officer suggests they have a drink. At this seeming moment of conciliation, though, a certain *lumpenproletariat* ressentiment emerges, in contradistinction to certain assimilationist narrative tendencies, when Frederick claims he will imbibe only if his men are so privileged. This anti-elitist tone also allows for the representation of similarities between American and German leaders. In one period-specific montage sequence, accentuated by Alex North's semidissonant score, cuts occur between the Brigade's mission and a German officer listening to Baroque music, bathing and enjoying a luxurious breakfast (signified by the obligatory egg in a cup) served by a well-dressed domestic. The mission succeeds and General Hunter congratulates Frederick, who hangs up in a familiar moment of mild rebellion.

These antiestablishment moments aside, *The Devil's Brigade* lacks the brutality, rebelliousness, edgy cutting, and odd camera angles typical of *The Dirty Dozen*. Hollywood's genius at diluting provocative content renders this a squarely traditionalist text. Nevertheless, the film ends on a note of ambivalence, unlike the rousing and commemorative denouement of *The Dirty Dozen*. Frederick proudly states in voice-over that the unit never retreated or lost a battle and created a myth but comments "too many died" in the process. He mentions the taking of La Defensa Mountain, notes the price, and despite indicating that this victory created a sense of pride, states "it wasn't much of a hill," which echoes the irony of *The Bridge at Remagen* and its "victorious" engagement.

This only mild ambivalence is characteristic of one of the most unambiguously "traditional" films discussed in this study. Interestingly, the reviews are no more unenthusiastic than for more interesting films such as *Anzio*. A typical account, provided by *Daily Variety*, refers to "stock scripting, sluggish direction" and claims it includes "the worst of *The Dirty Dozen*" ("Film Review: *The Devil's Brigade*").

Several motion pictures depart further from Aldrich's template yet still portray risky, small-group engagements. *Where Eagles Dare* (Brian G. Hutton), for example, also fits within the international intrigue milieu of its scenarist Alistair MacLean and is the most spectacular effort in the subgenre since it was blown up to 70mm with stereophonic sound, an intermission, and an overture in premiere engagements. The healthily budgeted production features two stars—the legendary Richard Burton and rising action hero Clint Eastwood—and extensive location shooting in the Austrian Alps. The mission's participants are ostensibly trusted British agents, and the OSS assassin Lieutenant Schaffer (Eastwood), not hard-scrabble misfits. Furthermore, the narrative carries themes of secrecy and subterfuge to a point where only the group's leader, Smith (Burton), and his immediate supervisor know the assignment's true purpose. In fact, the obligatory explanatory briefing is a deliberately inaccurate cover story designed to fool most of the characters. In this MacGuffin world, the narrative's real goal is to create sufficient pretext for treacherous, spectacular explosions and an exciting escape. This uncertain universe is remote from General Patton's idea of heroic, transparent warfare.

World War II trappings are employed to not only transform straightforward old-fashioned battle into a subgenre but also provide the setting for a new, sadistic form of action picture within the combat movie's traditionalist canon. Burton had played in the straightforward, classical World War II film *The Desert Rats* (Robert Wise, 1953) and would appear in the depleted, anachronistic *Raid on Rommel*. Here he goes undercover and passes the torch to the once-and-future Harry Callahan/Man with No Name. Schaffer/Eastwood exists to mechanically machine-gun Nazis while his granite visage blankly sneers. The narrative innovations of increased sadism and championing unfair combat practices in *The Dirty Dozen* were yoked to progressive ideological tendencies and suggested these treacherous missions might even regenerate sympathetic nonconformist or antiauthoritarian characters through violence. In contrast, the "heroes" of *Where Eagles Dare* are an elite spy, possessed of superior knowledge and employing secrecy because the men he leads are untrustworthy, and an American assassin united through murder (which may be an honest representation of warfare), not camaraderie. The film delivers the goods without any attendant liberal-humanistic baggage and signals the beginning of a newer right-wing action-oriented cinema, first hinted at by the James Bond films and soon firmly entrenched at the box-office.

The newfound representational freedom of post–Production Code maverick films perfectly suits the reactionary variant of Aldrich's innovative and often left-leaning narrative paradigm, although Hutton's staging of violent actions is bloodless in the older representational fashion. The film is noisy, not visceral. *Where Eagles Dare* turns mass slaughter into entertainment and champions repressive, hierarchical discourses. This seemingly odd combination of mild permissiveness concerning violence following strict self-imposed industry "censorship" and authoritarian content suggests the often-fractured, ambiguous meaning of terms such as "progressive," "innovative," "traditional," and "conservative." The straightforward division between this "conventional" war film and ground-breaking productions such as *M*A*S*H* or *Catch-22* is muddied,

Figure 2.3. The granite sneer of future action star Clint Eastwood blows us away in *Where Eagles Dare* (Brian G. Hutton, 1969).

complicating its positioning in terms of a critically constructed maverick/ traditional dialectic.

Such ambivalence completely characterizes *Too Late the Hero* (1970), Aldrich's ideologically complex return to the small-group combat movie, which immediately adopts a despairing tone during the credit montage in which American, British, and Japanese flags become increasingly tattered. The film also includes antiauthoritarian sentiments and harsh ironies yet still valorizes selfless patriotism and provides another redemption narrative.

This mission's leader, Lawton (Cliff Robertson), is another reluctant figure, like Craig in *Tobruk*, commanded to join a group of British disciplinary cases and destroy a Japanese transmitter in the New Hebrides. He protests bitterly to his captain (Henry Fonda), but must obey or face court-martial. The officer shows disdain for his underling's petulance and possesses clear moral superiority, furthered by the inherently noble presence of Fonda, hoping to save the lives of thousands of sailors.

The narrative's main antiauthoritarian representation involves the British soldiers' hatred of their leader: by-the-book, aristocratic Captain Hornsby (Denholm Elliot), who speaks derisively, and anachronistically, about long-haired antiwar protesters. The unit of "odds and sods," basically in subdued revolt, is represented by the caustic, unpatriotic and cynical medic Hearn (Michael Caine). Expectedly, considering a general rebelliousness in Aldrich's corpus, Hornsby is less sympathetic than these misfits except for the abject Campbell (Ronald Fraser) who loots enemy corpses and, surpassing any craven behavior previously represented in the subgenre, kills an injured compatriot, Thornton (Ian Bannen). Campbell is eventually tortured and killed for despoiling the dead, which seems fitting punishment even in a narrative avoiding traditional moralizing. This character's acts, though, only amplify the general self-interestedness of the other group members (and the subgenre's more scabrous tendencies). The film's increased nihilism stems from the negative presentation of both the mission's authority figure and his rebellious subordinates. At best, Lawton and Hearn are portrayed as brave and clever although cynical and selfish, whereas Hornsby is a noble fool and the rest merely loathsome. Furthermore, as expected, the mission produces not union but dissension, death, and vicious in-fighting.

The ambiguities and ironies flourish when the group reaches the Japanese encampment, where Hornsby gains in stature and proposes they heroically supersede actual orders. Previously, Lawton or Hearn's charisma and rebelliousness conveyed by Caine and Robertson, the film's two stars, echoed Aldrich's antiauthoritarian personality and created a solidly iconoclastic tone. Lawton's reluctance and cynicism suddenly seem petulant and selfish when he refuses, while Hornsby, previously an elitist martinet, bravely rushes in, but is killed. His eyes remain open in obvious symbolic accusation of both Lawton's betrayal and perhaps the viewer for favoring a handsome, charming rogue over a dedicated officer. Next, the truly craven Campbell, representing an exaggerated version of Lawton's selfishness, kills Thornton, and, with two other survivors, surrenders. The pursuing Japanese rig up a public-address system, itself a technological anomaly and surreal narrative device amid a jungle, and threaten to kill these prisoners unless Hearn and Lawton surrender.

The film's moral stance becomes more complex, as neither character will consider giving up, being unconcerned about the fate of cowards, yet the suddenly heroic American proposes returning to the base while Hearn suggests remaining until the Japanese will no longer bother following. After questioning patriotic impulses and foregrounding truly selfish, nihilistic characters, the film shifts its register and valorizes the suddenly noble Lawton, who speaks of the many American lives at stake. The struggle between cynic and idealist is again reconfigured and the movie's ironic title becomes apparent as Lawton dies, while the cynical medic survives to hopefully convey crucial information, although the film ends before this moment is shown. Otherwise the mission's pointlessness would be complete, which, oddly enough, may have been Aldrich's point vis-à-vis the ironic title, yet the character's silence would seem almost unthinkably cruel and perverse (and ultimately uncharacteristic since he is simply selfish, not malicious or a traitor) after such devastation. Nevertheless, *Too Late the Hero* ends with him speechlessly gasping for breath and refreshingly avoids the ideological comfort of unambiguously framing the mission as a necessary sacrifice.

Other Combat Zones

Ambivalent supposedly traditionalist World War II movies that generally qualify victory and somewhat rebellious small-group films synchronically echo an era when the American military and many civilians felt embattled by Cold War threats. Simultaneously, the nation's engagement in Vietnam, ostensibly to stop the world-wide spread of communism, faltered and continued losing public support. This raises the question of whether any movies dealt directly, rather than allegorically, with the period's current geopolitical struggles.

Two relevant films directly addressed contemporary realities within texts more thematically and stylistically conservative than the films discussed. Liberal discourses flourished best through the prism of World

War II while hawkishness uneasily prevailed, albeit to varying degrees, when representing Cold War–related military engagements.

Ice Station Zebra, released in Cinerama with overture and intermission in its roadshow engagements, resembles costly musicals such as *Hello, Dolly!* and *Doctor Dolittle* as the ultimate bloated dinosaur production tendencies wedded to fantastic, unrealistic, and clichéd narratives. Interestingly, its biggest fan was billionaire recluse Howard Hughes, the epitome of the out-of-touch, who would repeatedly call Las Vegas television stations he owned and request that it be shown (Kehr, "New DVDs"). The film stars the most 1950s-identified of square-jawed, traditional leading men—the synthetically named Rock Hudson (born Roy Fitzgerald)—but it attempts to be current through the admirably colorblind casting of football legend (and *Dirty Dozen* co-star) Jim Brown and by featuring Patrick McGoohan, who concurrently created and starred in the hip-paranoid TV classic *The Prisoner*. The plot is a compendium of generic clichés. For instance, a character's sudden death ironically follows his humanizing back story. Similarly, the Russian Colonel Ostrovsky (Alf Kjellin) speaks in the villainous and aristocratic cadences of a World War II Nazi and makes statements regarding "your vastly inferior forces" to the Americans and utters the hoary "I believe your expression is . . ." before saying the words "booby-trap." Based on Alistair MacLean's novel, the narrative has the generically expected twists eventually explained in clunky, expository speeches. The script also revels in an excessive technicist discourse such as "Coming onto track now." "300 feet I." "Make it twenty down" plus time-worn lines such as "I can't hold this much longer," which causes Captain Ferraday (Rock Hudson) to bellow "You've got to."

Ice Station Zebra is ironclad classical in style except for a few, noirish tilted angles (at times motivated by the submarine diving) conveying uncertainty. Establishing shots, some underwater, of the submarine seem excessively long but presumably dazzled viewers on curving Cinerama screens. Interestingly, mise-en-scène is, at times, inadvertently unclassical; the now-dated use of rear screen projection and clearly studio-built interiors unconvincingly simulating polar landscapes certainly break the cinematic illusion. These artifices are even noticeable when a DVD of the movie is viewed on a low-definition television. In Cinerama, their contrivance would be more obvious, almost serving as a metaphor for the artificial, unrealistic nature of roadshow spectacles attempting to magically recreate historical, fantastic, or exotic locales. Whether simulating Union Square in *Hello, Dolly!*, a pink sea snail in *Doctor Dolittle*, or the Arctic, such scenes, especially with the attendant publicity over their cost, instead attract attention concerning their relative success or failure

Figure 2.4. Captain Ferraday (Rock Hudson, bottom far right, crouching) and the treacherous Vaslov (Ernest Borgnine, to Ferraday's right) amid Styrofoam ice and against rear projection in *Ice Station Zebra* (John Sturges, 1968).

(as with *Ice Station Zebra*), at imitating reality. Meanwhile, maverick films such as *Bonnie and Clyde* or *The Wild Bunch* were praised for authentic period detail and gritty realism.

In contrast, the film's reinforcement of paranoid, anticommunist ideology does include a few nuances. The narrative of *Ice Station Zebra* presents an atomic submarine, commanded by Ferraday, heading for an Arctic weather observatory to retrieve a U.S./British spy camera capable of taking highly detailed satellite photographs and locating nuclear missile installations. Ferraday, though, is not a completely stock hero. He expresses a surprisingly prescient wariness about nuclear fission, which, despite seeming benevolent and providing an efficient power source, "doesn't like to be controlled." This hardly typifies the period's generally positive discourse on atomic energy. In another scene, Ferraday silences a praying crew member and says "we're trying to think." The opposition of faith and reason is amplified when the grateful subordinate thanks God for their deliverance and the captain states "I'll thank the electric boat division. That covers us either way." American anticommunist efforts were often led, during this period, by those of a liberal, scientific bent.

Per generic paradigms, often steeped in Cold War paranoia, the mission's true goal is hidden under a cover story and only revealed after the intermission. After the submarine arrives at Ice Station Zebra, hostile Russians, led by a commander who freely admits his violent nature, appear to literalize previous dialogue concerning "fingers on the button" (a widely understood Cold War phrase for potential nuclear apocalypse).

Adding to the tension is the presence of a Soviet spy. The audience is (mis)led to suspect the African-American Captain Anders (Brown), another familiar generic ploy, yet eventually discovers the culpability of Vaslov (Ernest Borgnine), an alleged defector. His villainy suggests the insidious patience of Soviet agents, which could stoke paranoid terror in American audiences. In a fatalistic, relativistic speech, though, Vaslov states that if they were born in different places, he and Jones would have differing political loyalties. This ambiguous dialogue might fortify the racism of any viewer briefly considering the possibility of a Russian working against communism, by suggesting that national loyalty trumps everything. In contrast, the sheer luck of one's birthplace, albeit within an inherently "good" or "evil" society, creates the potential for spectators to realize that only good fortune, not innate decency, allows them to claim and champion American identity.

Ice Station Zebra is not apocalyptic, and the struggle between democracy and communism proves a fortunate stalemate as the spy camera is destroyed. Since the device had filmed both American and Russian nuclear installations, either side could have used its contents for deadly purposes. The sinister Colonel Ostrovsky says "until we meet again" to Ferraday, which fatalistically winks at U.S.–Soviet relations as eternally antagonistic.

The film ends with a clearly deceptive press release calling the rescue of Ice Station Zebra's crew members an example of international cooperation. Alfred Hitchcock's Cold War thriller *Topaz*, released the following year, also tags on a euphemized newspaper headline contradicting clearly presented narrative events. The U.S. media, presumably under government orders, are directly presented as dishonest. This view would appear obvious to both leftist revolutionaries and paranoid Birchers. Either way, a fatalistic and cynical tone permeates even a traditionalist roadshow spectacle.

Spy narratives are, of course, inherently conspirational and position viewers as privileged to the "real dope," in contrast to a putative "average" citizen's duped perspective. Nevertheless, *Ice Station Zebra* continues the pattern started by a war film, *The Dirty Dozen*, where the covert and hidden is a source of pleasure. The spectator omnipotently understands secretive activities and war can be presented entertainingly. During the unpopular Vietnam War, a more traditionally vigorous, overt, and cheery approach might seem tasteless and unrealistic, as in the sole Hollywood film of this period actually set in Indochina.

John Wayne and Ray Kellogg's *The Green Berets* bears this distinction and proves to be an embarrassing, bizarre anomaly, since, despite occurring two decades later, it stays closer to traditional combat film paradigms than any of the era's World War II narratives. Wayne presents the Vietnam War in the unambiguous and simplistic manner of his earlier productions, where he represented American courage in the face of evil Asian tyranny or Native American savagery. Beyond the star's mere presence providing familiarity and invoking generic clichés, *The Green Berets*, like *Ice Station Zebra*, is a collection of well-worn narrative tropes ranging from speeches about democracy to sadistic and treacherous acts courtesy of the Viet Cong (standing in for "Japs" or "Redskins"), comic scenes of tired soldiers unwillingly wakened at dawn, and the presence of a scrounger character who pilfers supplies.

The film's representation of the Vietnam War is also dishonest, because the conflict is not framed as an internal struggle, but as an invasion by the North. This representation ignores the country's artificial partitioning by the U.N. in 1954. *The Green Berets* also inaccurately represents an actively engaged, competent South Vietnamese army staffed by gung-ho, noble officers. The fantasy extends to a notorious shot of the sun setting into the ocean, filmed in California, yet Vietnam only has east-facing beaches! (Abramson 206–9).

Interestingly, the narrative climaxes with a covert mission, per Aldrich's innovative paradigm, which involves many brutal killings of unsuspecting enemy soldiers. This slaughter does receive justification, unlike other films depicting deadly surprise attacks, since it follows numerous depictions of "Charlie's" vicious cruelty. Despite this semiaberration, *The Green Berets* bucks the tide of ambivalent combat narratives, which sometimes allegorized the Vietnam conflict, by directly dealing with the Indochinese situation itself but in the anachronistic syntax of World War II films and Westerns.

The film also was a hit when released in July, 1968, and returned $8 million ("Big Rental Films of 1968"). Many audiences found reassurance in its Manichean morality, yet innovative war movies from *The Dirty Dozen* through *M*A*S*H* also succeeded with viewers ("Big Rental Films of 1967," "Big Rental Films of 1970"). Concurrently, conservative productions such as *Tobruk*, returning $2 million at the box-office ("Big Rental Films of 1967"), and revisionist efforts such as *Catch-22*, which returned $9 million but cost $18 million, failed to turn a profit ("Big Rental Films of 1970," "Catch-22"). The era's mix of old and new, not single-minded radicalism, is again invoked by the success or failure of both traditionalist and maverick texts.

Nevertheless, the World War II spectacle ultimately provides a coherent, if highly ambivalent, group of (basically) pro-status-quo texts. The next genre—naughty sex comedies—evinces new incoherencies in a manner different from the dialectical maneuverings of war narratives.

3

Naughty Sex Comedies

THE "NAUGHTY" SEX COMEDY differs from the richer, long-lasting narrative traditions of the musical and war movie. The latter are putatively the era's quintessentially reactionary, bloated, and financially problematic productions despite their generous servings of synchronically relevant and progressive discourses and formal elements. In fact, these modes did fade away and lie dormant, yet periodically revive at the box-office, or with Oscar voters, or they receive critical acclaim. In contrast, "naughty sex comedy" is a term I use to describe a subgeneric cycle within a larger, generally recognized, long-lasting narrative mode. Furthermore, it existed for less than twenty years, when its limited concerns perfectly dovetailed with cultural developments. The subgenre engaged with and contained contemporary sexual mores, sometimes questioned the social order, and reveled in new-found representational freedom, yet generally upheld the status quo, albeit sometimes tenuously. Finally, these films come closest to resembling maverick texts, and even veer into R-rated territory eventually, through focusing on sexuality and seeming to reflect a new openness. In contrast to the war film and (to a lesser degree) the musical and especially the western, there is little of an actual maverick tradition here, because that would entail avoiding naughtiness for frank representation. Ultimately, the films are almost always vessels of containment, not liberation, and function as a further example of the residue of older moral attitudes once expressed less problematically by classical Hollywood productions.

The naughty sex comedy reflects, negotiates, and contains the so-called sexual revolution—and the concomitant loosening of romantic mores among the younger generation—and its threats to marriage, monogamy, and the nuclear family. These films take advantage of increased representational freedom to give viewers voyeuristic titillation. They also pursue complex, dialectical, sometimes incoherent, narrative developments before almost always restoring traditional values. Their concerns are fitted onto theatrical farce conventions involving mistaken identities, deceptions, misunderstandings, and characters often adopting disguises and evading and spying on their rivals.

∽

The subgenre's cinematic predecessors include risqué silent comedies, Ernst Lubitsch's sophisticated productions (*Trouble in Paradise*, 1932; *Design for Living*, 1933), and pre-Code Mae West vehicles (*She Done Him Wrong*, Lowell Sherman, 1932; *I'm No Angel*, Wesley Ruggles, 1933). The form's foundational texts are the comedies of two directors: Billy Wilder (*The Seven Year Itch*, 1955; *Some Like It Hot*, 1959; *The Apartment*, 1960; *Irma La Douce*, 1963; and especially *Kiss Me, Stupid*, 1964) and Frank Tashlin (*The Girl Can't Help It*, 1956 and *Will Success Spoil Rock Hunter?* 1957).

The naughty sex comedy climaxed in the early 1960s with such canonical titles as *Under the Yum Yum Tree* (David Swift, 1963), *Who's Been Sleeping in My Bed?* (Daniel Mann, 1963); *Sex and the Single Girl* (Richard Quine, 1964), and most notably the Doris Day cycle (*Pillow Talk*, Michael Gordon, 1959; *Lover Come Back*, Delbert Mann, 1961; *That Touch of Mink*, Delbert Mann, 1962; and *The Glass Bottom Boat*, Frank Tashlin, 1966), which focused on the star's alleged virginity.

By 1967, the subgenre was reaching exhaustion since its possibilities were played out. The Production Code's demise instantly allowed films to include nudity and frank talk about and graphic representations of sex. Smirking euphemistic movies were suddenly rendered obsolete. Nevertheless, during the Hollywood Renaissance, some filmmakers pressed on by combining qualities of the naughty film with genuinely candid discourse about sexuality.

For instance, the maverick classic *The Graduate* can also be accurately described as a naughty sex comedy in its first part where the affair between Benjamin Braddock, the title character, and his parents' friend, Mrs. Robinson, is the narrative focus. As noted in this study's introduction, though, the film's structure and, in particular, style have been discussed as paradigmatically innovative by many, including Mark Harris (Harris 313–15). The "naughty" aspects are immediately prevalent in the double-entendre discussion about "adequacy" and "seduction" by Ben and Mrs. Robinson or the famous, almost subliminal shot of her bare breasts (using a body double for Anne Bancroft; Harris 362), which is seemingly bold yet more accurately described as simply teasing in the manner of the subgenre. Similarly, the film critiques middle-class morality, and shows a marriage being invalidated even after vows are spoken (with a crucifix used to blockade a church door) yet ends, per Pomerance, with "heteronormative love triumphing over every obstacle to achieve blissful harmony and nothing more." The hero's rebellion is subsumed into "a conventional, even a bourgeoisie future" (Pomerance 192). The film's ending, though, is also famously open and ambiguous in the manner of European art cinema. Once again, a dialectical relation exists between maverick and traditionalist, and between a synchronic analysis stressing bold innovation with an interpretation suggested by the film's incorporation of more-conservative, familiar discourses, including its possible celebration of heteronormativity.

The subgenre's aesthetic will be more fully described before two major narrative variants—involving marital difficulties and the generation gap—are detailed that reveal the same dialectic, and a few stray titles are discussed within the mode's framework.

An Unlovely Aesthetic

The most obvious distinguishing characteristic of naughty sex comedies is their long titles. These may have an instructional tone such as *How to Commit Marriage* (Norman Panama, 1969), *How to Save a Marriage (and Ruin Your Life)* or *A Guide for the Married Man* (Gene Kelly, 1967). Others promise an exposé, as with *The Secret Life of an American Wife* (George Axelrod, 1968) or *The Marriage of a Young Stockbroker* (Lawrence Turman, 1971) or ask a "naughty" question such as *Where Were You When the Lights Went Out?* (Hy Averback, 1968).

Categorizing this group of films as a subgenre also requires understanding the concept of "naughtiness." The notion is inherently euphemistic. A media culture that forbade 1950s teleplays from using the word "pregnant" clearly preferred treating sex as naughty rather than an explicit reality. As censorship loosened and the sexual revolution began, some comedies developed a sniggering, double-entendre-ridden aesthetic to present risqué, farcical narratives. Such films are "naughty": provocative but not graphic, generally conservative texts in mod clothing. For instance, these movies lack nudity but feature women in outfits that accentuate their breasts and buttocks. Coitus is either suggested, imminent, recently completed, or simply referenced but never directly represented. Lurid go-go music accompanies fetishizing zoom-lensed close-ups of women's (clothed) bodies. Bob Ingram, in *Inter/View* magazine, perfectly defines the tone when noting "it's a little dirty around the edges . . . that cute simpering kind of sexless sexuality" (Ingram). In contrast, a later maverick sex comedy such as *Carnal Knowledge* features nudity, profanity, and characters explicitly, clinically discussing the minutiae of their sexual experiences.

In terms of narrative content these films, especially marital comedies, trade in characters actively practicing deceptions. Many lie simply by committing adultery and violating the implicit trust of a marriage vow, but some protagonists create complex false identities and back stories. This tendency exists in proto-naughty movies such as Tashlin's *Will Success Spoil Rock Hunter?*, where the title character (nebbishy Tony Randall) poses as Rita Marlowe's (Jayne Mansfield) "Lover Doll" in a publicity stunt, or *Pillow Talk*, which involves Brad (Rock Hudson) assuming false identities as both a Texan and a homosexual. Since these films tend to unrestricted narration, viewers always know everything, while characters, even the deceivers, are partially in the dark. The victim often becomes a love object who, in a reversal, discovers the scheme and enjoys retribution via another ruse. *How to Save a Marriage (and Ruin Your Life)* exemplifies this strategy's baroque possibilities as Dave (Dean Martin) pretends to date Carol (Stella Stevens), presumably his friend Harry's (Eli Wallach) mistress, hoping to prove *her* a liar. He realizes his error—she is actually an altruistic virgin—and feels guilty but now must create a fictitious dead wife to explain not consummating their newfound "love." Later she discovers this and takes revenge. Not coincidentally, Stanley Shapiro, who wrote the script for *Pillow Talk*, concocted this Byzantine scenario.

Naughty sex comedies also partake of stylistic peculiarities, many typical of the era. In fact, per Rick Altman's terminology, these films are semantically indebted to formal parameters (Altman, "A Semantic/Syntactic Approach to Film Genre," 684–85). A list of their characteristics helps define this mode.

1. These films sometimes begin with animated credit sequences, often accompanied by a title song, which relate to the narrative's overall philosophy. *A Guide for the Married Man* presents these elements separately by starting with cartoons portraying adultery as a venerable institution, and presenting famous quotes endorsing infidelity, before the titles proper where The Turtles sing about the necessity for a handbook to instruct husbands in successfully cheating. A series of images using puppets appears under the opening titles of *How to Save a Marriage (and Ruin Your Life)*. These figures ride on a merry-go-round, a grim treadmill-like image, and eventually, in the ending credits, are depicted as paired up, suggesting monogamy and marriage as inevi-

table destinations. A song, performed by The Ray Conniff singers, is more romantic and describes love's transcendent power which is at odds with the film's narrative and this repetitive, deterministic imagery.

Diegetic and non-diegetic music also play significant roles throughout these films.

2. Many of these naughty sex comedies attempt hipness by mildly acknowledging rock and roll. For instance, scenes occur in discotheques, as in *Cactus Flower* or *How to Commit Marriage*, which are initially unfamiliar, even exotic, environments to the main characters. Such moments suggest the sub-genre's interest in limited experimentation with new cultural forms and sexual identities. The beat and arrangements—electric guitar and Farfisa organ figure prominently—may signify "rock and roll," but the musical selections are either instrumentals written for the film or "covers" of mainstream pop. These are typically short, catchy, generic numbers not long-form psychedelic explorations or the proto-heavy metal of pioneering musical outfits. Furthermore, since lacking lyrics, the potentially subversive imagery and content of the period's innovative music is elided. Needless to say, despite the Greenwich Village locales, in the late 1960s New York of *Cactus Flower*, Walter Matthau is not dancing to "Heroin" by the Velvet Underground. When considering that the film's press brochure even refers to New York City as a "never-never land" in the same year *Midnight Cowboy* won best picture by portraying a seedy, deglamorized, dangerous Manhattan, the ultimately careful musical choices make perfect sense ("Broadway's Brightest Comedy Hit Blossoms on the Screen . . . *Cactus Flower*").

3. The films' nondiegetic scores rely heavily on "Mickey-Mousing"—an effect associated pejoratively with classical-era stylistic practices—where character movements are synchronized with or their emotions telegraphed by music (Bordwell & Thompson 282). Often the soundtrack will comically comment on events in the broad fashion employed by the era's television sitcoms such as *Bewitched* (where Samantha's twitching nose has a musical analogue) or *The Brady Bunch*. For instance, a loud, musical

cue repeats each time the lying husband, Paul (Walter Matthau), in *A Guide for the Married Man* shows up at home pretending his back is acting up (an excuse to scout out locations for adultery). In this film, and others in the sub-genre, martial music plays as characters steel themselves for seduction. Lurid go-go music (a combination of "rock" and "strip club" instrumentation and beat) is another staple. Whenever the sexy, bikini-clad Susie Steinberg (future Russ Meyer starlet Edy Williams) appears in *The Secret Life of an American Wife*, she is accompanied by leering burlesque-style scoring.

The mode's aesthetic also includes its cinematography and mise-en-scene.

4. Another stylistic element which directly comments on or emphasizes narrative proceedings involves visual tricks such as super-impositions, split screens and fast motion. The unreality of a fantasy sequence in *How to Commit Marriage* is conveyed by the first technique. Split-screening shows the various true events, involving swinging teen behavior, which contradict a parent's suppositions in *The Impossible Years* (Michael Gordon, 1968). A comic portrayal of stressful events is amplified by sped-up imagery in *How to Commit Marriage* and *I Love My Wife* (Mel Stuart, 1970).

5. The bright, flat, unnatural color of network programming predominates even when these productions are lensed by Classical masters such as Lee Garmes (*How to Save a Marriage (and Ruin Your Life)*), Leon Shamroy (*The Secret Life of an American Wife*), William Daniels (*The Impossible Years*), and Charles Lang (*Cactus Flower, How to Commit Marriage*). Naughty sex comedies, usually shot in Deluxe or Eastman Color, have the artificiality of Technicolor without its richness or subtlety. They look particularly old-fashioned compared to the realistic or imaginative cinematography of maverick comedies such as *The Graduate* or *M*A*S*H*. A high key, low contrast look removes depth or any chiaroscuro effects which renders the few cast shadows noticeable.

6. The employment of obvious studio sets furthers an anachronistic aesthetic in a period where actual locations were featured (*Easy Rider*), period realism fetishized (*Bonnie*

and Clyde, The Godfather), or a gritty aesthetic sought (*M*A*S*H*). In contrast, naughty sex comedies use undetailed, artificial-looking studio sets such as the Bensons' "Malibu beach house" in *How to Commit Marriage*, or soundstages even for "exterior" scenes as in a "Central Park" nightclub in *How to Save a Marriage (and Ruin Your Life)*. Rear-screen projection, increasingly abandoned by maverick films, furthers this hermetic quality. Critics, directors and producers accepted the technique into the 1970s but it currently looks dated (Turnock 157–62). Again, *How to Save a Marriage (and Ruin Your Life)* is exemplary since all its "New York" street scenes are shot on sound stages in front of back-projected images. Despite looking egregiously ersatz at present, *Daily Variety*'s critic declared "Strongest asset of the film is its production" before praising art direction, cinematography, and costumes, and inaccurately praising the (barely existent) "location shooting" ("Film Review: *How to Save a Marriage (and Ruin Your Life)*"). Paul D. Zimmerman's review in *Newsweek* avoids blithe tolerance of artifice, probably via awareness of the realistic look of the era's maverick films, and comments on "cardboard skylines of New York City" (Zimmerman).

Figure 3.1. Flat lighting, the ubiquitous and artificial-looking dark-walled office set of late 1960s Universal films, and broad acting from Edmond O'Brien and Maureen Arthur in *The Love God?* (Nat Hiken, 1969).

7. The subgenre's cinematography is also characterized by the omnipresent zoom lens, itself a synecdoche for the period's stylistic excesses. Often this device moves in on female characters' fetishized body parts—particularly breasts and buttocks. Such objectifying compositions are featured even without zoom lensing. For instance, Paul's sexy neighbor, in *A Guide for the Married Man*, is always introduced by a close-up of her twitching rear end. He even fantasizes about her in a degraded version of the Resnais-type flashback used by Lumet in *The Pawnbroker*, and Minnelli in *On a Clear Day, You Can See Forever*. Such displays serve a philosophy of "look but do not touch or cheat" in these films' sexual-revolution-appropriate defense-of-marriage initiative.

Love and Marriage

Eros and its alleged liberation during the 1960s is usually contained within the naughty sex comedy's subgeneric framework. In particular, the mode attempted to salvage matrimony—a key bulwark of the nation's status quo and prized value of the classical Hollywood cinema. Returning to Rick Altman's concept, semantics aside, the films' syntactical dimension relates to older ideological positions (Altman, "Semantic/Syntactic Approach," passim). Nevertheless, as a result, cause, or both, of the sexual revolution, the country's divorce rate skyrocketed in the 1960s and a discourse concerning adultery became prevalent in various cultural productions (*Historical Statistics of the United States* 49, 65). This seemingly lurid topic appealed to Hollywood, which explored infidelity in narratives that usually recuperate the institution of marriage, although as the subgenre develops, matrimony is increasingly questioned or jettisoned.

A Guide for the Married Man exemplifies the mode's presentation of adultery. The narrative is structured episodically as Ed (Robert Morse, star of the same year's similarly instructional musical *How to Get Ahead in Business without Really Trying*) explains the nuanced art of penalty-free cheating to Paul Manning (Walter Matthau). The film's title references his various suggestions for successful infidelity and promises a ribald romp, but protecting marriage trumps swinging. Ironically, even Ed's initial advisory tale of a nebbish (Wally Cox) who, after years of fidelity, snaps and randomly molests women, is framed as a warning. He claims that pent-up frustration, presumably the result of monogamy, could prove disastrous and hurtful to Mrs. Manning. Paul concurs although his genial, attractive, sexually willing wife, Ruth (Inger Stevens), hardly seems likely to spur the hysterical acts depicted in this cautionary vignette. Perhaps, then, infidelity is a response to the boredom represented in the film's first scene, which depicts her clad in a leotard, performing provocative bust-enhancing exercises, and then, shot from the back, undressing while Paul, reclining in a Production Code–era twin bed, is so engrossed in a book he denies her veiled request for sex. In a classic example of Barthes's "Operation Margarine," the text seems to criticize an institution—marriage—for frustrating the male libido or routinizing sex. A response (therapeutic adultery) is suggested but ultimately the status quo is deemed functional and admirable (Barthes 39–41).

A Guide for the Married Man also performs another Barthesean notion—naturalization (Barthes 125–27). The aforementioned pre-credit animated sequence depicts adultery, starting in the Paleolithic era, as a time-honored tradition and inevitable response to matrimony, something eternal, elemental. The titles show Paul's voyeuristic lust as today's version of the immortal urge to cheat. A series of zoom shots focus on his sexy neighbor's behind, while he also imagines businessmen turning into jiggling, braless women. This montage culminates with Manning squeezing into an elevator packed with giggling, sexily-clad ladies while looking both shy and titillated. The Turtles' eponymous theme song states, unequivocally, "What we need in the world today is a guide for the married man." Presumably modern husbands require instruction to fulfill their innate desires, which both fuel and are inspired by these constant scopophilic reveries. Four reasons—pent-up frustration, boredom, naturalized adultery, and voyeuristic temptation—rationalize infidelity and seemingly reveal the problematic nature of traditional matrimony. Nevertheless, the ideology of containment proves stronger.

A Guide for the Married Man follows the "titillate and moralize" aesthetic of DeMille and Fellini to outline many variants of infidelity and revel in new-found representational freedom. Paul even finds a playmate, but ultimately changes his mind and decides to remain faithful. Directly following this reversal, as if motivated by the character's choice and intended to reinforce and reward his moral correctness, he sees Ed, coincidentally occupying a room at the same motel, rousted by his wife while a flashbulb-popping photographer catches him in flagrante delicto. Direct punishment or, in Paul's case, illustration of potential chastisement for sinning, is a hallmark of the Production Code, which reveals the ultimately reactionary nature of this text that seemingly flaunts its naughtiness before retreating into the status quo. The film ends with a tamed version of the opening credits to disavow its earlier provocations. The businessmen no longer become women, Paul's secretary's dress does not reveal cleavage, and he declines to enter an elevator packed with women.

This retrenchment is plausible since the affable, pretty Mrs. Manning excels as a gourmet cook, mother, and willing lover. Other naughty sex comedies acknowledge matrimony's many imperfections and recognize infidelity as a potential solution. These films usually sentimentalize romantic love yet resignedly view monogamy and marriage as the logical, inevitable endpoint of mutual attraction.

How to Save a Marriage (and Ruin Your Life) avoids literally fulfilling its title's promise. The product of Stanley Shapiro, this is superficially the subgenre's most anachronistic entry and was immediately recognized by Pauline Kael as a retrograde story with Doris Day simply replaced by Stella Stevens (Kael, *Going Steady*, 21–29), an observation echoed by Paul D. Zimmerman in *Newsweek*, who also wrote "Rock Hudson is played by Dean Martin." His parting shot—"No one is going to stop Hollywood from producing garbage. But let's at least have today's garbage"—perfectly mirrors the typically withering view of traditionalist films by historians who even acknowledge their existence (Zimmerman). Surprisingly, the movie was well-reviewed by *Film Daily* as "one of the comedy delights of the year," and Shapiro's "masterful way in depicting the man-woman conflict" was praised ("The New Films"). Similarly, John Mahoney in the *Hollywood Reporter* ("consistently funny") and a reviewer from *Daily Variety* ("amusing") wrote basically favorable accounts (Mahoney "Film Review: *How to Save a Marriage (and Ruin Your Life)*"; "Film Review: *How to Save a Marriage (and Ruin Your Life)*," *Daily Variety* [here I reference two reviews with identical titles]). The film also features the aging Dean Martin, a fixture of the mode's "classic" era and almost synonymous with leering, double-entendre-ridden sexual humor. The strenuous narrative is structured as a farce of mistaken identities, misunderstandings, and elaborate deceptions, which would instantly terminate if the characters behaved truthfully or with a modicum of sanity.

How to Save a Marriage (and Ruin Your Life) is conventional stylistically and in terms of narration, and was clearly intended as simple comic fluff. Nevertheless, the film's pointed representation of love and marriage is bitter and cynical. Maverick productions criticize society and offer an alternative, even if only to glorify suicidal revolt. This film is ultimately conservative, since pessimism usually accompanies resigned acceptance of the status quo for lack of a better alternative, yet is scarcely an example of mainstream cinema propping up the social order. In fact, Shapiro's vision of America is not much different than that of the counterculture. The difference is his characters accept matrimony as the lesser of two evils. In particular, women view the institution as a security blanket in a sexist, capitalist economic order.

Marriage is described, via elaborate metaphors, as both a war and the equivalent of death—"the hangman's noose." Harry and Mary Hunter's (Eli Wallach, Katharine Bard) union is presented as a hellish series of arguments. He gives a lurid soliloquy about how "There's a war going on out there in the suburbs. Do you want to know what life is like in those split-level trenches?" Harry then chronicles a declining marriage as ending with capitulation or "Munich . . . peace at any price." Further humiliations include the "grim message" of aspirin on the night-table announcing "Have a headache! Don't touch" until the final reality: "You curl up in the fetal position and you pray for merciful sleep." Later, Dave (Dean Martin) comments on a newlywed couple where the woman is already nagging her groom by describing him as "sentenced . . . to death." Only in retrospect, as with Mr. Slotkin's (Jack Albertson) sorrowful memory of his late wife, is matrimony viewed romantically.

The clichéd and misogynist representation of Mrs. Hunter as a constantly nagging virago is hardly progressive, but this floundering marriage does dissolve, a denouement often forbidden by the Production Code. In keeping with changing social mores, divorce is viewed as a potential solution. Furthermore, Harry's mistress Muriel (Anne Jackson) is depicted as a skilled homemaker, not the usual materialistic tramp, who successfully ministers to her tired businessman lover. This characterization even leads to the potentially revolutionary idea of an adulterous relationship as therapeutic, a possibility only briefly envisioned in Wilder's *Kiss Me, Stupid*. Ultimately such a transgressive reality is foreclosed when Harry proposes to Muriel while Dave weds Carol (Stella Stevens). The opening credits' matrimonial merry-go-round will continue ad infinitum, not as a promise of bliss but paying lip service to a clearly unsatisfactory norm.

How to Save a Marriage (and Ruin Your Life) also ironically extols marriage as a safety net for women. In fact, Shapiro seemingly registers a feminist protest against economic insecurity and sexual harassment. In the first scene, female employees in Hunter's department store are overseen and sized up by male supervisors, who promise career advancement for sexual favors. Carol's thirty-three-year-old coworker, Marcia (Shelley Morrison) chooses the alternative to such treatment by marrying an older man. A wife, at least, is legally protected and can even profit by divorce. In fact, Mrs. Hunter states that twelve years of self-sacrifice grant her the right to "every penny he's got." Muriel's comfortable situation, as well as the luxurious apartment Dave procures for Carol (thinking *she* is Harry's girlfriend), might present a mistress's lot as a decent compromise, providing both love and shelter. Thelma's (Betty Field) reality dispels this notion when she discusses being dumped after a fourteen-year adulterous romance. Similarly, when Harry mistakenly thinks Muriel is cheating, he sunders their ties with a cold, businesslike termination letter. This provokes Carol to propose unionizing mistresses. She even writes up a contract for Muriel, including a pension, as protection in the event of future misunderstandings. Harry calls these demands "anarchy, socialism, creeping Trotskyism." The possibility of economic security for a nontraditional form of employment is provocatively raised but ultimately abandoned. Harry marries her and Dave weds Carol in a conventional finale. The suggestion remains that in a deeply unfair economic system, women should strive for matrimony as the least-objectionable option.

The only refuge provided by this bitter vision is through old movies. For instance, the script's clichéd metaphors, which describe its cynical worldview, suggest classical film genres. Military references are augmented by such phrases as "It's their range, honey," and "it's time to saddle up," reminiscent of Westerns. Furthermore, Muriel obsessively views classical-era weepies on television. She mentions watching a film where all the actors are deceased, which invokes the death of many Hollywood legends in the late 1960s, and notes how Kay Francis waits twenty years for George Brent. In contrast, she states that "I don't think any of the newer actresses would wait that long," which masks the contrivances of cinematic narrative into the spontaneous decision of performers, by suggesting that today's stars can choose not to pine for a man. The hangover of studio-era attitudes even infiltrates the film's more progressive questioning of matrimony.

Where Were You When the Lights Went Out? proves similarly defeatist on a smaller scale. The film energies are diffused, with only one couple's situation represented, since the narrative strays beyond the subgenre's parameters to include the attempted robbery of company funds by an unfairly treated executive, Waldo (Robert Morse). A sex farce involving Margaret and Peter Garrison (Doris Day, Patrick O'Neal) is linked to this caper by the great Northeast blackout of 1965.

Ideologically retrograde, the narrative connects female employment with male infidelity. Margaret wishes to leave a hit Broadway play to have children, recalling the dilemma of characters in musicals such as *Star!* and *Funny Girl*. She also tries to initiate sex with Peter. This active erotic desire furthers a self-reflexive discourse deliberately playing against Day's chaste persona, exemplified by the title of her character's successful play—*The Constant Virgin*—itself a reference to a joke ("I knew Doris Day before she was a virgin") by Oscar Levant, which Peter paraphrases. She tries to privilege family by breaking their mutual celibacy. Fulfilling the imperatives of bedroom farce, though, requires subsequent misunderstandings starting when Margaret returns home and catches Peter seducing a female journalist. The contagion of career is implicitly blamed because this reporter is only at their apartment to interview Margaret. Peter's exposure happens before this tryst is consummated, but his act starts a chain of wild, comic events resulting in her downing sleeping pills and eventually waking up next to Waldo.

Where Were You When the Lights Went Out? takes an odd narrative turn indicative of reactionary sexism when Margaret's innocence becomes (in a reflexive twist) the subject of extensive debate after Peter sees her new bedfellow. She even agrees, based on her "Yankee Doodle, middle-class morality" that cheating, even while drugged, would end their union. Presumably, divorce is less contrary to traditional values. The idea of working woman as threat to the status quo then resurfaces when Ladislaus Walichek (Terry Thomas), her voyeuristic producer, attempts blackmail. His character's excessive (and incoherent) perversity—he has a peephole into the actress's dressing room, yet makes comments suggesting homosexuality—couples with Margaret's bizarre morality to create an estranging effect in line with an overall tone of self-reflexivity, which might cause a sentient spectator to question the entire narrative's ethical foundation.

Nevertheless, the film presents her eventual reunion with Peter as joyous and even sanctified by pregnancy. Interestingly, Margaret continues to believe she has cheated even if unconsciously. The epistemic submission of women is secured in an odd moral economy where Peter's actual infidelity is ignored, while he lets Margaret believe she has strayed despite learning of her innocence. A deliberate lie by a would-be adulterer is acceptable, since she quits the stage. Her pregnancy is even naturalized and folded into a supposed region-wide baby boom nine months after the blackout.

Day's star persona can only be kidded so far, yet revealing its artificiality may simultaneously point out the laborious constructions necessary in this period to uphold traditional morality. For example, Waldo's larceny is also forgiven, and he receives a deserved promotion. A lie, in Peter's case, or truth is equally valid to maintain the status quo. Still, any film that shows that questionable means are sometimes necessary for this end, inadvertently reveals the same guilty conscience directly attacked by maverick productions critical of bourgeoisie ideals, such as *The Graduate* or *Easy Rider*. Some classical-era plots—*Stella Dallas* (King Vidor, 1937) providing a perfect example—doubtlessly require viewers' queasy acceptance of injustice to maintain order. In general, though, golden-age films *effortlessly* support the dominant ideology after seemingly debating its alternatives. In *Where Were You When the Lights Went Out?* the audience is presumably as blinded and powerless as the citizens of New York and will simply assume that the status quo's continuance requires minimal justification.

The Secret Life of an American Wife analyzes marital troubles and infidelity with less despair but more nuance than *How to Save a Marriage (and Ruin Your Life)* or *Where Were You When the Lights Went Out?* The latter depicts matrimony as bleak but inevitable. Axelrod's film is more conservative through valorizing romantic love and ultimately deeming marriage an acceptable institution. Progressively, it blames a numbing, suburban lifestyle for the main couple's problems and offers bohemian stimulation as a solution. *McCall's* critic perceptively noted this when titling their review "In tune with the times, the suburban middle class is taking a beating in films these days" and then invoking a classic piece of subversive art cinema, also about a housewife turned hooker, Buñuel's *Belle de Jour* (1967) ("In tune with the times"). The film's basically positive tone, in contrast to *How to Save a Marriage (and Ruin Your Life)* and *Where Were You When the Lights Went Out?*, is also recognized when their critic refers to Axelrod's film as "funny and sunny." An earlier title for the movie was *The Feminine Mistake*, which manages to invoke a progressive text yet seemingly blame the film's heroine (Untitled item, *Hollywood Reporter*). Even within production history, odd ambiguities surface.

Tom Layton (Patrick O'Neal again) is a stereotypically glib public-relations man who specializes in staging the classic three-martini lunches we see in cinematic representations of businessmen. His job itself is a classic signifier of the bourgeoisie's most illusory and superficial tendencies. In contrast, his wife, Victoria (Anne Jackson again), has read all eight volumes of Proust in French (although he only wrote seven!), is witty and articulate, and yet is bored, discontented, and insecure about her sexual allure. In an unusual move for the subgenre, she even receives narrative centrality, directly addresses the viewer (Tom's doubts are presented through talking out loud but without looking at the camera), enjoys a detailed back story, and is allowed long monologues and visualized fantasy sequences to explain her thoughts and feelings. Mrs. Layton suffers from a version of the "seven-year itch" that writer-director Axelrod infected the husband with in his famous Broadway sex farce. In contrast to that work's protagonist, who struggles against the desire to cheat, Victoria constantly worries about her desirability and immediately grabs an opportunity for self-affirmation through infidelity. Her anxieties climax when she "accidentally" appears naked in front of a young and oblivious delivery boy. Presumably, the male gaze prefers peeping to direct address. In contrast, sexpot neighbor Susie Steinberg (future Russ Meyer starlet Edy Williams) is a successful exhibitionist when represented in Victoria's neurotic imaginings as bikini-clad, buxom, and accompanied by tawdry go-go music. Laura Mulvey's idea of the female spectator assuming a transsexual identity is literalized as Mrs. Layton's subjectivity includes the male viewer's putatively objectifying and fetishistic views of this suburban temptress (Mulvey, *Visual and Other Pleasures* 132–33).

In a panic, Victoria poses as a prostitute hired by Tom for "the Movie Star" (Walter Matthau), an otherwise unnamed cinematic sex symbol. The mere fact that the woman is the adulterer is notable. Victoria's actions even prove therapeutic for her and this would-be cinematic lothario, who admits, far quicker than through psychoanalysis, that his screen and public personae are fraudulent (like Margaret's in *Where Were You When the Lights Went Out?*). The Movie Star's confessions reveal a lonely, ailing, and saturnine libertine. Not coincidentally, Tom soon arrives and announces his resignation as the celebrity's PR man while Victoria hides in his bedroom. This suddenly conscience-stricken character claims concocting witty quotes and procuring women for his client has taken its psychic toll. The narrative connects Victoria's deception and increased self-awareness with her husband's abandonment of a dishonest career. The film's finale completes a circular narrative structure by occurring in the same location, Tom and Victoria's bed, exactly one day after the first scene—at three minutes before the alarm clock rings at 7:00 A.M. This brief interlude functions like a pared-down, suburban version of Virginia Woolf's "room of one's own"—her sole instance of contemplation and solitude. The difference a day has made is clear. Tom intends to work "independently" and move the family back to New York. She approves and they prepare for sexual relations. Her guiltless charade as a sex-worker has kick-started their ennui-laden, suburban existence.

Cactus Flower is only mildly risqué. The presence of Ingrid Bergman, as the protagonist's ultimate love interest, and screenwriter I. A. L. Diamond—Billy Wilder's collaborator on earlier Academy Award–winning sex farces—bestow class on the production. In contrast, jokes about sexy stewardesses, randy characters such as a dumb floozy or an adulterous Spanish diplomat, and scenes at "The Slipped Disc" go-go featuring instrumental pop and rock connote "naughtiness." The film is significant through incorporating youth-culture discourses into the aging mode. The bifurcation is reflected in positive reviews in the *Hollywood Reporter* and by Roger Ebert, which both note the film's "familiar" qualities but find it pleasant and funny ("Frankovich 'Cactus Flower' Smash Comedy Boxoffice Hit"; Ebert, "*Cactus Flower*"), and in the contrasting negative accounts in *Vogue* and *Inter/View*. The former is another of these perfect synecdoches for the dismissive tone held toward traditionalist films when the critic—an actual historian, Arthur Schlesinger, Jr.—writes "The film is 'surefire' in the worst sense—laboured, mechanical, predictable" (Schlesinger, Jr.). The profanity-strewn, bile-ridden, highly informal review in *Inter/View* by Bob Ingram is at its least obscene when writing "It's a witless, pointless, tasteless mélange of all the American public has been taught to welcome. In short, 'Cactus Flower' is a long television situation comedy without the commercials" (Ingram). The last comment was intended as particularly withering, considering the low cultural status of television in 1969, especially for anyone even vaguely yearning toward hipness.

Initially, marriage also functions differently in *Cactus Flower* since the main character, Julian (Walter Matthau, a subgeneric fixture), is a swinging bachelor who only *pretends* he is wed to stall his girlfriend, Toni's (Oscar-winner Goldie Hawn), demands for commitment. At first, matrimony only seems relevant as an illusory source of problems, not a viable reality, an ironic turn since Julian created his false marriage to avoid difficulties. Nevertheless, two soon-to-be-wed couples are formed by the film's end. The second romantic pair represent the "younger generation" and suggest a sea change in the naughty sex comedy

The narrative's key dialectic opposes the affluent, dishonest bourgeoisie, represented by the middle-aged Julian, to the era's allegedly sincere, honest youth culture; the synchronic dimensions of the period attempt to update the subgenre. In the first scene, a "hippie" strolls down Toni's street putting flowers on automobile windshields, while she has daisy decals on her water heater and prefers leather pants to a mink coat. This generational divide may be expressed through such obvious signifiers but also involves genuine differences in values. A symbolic mending of the gap occurs when Toni and Julian each find a new age-appropriate mate after the latter's dishonest actions—in response to her truthful demands—ultimately reveal his latent but genuine desire. Interestingly, *Cactus Flower* avoids a more typical, dialectical synthesis in which the dentist and his mistress would reach a compromise between their contrary values.

Julian is a seemingly contented swinger—the "Dancing Dentist of the Copa"—who enjoys an ideal situation: he has a young, steady mistress and a wife-substitute in his brisk, competent secretary, Miss Dickinson (Ingrid Bergman). The façade's first crack involves his impotence with a "tall, built, spectacular-looking" Australian stewardess because he keeps envisioning Toni. Julian proposes marriage, but the earnest young concubine wishes to meet his wife, which results in Dickinson agreeing to impersonate "Mrs. Winston." An obvious twist reveals that the nurse has always pined for Julian. The initial stereotypical rendering of her as an "efficient" old maid referred to as "Sergeant" is, thankfully, subverted when Dickinson describes an annual trip to Cape Cod where she wears jeans and paints landscapes. Furthermore, the "spinster" is actually a divorcee, thereby not virginal.

The deceitful dentist has presumably achieved a more authentic reality with Dickinson while firmly upholding the social order as a now-married professional with an age-appropriate spouse. Meanwhile, Toni's sincerity can coexist with her more conventional desires. She pairs up with Igor Sullivan (Rick Lenz), a vaguely beatnikish playwright. Ironically, this cheery denouement is the result of Julian telling Toni one final lie, which he knows she will see through. Marriage and the status quo have again triumphed, but the dishonesty required to achieve this result suggests societal ambivalence toward traditional institutions. The preservation of paradigms associated with an older mode of production requires bad faith.

Not Your Parents' Naughty Sex Comedy

Bob & Carol & Ted & Alice falls outside this survey's parameters but requires mention for its influence on the subgenre by depicting adultery among younger, hipper characters and self-consciously discussing shifting societal attitudes toward sexuality. The film's realistic cinematography and extensive location shooting place it outside the mode's typical televisual/backstage aesthetic. Furthermore, Mazursky and coscenarist Larry Tucker's script is subtle and observational, not broadly farcical. Improvisatory, lengthy dialogue scenes develop complex characters and present the tastes, habits, and desires of two upper-middle-class couples eager to join the sexual revolution. The narrative focuses on their erotic curiosity but eschews naughtiness or dishonesty. The first scene, at Big Sur's famous Esalen Institute, directly presents bare-breasted women and naked hot-tubbing. Furthermore, when Alice (Dyan Cannon) tells a psychiatrist about an episode involving her son entering the bedroom and seeing her "ti-ti," a classic euphemistic phrase, the shrink is puzzled about this expression and states that in his household the word "vagina" is used. The characters, starting with Ted and excepting Alice, all have adulterous affairs but directly tell their spouses, and such honesty strengthens their (flawed but loving and genuine) marriages; eros is harmless and does not require containment. Granted, the characters speak in psychobabble about "games" and "truths" and seem vaguely ridiculous, especially in the famous (anti) climactic "orgy" scene, but they honestly, awkwardly try to transcend middle-class morality. Their attempt at group sex fails, but rather than Mazursky and Tucker striking the defeatist note of most allegedly traditionalist naughty comedies, the characters merely seem puzzled, and certainly are treated sympathetically, as they roam among a crowd in a Las Vegas parking lot to the strains of Dionne Warwick singing Bacharach and David's "What the World Needs Now (Is Love Sweet

Love)." This Felliniesque denouement is open-ended, but not incoherent or forced as with many sex farces.

The subgenre's newfound representation of younger and hipper characters, hinted at in *Cactus Flower*, continues with *I Love My Wife* and *The Marriage of a Young Stockbroker*, two films that flirt with maverick status as star vehicles for younger, "hipper," actors Richard Benjamin (*Catch-22*, *Goodbye Columbus*) and Elliott Gould (*Bob & Carol & Ted & Alice*, *M*A*S*H*). Nevertheless, these productions are also bursting with naughty moments, and feature basically traditional, married protagonists engaged in status-quo vocations. Both films evince a familiar bitter disillusionment toward marriage, without containing adultery or recuperating matrimony, and incorporate the progressive antimaterialist critique and female subjectivity of *The Secret Life of an American Wife*.

I Love My Wife is structured around the "progress" of Dr. Richard Burroughs (Elliott Gould) from childhood through marriage to postdivorce promiscuity. He is immediately pegged as a generational representative in the first shot—a World War II–era newsreel exhorting citizens to participate in a rubber drive—that he watches as a boy along with heroic images of Gary Cooper in DeMille's patriotic *The Story of Dr. Wassell* (1944). As with *A Guide for the Married Man*, the opening credits feature a series of vignettes, using some of the period's typical freeze frames and comic music, that alternates between pseudobaroque (harpsichord), jazzy (bongos and flute), and vaudevillian (muted trumpets, ragtimey piano). Many of these scenes vilify his overprotective, negative, and prudish mother, the narrative's first misogynist representation. Her fear of sex has produced a counterreaction in young Richard. For instance, he and his father daydream in church and imagine, in clearly marked subjective shots, the female congregants naked, which is reminiscent of, but more explicitly rendered than, Paul's naughty vision in *A Guide for the Married Man*. Both generations find refuge in fantasy rather than actual rebellion. Despite the presence of Elliott Gould, *I Love my Wife* shares the resigned, frustrated tone of more traditionalist naughty sex comedies, not the overt transgressiveness of a maverick text.

Richard's marriage to Jody (Brenda Vaccaro) furthers the narrative's depiction of entrapment. Their union's presentation mixes a progressive critique of money-obsessed and materialist professional life with a portrayal of Mrs. Burroughs that oscillates between misogynist cliché and sympathetically nuanced portrayal, while the main character's representation is increasingly unsympathetic and reveals the shallowness of the middle-class professional male.

In a bold move, Richard and Jody are introduced in *I Love My Wife* while haggling with an abortionist over money. This scene introduces a discourse critical of the medical profession's mendacity echoing the period's general bemoaning of the mercenary nature of many occupations and industries. Richard then changes his mind and basically, per his financial control, gives Jody permission to have the child. In line with stereotypical notions of femininity, his decision makes her ecstatic, and is the first step down the path to middle-class misery. Soon he is driving home to suburbia in rush-hour traffic, sprayed by the automatic sprinkler system, and tripping over children's toys. His new-found cynicism is apparent when he notes after a successful surgery that the patient can soon return to his "liquor store and Diners Club card payments." Richard's intelligence, and self-awareness, produce dissatisfaction with a comfortable existence some might envy. After selling out the interests of nurses striking for better pay, and being rewarded with a lucrative job, he sarcastically compares himself to Jimmy Stewart in an old movie. The remnant, here one of old Hollywood's most beloved figures, of earlier practice is invoked positively yet within a narrative of social criticism typical of the era's synchronic characterization as rebellious. The film offers no present solution and hits a peak of despair when Jody, in one of her vacillations between sympathetic and pitiful, feels guilty and cries out "What have I done to you?"

Multiple rationalizations are created for his inevitable infidelity, beyond escaping middle-class monotony. Mrs. Burroughs, per sexist cliché, gains weight and start nagging. A scene of Jody devouring Chinese spareribs—to unbelievably dated "Oriental" music unlikely in a maverick production—is topped by her cooking a frozen pizza while running several kitchen appliances, as if symbols of her material wealth and/or their white noise effect can amplify the soothing effects of gluttony. The character's appetite increases while her sex drive plummets after giving birth, another stereotypical representation. In a scene whose connotations require the viewer to interpret euphemistic dialogue—a sign that *I Love My Wife* is still a traditionalist naughty comedy often reliant on hinting, not frankness—she refuses to perform oral sex. In the ultimate insult, Richard screams at her: "You are my mother!" Jody has already gleefully embraced maternity, encouraged them to live with *her* mother, and is now associated with the overbearing prude who warped his childhood. Whether these connections suggest the film's misogyny or simply the protagonist's anti-Momism is unclear.

Eventually, though, Mrs. Burroughs's depiction does gain nuance as she becomes wiser (foreshadowed by her guilt over Richard's careerism), especially about the doctor's callow, undependable nature. Jody revitalizes by taking art classes at UCLA (where a bearded student asks for a date) losing weight and going blonde, the latter a classic signifier of desirability in the Hollywood imaginary. In contrast, Richard becomes increasingly unsympathetic: a stereotypical swinging doctor familiar from the era's *Playboy* cartoons. He eventually starts a serious affair with Helene Donnelly, an actress in television commercials. This situation impacts her husband, Frank, whose briefly depicted unhappiness hints at the actual suffering caused by infidelity, which is glibly dismissed or deliberately elided by most naughty comedies.

At this point, the film's "true" agenda is revealed—a critique of Richard's inability to commit. *I Love My Wife* shows the deadening combination of married life and status-quo materialism yet avoids a wholesale critique of matrimony by holding this unreliable, troubled individual responsible for his domestic woes. An alternative lifestyle choice, via his adulterous relationship with Helene, begins lovingly and contains a transgressive moment suggesting erotic possibilities previously unthinkable in a more typical naughty sex comedy. She brings out her vibrator, and despite the scene abruptly ending, is clearly preparing to masturbate while he watches. Richard is aroused yet also makes a possessive comment, redolent of patriarchal ideas concerning male ownership, about how others must watch her on television while he, using an objectifying expression, has the "real thing." Nevertheless, their unmarried romantic arrangement duplicates his deceitful marriage. Helene eventually echoes Jody's opinions concerning Richard's unreliability. This doubly reinforced judgment grants women rare moral agency within this subgenre and reveals the chronic childishness of American men as a pathology (here beginning in childhood) rather than fodder for leering humor. The film may conservatively, and predictably, lean toward resigned despair rather than progressive optimism, but still provocatively suggests that the problem with marriage may be bad husbands, not harmless, naturalized restlessness.

Helene's kiss-off speech is itself interesting in partly blaming Hollywood for American male immaturity. She states there is no "more" to life beyond reality, and that fantasy "is a blonde movie star on a 50-foot screen promising you love forever. But when the director yells 'cut' she goes straight home to the same problems you and I have." As a media insider, her words have currency. Considering that Richard is introduced at the movies watching Gary Cooper, this functions as an indictment of the culture industry. Interestingly, Richard's earlier speech mockingly comparing himself to Jimmy Stewart shows some awareness that cinematic narratives are idealized. Nevertheless, these stories have infiltrated his fantasies. More depressingly, classical Hollywood has been replaced by Helen's television commercials as the film's example of media influence. Even Jody resorts to unsuccessfully attempting to interest Richard by using the supposedly aphrodisiac feminine spray that her husband's lover advertises.

In the film's final scene, at a singles' bar to the accompaniment of the usual instrumental go-go rock, Richard feeds smooth pickup lines to a young blonde stewardess, a profession ridiculously overrepresented in naughty sex comedies. A direct presentation of his now-developed misogyny occurs when she asks which branch of medicine he practices and guesses "gynecology?" He is seemingly appalled and jokes "Not when I'm drinking," as if nauseated by even considering women as bodies or as vulnerable to illness rather than as objectified prey. The camera tracks backward, the credits roll, and their dialogue continues. This stylistic choice slowly suspends Richard in the cinematic analogue of the grammatical infinitive. His swinger's lifestyle is established and immutable. For once, matrimony and romance are not recuperated within a supposedly traditionalist title, since the "hero" is ultimately, irrevocably characterized as a shallow, immature philanderer.

A more optimistic text, suggesting that countercultural values and questioning can ameliorate bourgeois anomie, *The Marriage of a Young Stockbroker* follows another professional, Bill Halloran (Richard Benjamin), whose inquietude leads to acts of voyeurism. His ennui is amplified by witnessing a successful colleague rolled out of the brokerage after a fatal heart attack. The film is more critical of the workaday world than is typical of the subgenre, potentially interested in a female point-of-view, and unconcerned with resurrecting a societal status quo. Stylistically, László Kovács's (*Easy Rider*) muted, hazy cinematography and a pastoral folk score (furthering the paradigm started by Simon and Garfunkel's music in *The Graduate*) suggest the thoughtful, melancholic tone of a maverick production. The resemblance to *The Graduate* continues as *The Marriage of a Young Stockbroker* is also based on a Charles Webb novel and directed by Lawrence Turman, who had produced the earlier, more-celebrated film. In fact, Bill and his wife Lisa's fate temptingly suggests that of Ben Braddock and Elaine Robinson if they had reduplicated their parents' middle-class misery.

The Marriage of a Young Stockbroker also proves innovative by granting Lisa more attention than is typical for female characters in the subgenre. The emotions of a "trophy wife" are depicted in a respectful, nuanced manner similar to the sympathetically rendered protagonist in another Richard Benjamin film from the era—*The Diary of a Mad Housewife* (Frank Perry, 1970). Lisa is directionless, "numb," and feels "powerless." She leaves Bill and successfully applies to modeling school. This choice clearly conflicts with pursuing feminist enlightenment, yet seems to be an attempt at self-fulfillment despite simply trading domesticity for voyeurized objectification. Perhaps she wants male attention, considering that Bill's obsessive peeping focuses solely on other women. Interestingly, her reality as a housewife is also presented ambivalently. Lisa's daily routine is never described as drudgery, despair, or, per Betty Friedan, a waste of intellectual and spiritual potential, but as an ultimately unsatisfactory fantasy safe haven of pleasant pretense (Freidan 75–79, passim). In contrast, when Bill returns home angry and fatigued, even this illusion is shattered. Furthering the text's wavering tone, she finds his behavior repellent yet acknowledges that her husband's sour mood stems from working hard to provide for their needs.

This complex, borderline-feminist representation of Lisa Halloran's thoughts and desires is completely countered by the misogynist characterization of her castrating older sister, Nan (Elizabeth Ashley). This unsympathetic hypocrite tries to provoke Bill's voyeurism by "accidental" self-exposure while adjusting a revealing bikini top and asks "hypothetically" if he would like to watch her undress. Later, Nan forces Bill, her cowed husband, Chester (Adam West), and Lisa into impromptu group therapy. Feminist concerns over psychiatry as an institution that investigates and subjugates women are inapplicable here as the (female) doctor, another unsympathetic caricature, addresses Bill's "problem." Nan's borderline villainy also blunts Lisa's (valid) criticisms of his voyeuristic activity. Furthermore, she is clearly invested in dominating her younger sister, destroying the Hallorans' marriage, and replacing Bill with an eligible businessman, thus trapping Lisa in the materialistic status quo she has fled. In the patriarchal tradition, Nan's punishment finally occurs. She demands Chester "behave like a man" and stop Bill from reuniting with Lisa. He follows this directive and asserts masculinity by pushing Nan to the ground. This obvious comeuppance backfires when she retaliates by punching her husband in the stomach. A freeze frame as Chester doubles over in pain is the movie's last image; this period-specific technique creates a putatively comic effect yet any chuckles scarcely mask the previous unpleasant presentation of justified male aggression. Nevertheless, the moment's outcome fatalistically suggests that even violence proves impotent against Nan's imperturbable villainy.

The Marriage of a Young Stockbroker is subgenerically atypical in representing women's concerns. Nevertheless, the film's primary issue involves Bill's scopophilia, also depicted in a manner both progressive and conservative. His problem adds a reflexive dimension within a subgenre itself prone to the camera's objectifying gaze or showing male characters whose ogling serves as an aperitif for actual adultery. Bill is literally a voyeur in the clinical, psychoanalytic sense. He clearly suffers, yet from the film's first scene, viewers may vicariously and pleasurably gaze along with him. In the opening precredit sequence, point-of-view shots show

Bill watching a short-skirted girl, standing on literal display in the brokerage's window. The high-point of such identification occurs when he attends a pornographic movie and, in one pointed shot, the back of his head is framed between the image of two topless women on the theater's screen. The spectator is literally doubled by Bill. He even serves as a spokesman for scopophilia by comparing his activities to a mask allowing one the advantage of watching unwitting strangers in anonymity. This self-awareness almost anticipates psychoanalytic theories of cinematic voyeurism (Mulvey, "Visual Pleasure" 200–4; Metz 93–95). His statement defending peeping's merits is even proven true as his proclivity, in an intriguing irony, helps him detach from a stultifying bourgeois existence.

First, Bill follows a braless, tank-top-wearing blonde home. She lies on the bed on literal display and they have sex. The scene conveys melancholy as the woman reveals that she is on vacation from her job in a secretarial pool, that is, another escapee from workaday anomie. He also feels saddened by the experience and baffled by her cold, pragmatic postcoital aloofness.

Nevertheless, their tryst spurs a valuable epiphany: Bill gets a divorce and returns to find Lisa at Nan's country club. He enters the women's locker room to retrieve her, which narrativizes a classic voyeuristic male fantasy. This scene echoes the finale of *The Graduate*, where Ben impulsively interrupts a wedding and rescues Elaine Robinson. Bill, invading another "sacred" space, pulls Lisa out of the shower. He offers to establish a new, unmarried, relationship. Romance is recuperated, but not matrimony. They have sex in a towel closet to pseudo-religious music and stroboscopic, ecstatic editing. He is rewarded for following his roving eye while she is rescued from potentially repeating her previous passive status-quo marriage with the eligible, well-off suitor hand-picked by Nan.

As they drive away, Lisa sees Bill briefly notice a short-skirted woman and, similar to her calm response to his literal "locker-room" description of the sexual encounter with the blonde secretary, adopts a seemingly healthy, nonpossessive attitude. Her blasé reaction may tacitly deem male voyeurism and promiscuity to be harmless and best ignored. Could such a text comfortably represent Bill's indifference if she confessed a sexual dalliance and then asked him to reunite? *The Marriage of a Young Stockbroker* revels in scopophilic titillation and portrays peeping as, at worst, symptomatic of dissatisfaction with work and monogamy. Presumably, in the liberated relationship Bill's voyeurism has ultimately spawned, he may enjoy, albeit healthily, the traditional male prerogative of ogling, just as many men enjoyed the fruits of the era's "free love" ideology more than women. He benefits from the sexual revolution *and* transcends middle-class morality, along with his now-emancipated ex-wife.

These films, despite not achieving any sort of fame or canonical status, come closest to reflecting the periods' progressive attitudes of any of the titles discussed in this study. Interestingly, more seemingly conservative attempts also existed to create products dealing with adultery geared to older viewers.

Your Parents' (Self-Conscious) Naughty Sex Comedy

In 1972, as the period was ending, the Neil Simon adaptation *The Last of the Red Hot Lovers* (Gene Saks) and Billy Wilder's *Avanti!* eschewed the partial revivification and revisionism of the subgenre provided by *I Love My Wife* and *Marriage of a Young Stockbroker*. Instead, they reverted to portraying middle-aged characters. The resigned tone characteristic of earlier entries like *How to Save a Marriage (and Ruin Your Life)* returns but in a bittersweet, less depressed key, while the institution of marriage is basically preserved. These autumnal narratives also suggest that the mode's self-conscious, final phase has arrived. Infidelity and promiscuity are viewed as commonplace, well-known activities, associated with youth culture and hipness. Simon and Wilder portray would-be swingers who have read about the sexual revolution and wish to participate. These films treat society's new-found permissiveness as a topic of discourse or fad rather than the spontaneous result of unhappy marriages, and self-reflexively present characters that discuss and attempt adultery, just as the mobsters on *The Sopranos* can quote from *The Godfather* movies and know the gangster film is an established Hollywood genre.

The Last of the Red Hot Lovers follows a middle-aged, Jewish businessman trying to be au courant, which mirrors the situation of a deeply conventional playwright like Simon tackling a racier topic than usual. One tries out adultery, the other writes a farce *about* infidelity. Ironically, the fading naughty-sex-comedy mode only apes hipness, and thus Simon jumps on a square bandwagon. Befitting its ultimate conservatism, the film also upholds monogamy with, unlike earlier titles, only a bittersweet resignation as Barney, happily married, is not really interested in sex but had hoped a meaningful experience might ameliorate his midlife crisis. The character's belief in "decency" prevails.

The narrative's protagonist and spokesman, Barney Cashman (Alan Arkin), is only a restaurateur, not a Broadway fixture, but still financially successful, as suggested by his surname. *The Last of the Red Hot Lovers* starts with a subjective shot from this character's point of view as he rises in the morning. His wife is only a shape next to him and never shown throughout the film, and is therefore easily idealized. He notes that her skin looks great for a woman of forty-three, which avoids the misogynist representation of Jody's body in *I Love My Wife*. He narrates these thoughts in interior monologue and the viewer is simply privy to his mental states, but not addressed directly as in *The Secret Life of an American Wife*, which also begins with the protagonist waking before his spouse and ruminating on infidelity and dissatisfaction. The credit sequences then show images, imitating magazine advertisements, of cavorting, sporty young people, such as a pretty girl kissing a race-car driver, accompanied by Neal Hefti's lounge jazz score. As he drives to work, stuck like Richard Burroughs in rush-hour traffic, Barney muses that beautiful blondes are suddenly ubiquitous, whereas when he was a teenager there were ostensibly only six attractive women in the world.

His main reason for adultery is a variation of "the seven-year itch"— a midlife crisis caused by growing awareness of mortality. Concerned with his legacy, Barney states "The sum total of my existence is 'nice.'" The fact that a parking lot attendant recognizes him each morning only by the car he drives provokes his ennui about the fact that mere monetary success lacks grandeur or significance. Barney wants only one adulterous experience to prove that he has truly "lived," and expects a profound and meaningful event. His first "conquest" is Elaine (Sally Kellerman, fresh from Altman's maverick classics *M*A*S*H* and *Brewster McCloud*, 1970), a literal materialist and cold-blooded libertine who denies any reality beyond what is directly, physically experienced. She ably parries his existential queries about mortality by saying that everyone is dying. Barney's scruples vex Elaine, who leaves without consummating their affair. Simon deserves credit for not vilifying her but, dialogically, convincingly presenting her viewpoint. She is also clear about her desires, unlike the clumsy, inept Barney.

Of course, Cashman does not really want to cheat, nor does Simon wish to write a typical naughty comedy. The character uses his mother's place for his attempted trysts. Choosing this environment might reveal a bad conscience by invoking a classic signifier of guilt—the Jewish mother. A perverse Oedipal reading of this decision is also possible. He cannot handle Elaine's coldness. Barney is also put off by Bobbie (Paula Prentiss), a kook similar to Doris (Barbra Streisand) in *The Owl and the Pussycat* (Herb Ross, 1970), as both describe encounters with implausibly, randomly constructed "perverse" characters. For instance, Bobbie lives with Wilhelmina, a Nazi who sleeps in leather pajamas, uses a whip for punishment, but more in keeping with a masochistic personality and thus rendering the entire characterization unbelievable, also has her name scarified into her flesh. These "kinks" are more reminiscent of a gag writer's ideas than a believable description of alternative sexualities.

Finally, he is propositioned by his mirror image—Jeanette (Renee Taylor), a married member of the Cashmans' social circle. This character's curiosity is piqued by her husband's descriptions of a "new, guiltless society." Her existential crisis—wondering if any decent people exist—spurs a desire for adultery, but she too cannot follow through and sleep with Barney. Ironically, poor Cashman is finally ready to cheat and angrily shouts that he knows "Where it's at. I'm in!" using the period's spatially indeterminate term for hipness. Eventually, though, he aligns with her search for goodness. She leaves, and he calls Mrs. Cashman and suggests a rendezvous at his mother's apartment. Fantasy adultery with your spouse—who is dubious about this proposition and does not definitively agree to participate when the film ends—is the best result when one only cheats to solve existential crises or keep up with the countercultural equivalent of the Joneses. The quietistic resignation of *The Last of the Red Hot Lovers* lacks even the unwitting bitterness of earlier naughty comedies.

Billy Wilder's quirkily romantic *Avanti!* also features a character aware of the sexual revolution's allure, but is more traditionalist via a classically elegant narrative structure and subdued visual style with truly attractive and tasteful cinematography. The opening credits—simple yellow titles against aerial shots set to romantic, Italian music—are old-fashioned. Since directed by a past master of envelope-pushing morality tales, the film is also seemingly progressive, via its unequivocal valorization of adultery. Only George Axelrod, Wilder's collaborator on the seminal naughty text *The Seven Year Itch*, presents infidelity as sympathetically during this period in *The Secret Life of an American Wife*. *Avanti!* revisits the auteur's earlier concept of therapeutic cheating presented in *Kiss Me, Stupid*. In both films infidelity also strengthens the status quo and proves to be a good business decision. Here a major director, who had earlier pushed against the representational limits of an earlier period, is now freer to express his philosophy without censorship per the new ratings system. Wilder also uses adultery in *Avanti!* as part of a dialectical process in which Americanism itself is also recuperated along with its marital and economic traditions.

The film's protagonist, American tycoon Wendell Armbruster, Junior (Jack Lemmon), has arrived in Italy to claim his father's dead body and immediately meets Pamela Piggott (Juliet Mills), the grieving daughter of Armbruster Senior's long-term mistress. In contrast to attenuated farce construction, Wilder and I. A. L. Diamond's scenario quickly reveals that the father and his lover vacationed at the same seaside resort for over a decade and perished together. Their children will eventually follow this pattern and start an affair, coaxed along by the magical Italian setting.

The continental locale's relaxed and charming lifestyle allows Armbruster, as a proxy for American values, to be redeemed. At first, the character is stereotypically rude, and impatiently complains about inefficient

Italian customs such as the three-hour lunch. Predictably, he surrenders to the film's equally clichéd depiction of Italy as a haven of good food and *amore*. A less-flattering, even racist representation involves a jealous, hysterical, and mustachioed Sicilian chambermaid. By the film's end, an ambassador, Blodgett (Edward Andrews), has filled the spot of vulgar, pushy American. Armbruster can now represent the open-mindedness of a nation that once welcomed immigrants hoping to innovate and flourish.

This "melting pot" discourse is presented via the hotel's valet, Bruno (Gianfranco Barra), hoping to re-enter the United States after deportation for excessive patriotism—hitting a hippie antiwar protester who called "his" president, presumably Nixon, an unspecified dirty word. Bruno has a clever idea: blackmailing Armbruster, whose political pull could result in an entrance visa. Clearly, irony and humor are paramount here, not trenchant political analysis, but the idea still resonates that America offers such promise that even a recent immigrant would feel protective of the president's reputation, although exiled for his troubles, and then try to return by employing an extreme form of capitalism—the shakedown. Bruno's peeping also introduces naughtiness to a narrative that is usually either frank or refined. For instance, a scene of Armbruster and Piggott's skinny-dipping is presented as natural and innocent until other potential voyeurs (the crew of a passing fishing boat) cause him to cover her bare breasts with a black sock. The fishermen's lusty cheers and this absurd concealment invoke a smirking, "naughty" tone.

Figure 3.2. Wendell Armbruster, Jr. (Jack Lemmon), and Pamela Piggott (Juliet Mills) enjoy therapeutic adultery in *Avanti!* (Billy Wilder, 1972). Naughtiness only exists once nakedness is concealed.

This immigrant proletarian is the true capitalist, since he is clever and ruthless, but carries his entrepreneurism too far and ends up murdered by the jealous Sicilian maid he has impregnated. Meanwhile, Armbruster gains a new, more-refined awareness of how adultery and the sexual revolution ultimately prove compatible with two other American status-quo institutions: business and marriage. He already understands that permissiveness is an easily commodified product, having seen *Carnal Knowledge*, and visits a topless restaurant when on business in Los Angeles. Most notably, Wendell states that silicone is one of his company's biggest-selling products. Similar to Barney Cashman, he also wants to directly sample the sexual revolution and calls himself a "groovy cat" and "tuned in." Armbruster even sees therapeutic value in casual sex with a secretary or stewardess, again re-enforcing a subgeneric worldview in which these two jobs are the sole professions available to female characters. Similarly, as a male spectator, he encourages secretaries to wear hot pants.

The key idea here is these acts are either profitable consumer transactions, reify a power imbalance, or are at least contained if one only swings "for a couple of nights" and afterward says "Aloha!" In contrast, his father's long-term, affectionate infidelity proves morally incomprehensible and places Wendell in situations suspicious to his wife. In fact, the biggest problem with adultery would involve any potential impact on Armbruster's marriage to a wealthy business heiress, portrayed as a logical, professional alliance furthering the tycoon's career plans. His merely mildly nagging wife is symbolically important yet never shown or heard. Mrs. Armbruster is represented indirectly through a series of phone calls where the audience only hears Wendell's reactions. Ultimately, the father's contained but passionate relationship provides a successful precedent unlikely to destroy his marriage or business. Armbruster decides to pursue a future romance with Pamela, at the same hotel, the following summer. Clearly, American innovation can extend to "doing as the Romans do" when in Italy and enjoying harmless, therapeutic infidelity. As the subgenre waned, Wilder's film neatly performs a dialectical synthesis of progressive attitudes toward sexuality and status-quo values.

Family Values

A smaller group of films negotiated the sexual revolution through discussing the "generation gap" between middle-aged parents and their teen offspring. In particular, the subgenre presented the schism between status-quo marriage and monogamy, and youth culture's liberal ideas about sex, culture, and politics. This potentially threatening permissiveness spawned cinematic responses that comfortingly neutralized such developments, while often criticizing bourgeois hypocrisy, and treated the "kids" with sympathy and even provided comfort by showing their willing acceptance of status-quo values. Once again, traditional morality's residual power continues even in films seeming to synchronically partake of a newer, hipper social landscape.

The Impossible Years attempts to achieve contemporary relevance by detailing student protests, without taking a definite position, and performing a consistent critique of bourgeois morality. The narrative also depicts liberal college psychology professor Jonathan Kingsley's (David Niven) odd hysteria over his teenage daughter Linda's budding sexuality. In fact, the film mirrors his unnatural obsession with her virginity, which often seems an excuse to revel in the era's newfound representational freedom for "naughty" rather than liberating purposes. *The Impossible Years* concludes with a traditionalist upholding of marriage, per the subgenre's general ideology, which incoherently blends with its already uneasy mixture of social commentary and leering voyeurism. Perhaps this is why a film obsessively focused on sex and virginity was actually given a G rating by the MPAA.

Similarly, Kingsley's feigned hipness clashes with "square" beliefs. The film starts with a shot of students protesting, a seemingly relevant beginning. Kingsley is then introduced watching the proceedings from a classroom window and then turning to tell his students that campus revolt exemplifies a venerable tradition of youthful rebellion. This comment is both tolerant and simultaneously consoling through converting the demands of 1960s protesters, which usually involved specific anti-imperialist or anticapitalist messages, into a predictable, conventional occurrence. Furthermore, the demonstration's purpose is also vague. The marchers demand "free speech" without the narrative providing any specific context or goal such as American withdrawal from Vietnam. One protester even carries a sign saying "Stamp out hippies," which indicates the script's desire to include a joke is more important than accurately presenting student unrest.

Kingsley's more conservative attitudes are revealed following Linda's arrest for carrying a sign, photographed from the back with its contents never revealed, containing an unnamed yet "obscene" expression. He claims free speech and pornography are completely different matters. In line with the protest's hazy representation, viewers are unable to evaluate his judgment's validity since they are denied information about the placard's actual words. The professor's statement echoes conservative, juridical voices, not the tolerant attitude suggested by his initial statements as a seemingly hip, liberal instructor. Most significantly, the "free speech" demonstration contextualizes the increased libidinal content of such films within a general trend toward contemporary relevance, but just as the particular dirty word on Linda's sign is never revealed, naughty sex comedies also use eroticism as bait for potential spectators' titillation yet show little and eventually uphold convention. Renata Adler, in the *New York Times*, points out this elision and speaks of the film, per the typical critical understanding, as a "peculiarly joyless, fumbling dirty" comedy (Adler).

In contrast, *The Impossible Years*, despite an ultimately conservative resolution, certainly takes an unambiguously critical look at Kingsley and his status-quo values. The period's progressive discourses consistently attacked middle-class dishonesty and inauthenticity. These are the main flaws of a character who consistently and obsessively meddles with and investigates Linda's behavior. Ironically, he condescendingly ridicules "fuming, frustrated" parents who complain about their children but themselves need psychoanalysis. The professor's calming equanimity quickly shifts when he learns his neighbor's son has designs on Linda. He responds by imposing multiple punishments, and even runs out of ideas for new deprivations. The results of his enlightened parenting are her truancy from school, slovenliness, frustration, and confusion, although the point is made that these are normal teenage behaviors.

Beyond flagrant hypocrisy the professor also inevitably relies on alcohol when angered or nervous and represents the careerism so disdained by the era's liberal thinkers. He is mostly upset about Linda's arrest since such bad publicity might negatively harm his campaign for a promotion. Kingsley also collaborates with a professor, Merrick (Chad Everett), whom he dislikes but recognizes as an ambitious, savvy operator likely to further his academic progress. This hypocritical protagonist is the perfect central figure for a film suffering from bad consciousness that feigns a critique of bourgeois values, but cannot coherently represent student unrest and also exemplifies problematic attitudes toward and representations of sexuality.

The narrative focus on Linda's virginity couches its lurid presentation in parental concern and combines the sex comedy's "naughty" tone with a conservative resolution. In the post-Code era, the naughty films can explicitly investigate, and fret about, the endangered maidenhood that more obliquely motored earlier Doris Day vehicles. For instance, Freddie is shown aggressively trying to remove Linda's bikini top in a brief flash-forward, a device used by next year's maverick classic *Easy Rider*, which interrupts Kingsley ruminating about his daughter's sexual development. Again, Renata Adler observed "that dirty jokes between two generations of a single family are inevitably in the poorest taste imaginable" (Adler). This narrative prolepsis seemingly visualizes, using the cinematic grammar of subjective fantasy, the professor's fears while suggesting that he vividly, perhaps perversely, imagines Linda's erotic activities under the guise of worried speculation. In contrast, other instances clearly are objectively independent of his predictions, by revealing the character's fatuous assumptions as unrealistic. For instance, he views her trip to Catalina positively and talks about the value of "fresh air" and healthy exercise. A shot of Linda in a smoky nightclub quickly undercuts Kingsley's statement.

Therefore, the film's leering shots of fetishized and jiggling breasts and buttocks certainly extend beyond the professor's imagination, although the frank candor of a ground-breaking production such as *Carnal Knowledge* proves more impossible than even the teenage years. Freddie Fleischer's complaint about how a night of kissing, without any consummation, can cause physical problems and griping about taking cold showers, provides some honesty by noting male sexual frustration. Nevertheless, during the same scene, Linda discusses a geometry problem and traces a spherical shape in the air. This prompts Freddie's response with the classic hand gesture in American pop culture for "big breasts," which returns to the subgenre's traditional use of winking double-entendre. Later, Dr. Fleischer tells Kingsley that Linda is no longer a "spinster," which invokes the mode's euphemistic tendencies.

At this point, the narrative again presents the professor's extreme denial of reality, which, in tandem with drunkenness, leads him to speculate that Linda's condition is the result of exercise. Per the naughty comedy aesthetic, the idea that she broke her hymen playing sports is presumably clear to most audiences yet not stated explicitly. During this scene, Kingsley confesses to Fleischer about courting his future wife when they were teenagers, which resulted in an unplanned pregnancy and early wedding. The consolation that such youthful rebellion predates the 1960s, combined with his subsequent professional success, ultimately enfolds the film's leering depictions into the status quo's normal pattern. In fact, the status quo seems safe since Merrick has actually already married Linda. Since he is a clean-cut professor—and helps Kingsley obtain a promotion—the narrative seems closed with order restored.

Nevertheless, *The Impossible Years* ends ironically and suggests the film's previous ideological incoherence resists an easy resolution. The last image shows Abby, the family's younger daughter, running upstairs to "study" with a boy who, in tandem with the camera, gazes lovingly at her twitching, bikini-clad ass. Kingsley chases them until a freeze frame seemingly eternalizes this possibly endless struggle between parents and children while the end credit appears. The action resumes and the characters run out of the frame. Presumably this new situation will also be resolved, but the ease with which the patriarch's panic is reinvigorated suggests that further perverse ordeals will precede a hopefully satisfactory outcome. Kingsley, as a representative of both academia and the middle class, has seemingly gained wisdom and accepted 1960s youth culture's differing values yet instantly responds with hysterics. Of course, characters' repetitive stupidity is a fundamental principle of many screen comedies. More consolingly, this seemingly immutable idiocy is itself another predictable development, similar to youth protest and libidinal activity, and should eventually revert to tolerant acceptance, especially if the status quo triumphs and Abby continues the familial pattern by marrying an esteemed professional.

The Impossible Years perfectly exemplifies an odd, incoherent oscillation that occurs in many naughty comedies between moments openly critical of societal hypocrisy and those espousing the conservative attitudes that have just been found lacking. Dialectical synthesis between progressivism and the traces of traditional values is shaky when a film lewdly objectifies a seventeen-year-old girl's body while supporting matrimony and family. The freeze frame suggests a narrative denied the smooth resolution of the classical era, a story that can only pause before potentially repeating its incoherent ideological position.

How to Commit Marriage, a late star vehicle for screen legend Bob Hope, initially resembles a divorce narrative: Frank (Hope) and Elaine Benson (Jane Wyman) decide to separate after twenty years. The film's real stake concerns the generation gap and the movie ultimately attempts the same consoling message of *The Impossible Years*, that is, that today's youth are just as square as their parents and also want marriage and family. *How to Commit Marriage* also proves incoherent but in a different fashion. *The Impossible Years* uneasily blends prurience, liberal social critique of bourgeois values, and traditional moralism. The parental stupidity depicted, though, is ultimately harmless, while in *How to Commit Marriage*, the older generation directly threatens their children's old-fashioned values. The film's incoherence stems from its concomitant need to valorize the Bensons, despite their presentation as contagious hypocrites, and even reward the couple's (deceptive) actions since their compulsive dishonesty ultimately preserves the next generation's commitment to traditional morality. This sleight-of-hand works by shifting blame to another "bad" parent—Oliver Poe (Jackie Gleason). Unsurprisingly, such ideological instability ends, as with *The Impossible Years*, in another frozen moment, where the two fathers are literally trapped by a mudslide symbolizing their corruption.

Figure 3.3. Frank Benson (Bob Hope) and Oliver Poe (Jackie Gleason) literally trapped by middle-class chicanery in *How to Commit Marriage* (Norman Panama, 1969).

The plot strand involving the Bensons' marriage requires a conservative, status-quo-affirming, easy resolution. The couple's inevitable reunion is both a collateral benefit of their more narratively central salvage work of protecting the next generation and required as proof that marital contentment remains possible. Frank and Elaine initially establish new relationships. These function as subplots compared to the main project of restoring the younger generation's traditional values.

As noted, the kids themselves are all right at first. Unsullied by the 1960s, the short-haired David (Tim Matheson) and wholesome-appearing Nancy (JoAnna Cameron) meet the Bensons and state their desire for a church wedding with all the trimmings. Furthermore, he plays avant-garde jazz and classical music, not a mainstream vocation but uncontaminated by the counterculture, and has been accepted to Julliard. Frank's main worry about his potential son-in-law is that a career in serious music is unprofitable. This concern, coupled with the shadiness of Benson's real-estate business, introduces an almost Marxist suggestion that capitalism is both dishonest and threatens high cultural values.

At the young couple's wedding, during the moment when a minister typically asks if anyone present objects to the union, Poe reveals that the Bensons are divorcing. When Elaine says love can endure, her daughter agrees, but does not require matrimony (which she calls "a fraud") and moves in with David after canceling the ceremony. This point of departure, arguably similar to the climax of *The Graduate*, where another failed marriage ceremony produces a romantic couple, might provide the narrative with a progressive denouement and show a realistic response to parental hypocrisy. Poe's contagion continues, though, and produces its antithesis in the Bensons' status-quo preservation efforts

Mr. Poe is a complex, dangerous, and irreconcilable corrupting figure. A status-quo exemplar through his wealth, bourgeois status, and staunch commitment to alcoholism, he also holds a dim view of matrimony, which he euphemistically calls "bushwa," and openly flaunts his mistress, Laverne (Tina Louise). He also hates Benson for selling him a house which was immediately inundated by a landslide and is supposedly still, twenty years later, being dug out.

He does possess an odd integrity when cataloging the world's rotten attributes in an almost free-associational beat-poem speech decrying "famine, pestilence, peek-a-boo bras . . . computer dating, diet cola, air pollution . . . zip codes." All these horrors share one thing: "They're all married." This incoherent statement either equates such problems *with* marriage or suggests they *are* "married" through their similarities. This latter idea oddly equates truly horrific situations with examples of both consumerism and permissiveness (two topics of concern but usually for those with opposed ideologies). His response to the fallen world—typical of many cinematic sociopaths who use the "life is a jungle, eat or be eaten" defense to rationalize their selfish cruelty—is that the individual must first understand "the venal sound of the hypocrites, liars, the sycophants" and then steel themselves with money, liquor, and women.

After the failed wedding, his mocking nihilism seems triumphant. Poe then recruits the couple into a successful rock band, the Comfortable Chair, which he manages, and the darker side of the character's realist philosophy appears. When Nancy becomes pregnant he bribes the band's spiritual adviser—a thinly veiled parody of the Beatles' guru Maharishi Mahesh Yogi known as the Baba Ziba (comedian Irwin Corey)—into requesting the couple put up the child for adoption. Encouraging an abortion is beyond the text's ideological imaginings and would render Poe too villainous. This suggestion might destroy Poe's moral agency but would also render him unredeemable, foreclosing a necessary possibility since comic narratives typically end with harmony between major characters. Frank had already worried that David's earlier musical career was unprofitable. Now the darker forces of capital have seemingly trounced family values. Rock 'n' roll, a supposedly liberating music, is simply a business, while the Eastern spiritual practitioners associated with the period's open-minded youth, and viewed as threatening to traditional religions, actually worship at the tycoon's purse strings.

This unstable synthesis of money and cooptable counterculturalism is anathema to the film's traditionalist values, so the narrative concocts another dubious alliance by reuniting the Bensons and having their dishonesty, previously viewed as dangerous, ultimately restore marriage and family. Presumably these qualities are worth lying to protect, although fibs also undid David and Nancy's wedding.

Poe is not easily defeated. Again, the film displays ambivalence in presenting a character probably similar to the studio bosses who financed *How to Commit Marriage*. Certainly, his clever resourcefulness exemplifies the entrepreneurial spirit typically favored in American films. In an interesting development, he hustles Frank at golf by offering to put money on a chimpanzee he has taught to play the game. A scene like this is obviously only intended as absurd comedy, but once again Poe both mocks a status-quo-associated institution—a sport deeply enmeshed with Hope's public persona—and profits from manipulating the system.

Nevertheless, Poe also personifies rampant avarice, a characteristic rarely explicitly valorized in mainstream films, which instead champion populism and decency. The tycoon's unstable mix of (bad) conventional values and quasiprogressive social critique is untenable. The hypocritical Bensons may also shoulder blame but then seek to restore order using any means necessary. Using the same crooked approach as Poe, Frank tries bribing the Baba Ziba to reverse his advice that David and Nancy give up their child, but instead unwittingly bargains with the spiritual leader's assistant. In a gesture completely inexplicable to Benson, reflecting the egalitarianism of Eastern spirituality, a subordinate occupies the venue's best dressing room. Frank then buys the assistant's clothes, reinforcing his faith that money can solve problems, and addresses the faithful. He tells the young couple of his "new" vision where they raise their child and instructs them to "get married and be miserable like everybody else." This statement is a synecdoche for the film's conservative, resigned attitude, which renders unfeasible such possible developments as postdivorce fulfillment and unmarried cohabitation, and presents the Baba Ziba—a potential figure of enlightenment and non-Western religious philosophy—as an empty signifier whose robe, beard, and seemingly profound (but nonsensical) speeches, masking an intellectual void, are easily imitated by a fraud like Benson.

Following this twist, Poe suddenly states that he has been a bad father, encourages the children's marriage and parenthood, and announces his engagement to Laverne. Contagion is seemingly contained. This reversal's implausibility and abruptness almost seems a self-reflexive commentary on such last-minute conversions in earlier, classical films. Sure enough, this epiphany is another desperate masquerade, this time orchestrated by Poe's mistress who threatens to leave him and succeeds in "reforming" this unstable, complex antagonist. Evidently even nihilists need security, and he caves in to her demands rather than remaining consistent to his putative nonconformism and starting over with a new lover.

The narrative's denouement, though, criticizes the shoddiness of such contrived arrangements that clumsily restore social order. As the two patriarchs toast their truce with expensive brandy, a storm causes the hillside to collapse on the mansion Poe has just purchased from Benson. The final shot of *How to Commit Marriage* reveals the two middle-class icons up to their necks in mud, hopelessly immobilized in the dirty, dishonest status quo. The film ends with another uneasy, eternalizing and frozen moment similar to the last images of *The Impossible Years*.

How Sweet It Is (Jerry Paris, 1968) also employs a contorted narrative to provide its consoling message, and is another sex-obsessed yet G-rated movie. The film follows Grif and Jenny Henderson (James Garner, Debbie Reynolds), their teenage son Davey, and his girlfriend Bootsy to Europe on vacation. The Hendersons are a healthier and happier unit and require less recuperation to restore the family's equilibrium than in *The Impossible Years* or *How to Commit Marriage*. They suffer some generational challenges, mainly between father and son, which are interesting as reflections of period discourses on social values and masculinity. The film's more conservative valence is expressed when a few convenient targets—overprotective mothers and (to a lesser degree) European libertinism—are blamed for domestic troubles, but the film shows faith in both youth and (eventually) parents. The narrative is also more centered on the parents' marital challenges. The depiction of teen eros and romance is mild and unworried; the naughtiness involves the grown-ups.

The main generational conflict, such as it is, occurs between father and son over social issues. In an earlier scene, Grif wonders if the boy is sexually active, albeit without the obsessiveness of Kingsley in *The Impossible Years*, but mostly inquires because Jenny wants reassurance. The issue is tabled when Davey indicates indirectly that he is still a virgin. Mrs.

Henderson will continue to meddle but only affect her marriage, not the boy. Grif's insistent masculinity and social values, though, will create some friction, but have little impact on his son, who appears comfortable expressing countercultural attitudes and nontraditional masculinity.

Similar to Linda in *The Impossible Years*, Davey protests on campus but his "cause"—making P.E. classes optional—hardly reflects the era's significant issues. Reassurance of his "normal" vigor and masculinity is even provided, since young Henderson is a track star, but expresses concern for students forced to unwillingly participate in athletics. The demonstration is a timid analogue to those against making young men serve and die in Vietnam. Davey also wears a peace sign medallion and, along with the film's other teen characters, constantly talks about and uses the word "love," again in a defanged manner, since such consistent, generic usage renders the term a meaningless signifier of liberalism similar to the Baba Ziba's robe and beard.

Nevertheless, Grif has mild complaints about this mild rebelliousness, particularly when it defies traditional masculinity. He demands that Davey stop fiddling with the medallion and talk with him "like a man," and proves to be unamused when Jenny describes the boy's hair as "pretty." In another scene, Grif describes his generation's form of rebellion as writing "Kilroy was here" on available surfaces, and then reminisces about helping Davey construct model airplanes. These activities share militaristic, hence traditionally masculine, connotations, just as the son's counterculturalism is feminized. The "Kilroy" reference invokes a form of communication used by World War II participants when entering previously occupied territory, while the miniatures built by Grif and Davey are fighter planes. In a line obviously intended humorously rather than literally, he states that his son currently would only be interested in sniffing the modeling glue, thus reinvoking the counterculture by linking Davey to its alleged drugginess. His most overt statement supporting violence—the linking quality of militarism and machismo—is when Davey blathers "Love's all over the world. It protects us all." Griff responds with "I've been all over the world. Take a gun." The ugly American is still alive and kicking.

None of these cultural-political generational debates are presented too seriously. Since cowritten by Garry Marshall and directed by Jerry Paris, both future sitcom creators, these comments simply bounce off their recipients. In fact, Grif does a good job as chaperone, and father and son even have a "first drink" together in Italy. Mr. Henderson's only "serious" paternal advice occurs during this scene. He states that, with the exception of Jenny, women are untrustworthy and should be fooled. Davey never directly follows this advice, but he unwittingly proves

Grif's philosophy and learns about manipulating female psychology. For instance, Bootsy behaves disinterestedly until he inadvertently visits a brothel, which provokes her jealousy. Grif might recommend deliberately causing this situation, whereas Davey only stumbles into it, but still the father's presence fulfills his desire to "make a man," and a representative of a deceptive status quo, out of the boy. This result would be unlikely if Jenny accompanied the tour. Therefore, the son benefits from, but does not foster, deceit and can retain his "honest" liberal attitudes while meeting with his dad's approval. The intergenerational relationship resolves perfectly in the film's last scene, where Grif, now wearing a peace-sign medallion indicating his participation in the dialectical synthesis of cultural values, and David playfully frolic on the French Riviera. Jenny also appears in this shot, signaling the end of a much longer redemptive process stemming from her problematic behavior.

Grif grants his son autonomy, and basically acts blamelessly since he never considers adultery. In contrast, Jenny's representation exemplifies traditional misogynist notions concerning overprotective mothers. Furthermore, she is culpable for much and almost cheats. At first, she seems like a hip, tolerant parent, especially about Davey's politics, a topic presumably irrelevant to a woman anyway, at least per sexist logic. Father–son conflicts are raised but eventually fizzle into impotence, but her smothering nature creates genuine trouble. Jenny pulls strings to send Grif on a photo assignment documenting the youth group's European tour.

Interestingly, Davey barely notices her meddling, which instead infects the Henderson's marriage. Refreshingly, parental misdeeds, which affect their children in *The Impossible Years* or *How to Commit Marriage*, only harm the older generation in *How Sweet It Is!* Trouble begins immediately when Jenny decides to accompany the group on their trip. European libertinism, represented via a suave French millionaire, Phillipe (Maurice Ronet), amplifies Mrs. Henderson's unreliability by opening the Pandora's box of middle-aged, bourgeois, American female sexuality. Insecure about her desirability and fearing Grif's interest in the tour guide, she encourages Phillipe's courting, which includes the purchase of a bikini. He employs a scowling Marxist butler (Marcel Dalio, intertextually recalling the Popular Front) who speaks of communist victory in the upcoming French elections in a fascinatingly coincidental invocation of May '68 and reminder of the leftist values feared by Grif. Jenny returns from an unhappy "surprise" visit with her husband, who calls her "old girl," and prances around a swinging pool party in the bikini, chest thrust out and seeking attention. No one bites, which increases her hysteria.

In a running gag, she appears in this bathing suit for several scenes and uses it to both shock and delay pursuers or to hopefully solicit an affirmative response. Jenny's shenanigans culminate with arrest until a pimp pays the bail and takes her to his brothel, where she meets Davey. Mother and son are thrust into a room together in the film's creepiest moment, where overprotectiveness has invoked its logical conclusion: incest. Jenny throws off her coat and asks Davey his opinion of her appearance. He says she looks fine, but not like a "real mom," a charitable, and boundary-respecting response considering her frenzied behavior. Clearly, the American matriarch has some explaining to do as attempts to monitor teen desire lead to imperiling a solid marriage and her exposure to contaminating European influences. Davey, in contrast, has immediately tried to leave the bordello and, as noted, requires little guidance beyond inadvertently following some paternal advice.

The most surprising element of the film involves both showing adults with a healthy sex life and placing them in the position of transgressors. Once again, the crazed mom's possessiveness causes trouble.

The Hendersons suffer consistent interruptions in their erotic activity, which reverses the typical situation where adolescents seeking privacy resort to parked cars and deserted locations. The film's first scene shows Grif and Jenny in postcoital bliss. Suddenly, they hear something downstairs. An edit occurs to a subjective tracking shot—a cinematic device already associated with a killer's viewpoint by 1968—as an unidentified character grabs a kitchen knife and climbs the stairs. The intruder is Davey home from work early, looking for a snack. They cover up and he exits feeling ashamed and foolish. This again reverses viewer expectations, since parents are usually presented as self-conscious witnesses to teen eros. Possibly Oedipal in meaning, or linking differing forms of hunger, the scene is also either a harbinger of later, quasi-incestuous moments in the narrative or a refreshingly frank presentation of an event that occurs in many families yet was unimaginable in the classical Hollywood cinema. The Hendersons' healthy sex life continues to be interrupted. On the boat to Europe, Grif and Jenny visit the ship's make-out spot. This scene shows the disturbing nature of mature sexuality, as the teenage habitués of this lovers' lane hastily shut off a forty-five record (of the usual generic instrumental rock) and stop kissing until the adults leave.

By the release of *How Sweet It Is!*, the naughty comedy's imaginary seems inured to teenage sexual behavior, especially when innocent and level-headed, but still demonizes women and foreigners. Whether because farce construction requires obstacles or as payback for parental meddling, the expression of middle-aged, marital passion is stifled, which perfectly suits a subgenre where representations of erotic, satisfying marital relations are rare. The film proves relatively progressive through briefly depicting (and preserving) the Hendersons' passion and for again portraying the period's youth as admirable and healthy albeit future exemplars of the status quo. Similar to *The Impossible Years* and *How to Commit Marriage*, *How Sweet It Is!* reconciles traditional values with social critique.

Love Gods and Stray Cats

Beyond marital and generational sex comedies, two stray titles are worth noting. Each perfectly exemplifies the ideological complexity and incoherence present in the subgenre's narratives and provides a reminder of the nervous but constant negotiation of social change in even seemingly inconsequential or escapist fare. The first, *The Love God?* (Nat Hiken, 1969), satirizes the sexual revolution, connects eros with business, and presents the opposition of "naughty" and "frank" content. The second, *The Owl and the Pussycat*, attempts to modernize the subgenre and replace its euphemisms with candor.

Another text directly foregrounding virginity, *The Love God?* initially appears to be merely another cheaply made vehicle produced by Universal featuring then-popular television star Don Knotts of the *Andy Griffith Show*. Normally these were G-rated family comedies parodying genres such as the Western in *The Shakiest Gun in the West* (Alan Rafkin, 1967)—a remake of the Frank Tashlin–scripted *The Paleface* (Norman Z. McLeod, 1948)—or science fiction in *The Reluctant Astronaut* (Edward Montagne, 1967). In contrast, *The Love God?* represents current social issues and spoofs the sexual revolution, the Playboy aesthetic, and erotic media.

Knotts plays bashful, bumbling, naïve small-town editor Abner Peacock, whose ornithological gazette, *The Peacock*, is saved from bankruptcy when a publisher of adult magazines, Osborne Tremaine (Edmond O'Brien), bails him out hoping to distribute his "smut" under a new title. A series of contrivances ensues, but basically Peacock must pretend to be a womanizer and sex symbol in the Hefner mode. This narrative device of creating a false sex symbol, and other moments, are directly lifted from *Will Success Spoil Rock Hunter?* (both film's titles even end with question marks) just as Tashlin's script for *The Paleface* was retooled, but at least credited, for *The Shakiest Gun in the West*. Both stories deal with a mild-mannered character who adopts the role of sex symbol for publicity and economic gain. The films' similarity even extends to the inclusion of musical numbers commemorating the characters' triumphant rise to fame and fortune. In *The Love God?* the celebratory tune is "Mr. Peacock," in *Will Success Spoil Rock Hunter?*, "You've Got It Made."

The Love God? was released a year after the motion picture ratings system replaced direct, albeit self-imposed, censorship of movie content and during a period where court cases increasingly allowed the publication of sexually explicit literature and magazines. The film directly presents contemporary discourses concerning sexual representation and the related idea of how such erotica, particularly if cleverly or deceptively marketed, can turn a profit within a capitalist economy. As with the generational comedy, the narrative also suggests society's fundamental innocence and traditionalism; a "purity" more comfortable with naughtiness than frankness, even when the topic *is* virginity.

Needless to say, *The Love God?* itself is pretty tame, although rated M (the equivalent of today's PG and PG-13 categories) unlike other Knotts vehicles. The photographs in Tremaine's "scandalous" magazine are cheesecake shots of models in lingerie accompanying lurid "fallen women" or "true crime" tabloid-style fiction, which are directly depicted without earning the film an R or X rating. In other words, these are "naughty" images, not the bolder representations of *Playboy* or other 1969 releases, such as *Midnight Cowboy* or *Bob & Carol & Ted & Alice*. In an unwittingly self-reflexive line, a judge calls Mrs. Tremaine (Maureen Arthur again) "a coarse, overdeveloped caricature of a woman." This could easily describe the characters Arthur plays in *How to Commit Marriage* or *A Guide for the Married Man*, or many female roles in naughty comedies.

Tremaine's legal problems allow narrativization of the period's discourses concerning erotic representation, presented via a cartoonish depiction of ideologically polarized positions. The "Council for Constitutional Liberty," a thinly veiled representation of the ACLU, come to his defense, as do students carrying "Free Peacock" signs, who say things such as "You're cool, baby." Even French citizens, shown in fake newsreels satirizing the prior year's May demonstrations, join the cause. In opposition are parents carrying "Protect Our Children from Smut" placards. One indignant mother yells "Go back to Russia" at poor Peacock, thus conflating two conservative positions.

Abner wins the case but objects to his defense lawyer, Darrell Evans Hughes (James Gregory, broadly parodying his already pompous, satiric performance as Senator Iselin in *The Manchurian Candidate*, John Frankenheimer, 1962) describing him as "filthy" and "dirty." Hughes's argument, a caricature of the typical "free speech" defense, is that even, in fact especially, degenerates deserve legal protection. The approach is successful, but the victorious Abner wants to hold a press conference and dispute this characterization. Interestingly, both Hughes and the prosecuting attorney oppose Peacock's plan. Is justice a game with a rigged outcome? Not exactly. *The Peacock* magazine is a potential cash cow and Abner's uncle also discourages his planned statement. The shame of bankruptcy proceedings had previously loomed large in this relative's imagination. In contrast, producing erotica is acceptable since it is lucrative. The status quo runs on profits and even supposed courtroom antagonists will concur in the interest of economic gain.

Abner's obliging and easily manipulated nature causes him to enact an odd charade. Echoing Hughes's earlier words about his emaciated physique expressing depravity, equally descriptive of Knott's body and thus rendering the actor believable in this role, the timid bird lover is cast as a libertine. Abner appears in public surrounded by women—the Pussycats—and opens "Peacock" clubs all over America. The parallels to Hugh Hefner are obvious. Two interesting suggestions occur. The first, similar to the perverse idea in *The Manchurian Candidate* that Joe McCarthy was a communist, is that Hefner might be a virgin. Second, the publisher's famed open approach, conveyed in his issue-spanning essays on "the Playboy philosophy," is here shown as a marketing decision.

A famed magazine editor, Lisa LaMonica (Anne Francis), decides the new publication will be "clean" (Hefner always referred to his centerfolds as "the girl next door") and "frank," not lurid and smutty. She echoes the period's alleged liberatory attitudes when stating, "After two hundred years of sexual frustration that began when the first Puritan stepped off the Mayflower, this country is exploding in a sex revolution and Abner Peacock is the flag bearer . . . the great emancipator who is

Figure 3.4. Abner Peacock (Don Knotts), a would-be Hugh Hefner in *The Love God?* (Nat Hiken, 1969). Note the period-specific superimpositions and costumes.

going to take them by the hand and dance naked in the moonlight." LaMonica claims great authors will write about sex in *The Peacock*, and top photographers will shoot the most famous women's naked bodies to create "a status symbol for swingers." It's an honest approach, unlike Hollywood's typically incoherent, double-entendre-ridden naughty comedies, yet fueled by a masquerade.

Furthering the presentation of this enterprise's essential fraudulence, though, is the presence of criminality behind the façade. The magazine's silent partner is a hood named "Ice Pick Charlie" (B. S. Pully, famed as "Big Julie" in both film and stage versions of *Guys and Dolls*). Abner's Casanova persona functions as another pose, but one concealing innocence, not larceny. The idea of Hefner as a naïf seems like a willfully blind, disavowing notion typical of reactionary wishful thinking. Nevertheless, used for satirical purposes in *The Love God?*, this narrative device also unveils America's sham licentiousness and, by proxy, that of many naughty sex comedies. The "real" Peacock is a thirty-something virgin, has a long-standing engagement to Rose-Ellen—a church organist and minister's daughter—and shows more interest in ornithology than women. When alone in his "Penthouse" with the Pussycats, he teaches them bird calls and is first shown impersonating various avian species while accompanying a church choir. Fittingly, the last one imitated is the American eagle, which reemphasizes his patriotic, small-town values. He also makes bird noises when nervous. Clearly, his libidinal function has been given sublimatory wings.

The virginity question provides *The Love God?* with its strangest, most singular dimension. Many male figures in classical cinema were presumably "pure," such as Jefferson Smith (James Stewart) in *Mr. Smith Goes to Washington*, Andy Hardy (Mickey Rooney), or Jerry Lewis, whose persona resembles Knotts's in most of his star vehicles. Similarly, Rhett Butler in *Gone with the Wind* or Rick Blaine in *Casablanca* are implicitly sexually experienced. In contrast, *The Love God?* places the topic up front and openly interrogates the hero's celibacy, a previously tacit subject whose candid discussion in Otto Preminger's *The Moon Is Blue* resulted in denial of an MPAA Seal in 1953 because Maggie McNamara's character described herself as a "virgin." By 1969, the word was permitted, and the film simply rated M, within a cinematic context where graphic violence and nudity had become normative. Nevertheless, after Abner proposes to his long-suffering fiancée, the word's discomforting almost-taboo nature arises. Rose-Ellen's minister father, afraid others will believe Peacock's public persona, tells him to openly proclaim his chastity. He begins hysterically stammering until finally, albeit audibly, whispering the word "virgin" into the patriarch's ear. Similarly, when practicing (alone) for a press conference to admit his true nature, Abner again cannot utter this two-syllable description. His press aide speaks the word openly, causing Mrs. Tremaine to state "That's the dirtiest thing I've ever heard in my life."

Presumably a simple joke in the script, her words also echo the odd hypocrisy of American culture, which prefers half-naked truthfulness. The Tremaines represent naughty, not explicit culture, as exemplified by most risqué cinematic sex comedies. An interesting ideological incoherence is produced since the couple are similar to Abner in commitment to family—Tremaine constantly uses his wife as a model and is upset when the new *Peacock* magazine nixes her appearance in its pages. Presumably she is too ersatz or connotes a more old-fashioned form of erotica; the latter quality would again pair her with Abner as she too exemplifies a "tradition." In contrast, his public acknowledgment of virginity would ruin the Tremaines' financial stake in the magazine, while a direct statement, even a proclamation of chastity, counters their commitment to veiled representation, perfectly served by distributing "smut" under cover of a birding gazette. This unmasking also would work against the same honest approach expressed in the pages of the new Peacock magazine, by exposing this frankness as a lie via Abner's innocence masquerading as libertinism.

The word "virgin" is costly and difficult to utter, just as in *The Impossible Years* where the weird euphemism "spinster" was employed. The film, per the subgenre's tendencies, must equivocate again since an ending of financial ruin violates the biggest Hollywood taboo—questioning the validity and triumph of capitalist entrepreneurialism, even when its hypocrisy is depicted as in *How to Commit Marriage*. To stop his press conference, Miss La Monica convinces Abner they had sex, and he responds in typical fashion with a marriage proposal. She substitutes Rose-Ellen at the altar, but the film ends with Abner convinced he is devirginized. Presumably his contamination, via innocence, of the Peacock magazine is averted, yet he still can marry his wholesome hometown sweetheart.

Incoherence continues to reign. American cinema ostensibly valorizes wholesomeness and virtue (traits ultimately recognized as dramatically uninteresting), yet as with the period's sex comedies, wishes to have it both ways and also flaunt a certain harmless naughtiness, often within the same narrative. In contrast, "honest" films such as *Bob & Carol & Ted & Alice* and *Carnal Knowledge* allow Hollywood to profit from direct, mature representation, just as Peacock's magazine thrives. *The Love God?* distinguishes itself from the maverick tradition, viewed as essentially dishonest via Abner's masquerade, yet also ends with a business that monetizes candid representation being protected through yet another ruse. The narrative's quick ending, involving yet another freeze frame, leaves his swinger reputation untarnished.

The Love God? is ultimately a reassuring title. Behind frankness lie innocence and profit, two American values. While *A Guide for the Married Man* and *How to Save a Marriage (and Ruin Your Life)* recuperate matrimony and *How Sweet It Is!* closes the generation gap, this film reveals that licentiousness and pornography are merely a deceptive masquerade, part of the economic order rather than forces of contagion. This tactic proves the cleverest strategy for containing potential threats to marriage and monogamy through their alleged contaminant's presentation as a paper tiger rather than a leering wolf at the door.

The Owl and the Pussycat, on the surface, contains enough hip trappings to seemingly place the text beyond the naughty sex comedy's domain and possibly within the maverick construction. The script, adapted from an off-Broadway play, is by Buck Henry, previously lauded as screenwriter of maverick classic and "naughty" comedy *The Graduate*. The male lead, George Segal, has a nebbish/bohemian persona, partially discernible in this film through the character's mustache and glasses, later epitomized by his role as in Paul Mazursky's hip counterculture romantic comedy *Blume in Love* (1973). The female star, Barbra Streisand, may have adorned many of the period's bloated musicals and worked within a traditional, pre-rock-and-roll performance tradition more reminiscent of Judy Garland than Grace Slick, but she also possessed a fresh, blatantly ethnic, palpably neurotic and untraditional screen personality. Stylistically, the film uses realistic-looking sets and New York location shooting emphasizing the city's seediness, as did maverick classics such as *Midnight Cowboy*. Veteran cinematographer Harry Stradling had previously lensed Streisand's three big-budget, traditionalist musicals (*Funny Girl*, *Hello, Dolly!*, *On a Clear Day You Can See Forever*) and the Oscar-winning, highly costly *My Fair Lady*, along with darker, black-and-white fare such as *Suspicion* (Alfred Hitchcock, 1941) and *A Streetcar Named Desire* (Elia Kazan, 1951). He died during production and was replaced by newcomer Andrew Laszlo ("Harry Stradling"). Despite Stradling's seemingly old-fashioned aesthetic, their joint effort produces a far more realistic, less garish look than many sex comedies.

The Owl and the Pussycat is also festooned with mild swearing such as "bastard," "slut" and "bitch," all currently acceptable on television. Furthermore, the film catalogs fetishes and "perversions." These contemporary-seeming qualities, though, are immediately belied since the film waters down its source material—a Broadway play about an interracial romance involving a black prostitute. *The Owl and the Pussycat* instead attempts to transcend "naughtiness" by directly discussing sex and focusing on characters atypical of the subgenre's bourgeois milieu, yet still culminates by establishing heterosexual monogamy

The narrative details the comic, romantic mismatch of Felix (Segal) an intellectual, would-writer, and his neighbor, Doris (Streisand), an "actress" and prostitute. Her character's profession allows the film to discuss sexual behavior. Nevertheless, the presentation of deviance is often merely quirky and incoherent although some social analysis occurs concerning prostitution as economic institution. Furthermore, the film indulges in the sort of fetishistic objectification reminiscent of the subgenre's least progressive tendencies. The main ideological stake, though, involves a power struggle between the characters and the traditional and unconventional notions of gendered behavior inscribed into their representation. A status-quo-affirming resolution is with difficulty reached, reminiscent of other naughty comedies' narrative contortions, and reveals an underlying, tenuous conservatism despite the film's strenuous attempts at modishness.

Doris describes "kinky" clients, such as a man who enjoys watching a parrot walk on her naked back. The kicker involves a customer who dresses in a smock and rolls hard-boiled eggs across the room while Doris, wearing a raincoat and tied to a chair, yells "Bombs away!" Rather than describe any actual "perversions" the script simply accumulates odd behaviors and combines them in a sort of mix-'n'-match fashion bearing scant resemblance to the activities of real-life fetishists. These fantasies are even bereft of sexual contact or orgasm, and simply function as signifiers of the film's kookiness. In fact, such representation defuses, through rendering this type of behavior merely silly, the actual threat of truly diverse iconoclastic sex acts such as sadomasochism or transvestism.

In contrast, Felix does bring some intelligence to the narrative's discourse about prostitution via the Marxist statement that she is a model capitalist who takes a natural resource, adds the cost of labor, and sells the product at a reasonable profit. Doris also shows awareness of the typical notions surrounding the profession when wisely discussing male insecurity and misogyny. The film often proves less astute.

For instance, *The Owl and the Pussycat* consistently objectifies women while displaying ignorance about sexuality. Doris wears a nightie with hand-prints drawn over the breasts when she tries to bed down at Felix's. The garment's design clearly creates a display, while literally including the male subject's groping hands, and by including her name on its seat, resembles brands that identify cattle. The obvious, blatant fetishism of the outfit almost achieves a self-conscious reflexivity, but the camera also consistently ogles Streisand's breasts and buttocks, although a topless scene was removed per her contractual agreement ("*The Owl and the Pussycat*: Trivia"). Felix himself enjoys voyeurism when spying on Doris and a john through binoculars. She later calls him a "peeper," and a "fag," and then suggests he might enjoy wearing her nightie. Typical of the film's occasional cluelessness, these three activities—voyeurism, homosexuality, and transvestism—are unrelated outside of the unhinged discourse of ultraconservative religious fanatics, yet the film itself avoids any ideological position via this weird conflation and simply uses sexual expressions and perversions as bawdy window-dressing similar to her clients' fetishes.

The power struggle between active and passive or subject and object that voyeurism and objectification suggest, narrativized through a battle of the sexes between Felix and Doris, is the film's primary concern. He attempts to assert both traditional and atypical masculinity. She alternately humiliates and nurtures. The split in *The Owl and the Pussycat* between hip, progressive tendencies and a retrograde presentation of sexuality tentatively approaches synthesis as the protagonists' relationship progresses.

Felix and Doris's characterizations suggest the subgenre's increased awareness of societal shifts in gender roles. Despite his peeping, he is not a macho pig but a sensitive intellectual who disdains the primitive side of sex. More conventionally, Doris is initially depicted as a stereotypically brash, uncultured whore, but also possesses intuitive psychological insights that help him achieve a more actualized reality. Much scrapping and reassertion of conventional sex roles occurs first.

Figure 3.5. A zoom-in focuses on Doris (Barbra Streisand) in classic fetishizing/voyeurizing fashion in *The Owl and the Pussycat* (Herb Ross, 1970).

At first, Doris threatens Felix in scenes that refreshingly show confident female sexuality and male vulnerability but also invoke misogynist notions associating assertive women with emasculation. She immediately turns the tables by watching as he tries to undress and go to bed. Doris then fixes the erstwhile voyeur in his own binoculars. He finally drops the concealing garment, to prove nonchalance, following her taunts about being ashamed. Despite claiming there is nothing wrong with him, a disavowal at odds with her subsequent undermining of Felix's masculinity, Doris laughs hysterically on viewing his penis, suggesting potential inadequacy. The voyeur is exposed and lacking, a potential moment of well-deserved feminist revenge that could empower, frighten, or enrage spectators depending on their sex and/or social attitudes. Furthermore, he proves powerless when Doris asks him to frighten her and cure a case of hiccups. Felix's attempts initially fail, but when he finally succeeds, she is startled and slaps him around in a display, repeated throughout the film, of her physical superiority.

Later Doris becomes sexually aggressive and Felix states that "I am not an animal . . . I am intellectual." She calls him "baby" and he protests "I am not 'baby.' I am Felix." This reverses typical gender norms expressed in narratives such as *Some Like It Hot*, where a female character complains about aggressive male sexual interest, and claims identity beyond her desirability. He seems both sensitive and sniveling. Doris responds by suggesting he simply pretend she is a boy. Whether his character expresses a nonnormative sexuality or an inadequate maleness needing restoration is at first unclear. Felix's conventional masculinity, perhaps responding to animal instinct and eschewing impotent civility, revives when they argue over who will be on top during sex. He demands the dominant role out of "a simple respect for tradition," and they proceed. Interestingly, after such voluminous talk, *The Owl and the Pussycat* elides any graphic representation of love-making by fading to black. The representation of erotic activity is fundamentally similar to the depiction of adultery in *The Secret Life of an American Wife*.

After some friendly "pillow talk," Doris soon tries to regain dominance via displaying superior knowledge when he poses a vague question about their sexual encounter. She gets angry and then states that his real curiosity is that of all johns—an interest in how they "rate" in comparison to other customers. His reply reasserts a nonhierarchical, modern attitude to erotic pleasure as he feigns ignorance concerning the existence of rankings, and then sarcastically calls her "teacher," an appellation that a character who conspicuously idolizes high culture can only employ to demeaningly contrast Doris's profession with actual pedagogy. She counters about not "handling beginners," to emphasize her greater sexual experience—a sore spot throughout their courtship and power struggle. Felix's vain attempts at voyeurism, and subsequent complaints to the landlord, have resulted in her constant and threatening, yet also therapeutic, presence resembling that of a magical helper conjured from his erotic imaginary. Doris then predicts his second question, concerning her supposed inurement to sexual pleasure. She suddenly echoes *his* earlier lines about dehumanization. The idea that Felix, or any client, would assume she was a deadened "piece of wood" prompts her own protest against being treated like a "thing." Doris claims "I am a person."

The film could end here and both restore her dignity and valorize the character's wisdom and ability to revive Felix's masculinity, while preserving his sensitivity and passivity as challenges to typical male hegemony. The forming of a romantic couple ultimately occurs but only after she breaks him down once again, and is seemingly chastised for this violation of traditional femininity, before his phoenix-like restoration, in which both characters' happy fates function to synthesize traditional and modern gender identities.

In an almost textbook example of backlash against female empowerment, Doris is next seen dancing in a Times Square go-go bar (to a band playing generic instrumental rock!) but is ignored by customers. Usually a strip bar's patrons want to ogle semiclad women, hence this implausible scene is only readable as her character's punishment. Stripping may deny voyeuristic pleasure through its overt presentation of the woman's body, but is a paradigmatic form of female spectacularization and hardly troubling to the patriarchal order. Doris's disturbing transgressions against gender norms with Felix seem to be the real problem requiring her abasement. In contrast, the women unwittingly walking up an open staircase at his bookstore attract much male voyeurism from passersby. Meanwhile, Felix sees her image on a poster for *Cycle Sluts*, an adult movie, and enters a tawdry porn theater. Unlike Bill in *The Marriage of a Young Stockbroker*, he finds the experience sickening. His reclamation of manhood, contrary to the film's objectifying gaze, does not require voyeuristic pleasure.

Once she and Felix reunite, her taming has seemingly resumed and chastisement ended. Similar to Shirley MacLaine's hapless whore, Ginny, in *Some Came Running* (Vincente Minnelli, 1958), Doris starts improving her vocabulary. Suddenly, she is again gaze-worthy; presumably refinement is normative enough as a woman says "woo woo" to her and a group of men drive by in a car and make sexual comments. Here she again tips the scale by boldly refusing these admirers—she tells them to "fuck off"—who chase Felix and her. She regains power over Felix at this point, though, as he becomes feverishly incoherent. Felix describes a sexless relationship with his previously unmentioned fiancée—a career-obsessed concert pianist. This musician outstrips poor Felix in artistic success while denying his erotic fulfillment. Such bodiless and lofty figures are usually male in the cultural imaginary, women presumably proving too emotional and earthy for such aesthetic dedication. Doris, in comparison, is only relatively problematic and once again ministers to the unhappy protagonist and literally tucks Felix in to bed. Her nurturing and comprehension arouse Felix's anger and libido and they have sex again.

The final scene provides one more oscillation. In a seeming retrenchment, Felix again champions intellect over physicality. His miserable identity's obduracy has defied Doris's therapeutic efforts. Felix, mirroring the fantasy scenarios she performs with clients, then suggests she might actually be happy as an animal—his pet. He throws a stick and orders her to fetch. He then demands her "paw," which he kisses. She slugs him and another potential stalemate is reached. Nevertheless, this is a climactic moment. Each character is broken down, revealed as a phony, and can slowly move toward the status quo. Felix admits he is really named Fred and works in a bookstore. The character's intellectual ambitions are discarded by literally tossing his typewriter down a hill in Central Park. Doris tells him her real last name—Wilgas, not the fancy "Waverly" she had been using—and confesses her "acting" career has consisted of two television commercials and that she "was" a hooker. The sexually fulfilled and monogamous identity potentially attained by the couple will preclude such a vocation. They each state that they need a place to live and the film ends.

A further sign of a narrative resolution presenting assimilation to societal norms, where reproduction of the species can occur, is that Felix's libido, despite his half-hearted protests against dehumanizing promiscuity, clearly becomes normal and fully restored. Certainly, this open-mindedness toward sexual liberation is in keeping with the film's progressive dimensions, yet the character's abandonment of high-culture pretensions, associated with sterility, reveal the text's conservatism, since he can join the workforce and potentially have children, the latter being forbidden by his erstwhile fiancée. Doris has pushed and emasculated him and been duly chastised, but her efforts eventually produce a happier, more honest man. Amid such a confessional relationship, she can also admit her real profession yet attempt transcendence by becoming more cultured while also achieving heterosexual monogamy.

The dialectical synthesis of each character's virtues takes a while since the text's nervousness over Doris's emasculation of Felix, despite its comic potential, requires her constant rebuke and his steadfast resistance. Ultimately, though, she can triumph yet get taken down a peg.

The last image of the two walking through Central Park is deeply traditional. Despite all its hip trappings, *The Owl and the Pussycat* concludes comfortingly by protecting the status quo of committed monogamy and allowing for the possibility of marriage and family without completely sanding down the two protagonists' untraditional qualities and quirky foibles. As with *The Love God?*, traditional values are revealed beneath promiscuous window-dressing.

This entire subgenre, from comedies of infidelity to generational sagas to miscellaneous entries, often conveys a grim view of love, marriage, and parenting in American society. In contrast, positive transformation among (occasionally) decent characters occurs as well. While tipping toward the mainstay of monogamy, many synchronically relevant questionings of such institutions also permeate these texts. This odd, uneasy balancing act will again be performed by the period's Westerns.

4

The Last Roundup

In the canonical maverick title *Midnight Cowboy*, the Western is invoked as American society's quintessential pop culture text and myth system. This genre has been mentioned at other points in this study, usually glancingly, and fittingly provides the last example of a narrative tradition readable synchronically as addressing major sociopolitical and aesthetic shifts, since the period's Westerns reiterate some cultural issues negotiated by other cinematic genres. The mode also has specific obsessions, some of which even survived its temporary demise by finding a new host in the urban action movie.

The Western is well-known enough to make lengthy introduction unnecessary. The genre reached its classical phase in the late 1930s, and Hollywood continued to release straightforward titles with Manichean morality and status-quo values into the 1960s. Meanwhile, after World War II, revisionist efforts began altering the mode's long-cherished (although endlessly mutable) paradigms. These included psychological or adult Westerns such as *Pursued* (Raoul Walsh, 1947) and *The Left-Handed Gun* (Arthur Penn, 1958); the brooding, Freudian dramas of Anthony Mann such as *The Naked Spur* (1953) and *The Man from Laramie* (1955); and John Ford's increasingly ambivalent *The Searchers* (1956), *The Man Who Shot Liberty Valance* (1962), and *Cheyenne Autumn* (1964). Two important figures added to this countertradition: Sergio Leone, whose first films (*A Fistful of Dollars*, 1964; *For a Few Dollars More*, 1965; and *The Good, the Bad and the Ugly*, 1966) were technically Italian productions filmed in Spain and aimed at an international audience but set in America, and the television-trained Sam Peckinpah (*Ride the High Country*, 1962; *Major Dundee*, 1965).

These auteurs created the key maverick texts of the genre's twilight in 1969 with, respectively, *Once Upon a Time in the West* (filmed in the United States) and *The Wild Bunch*. These iconoclastic productions vividly rendered a vicious frontier featuring generically aberrant representations of law and criminality (and their dialectical relationship), masculinity, violence, cultural myths, and the role of children, women, and family. Furthermore, in line with Richard Slotkin's notions, these movies often functioned as metaphors for the war in Vietnam (Slotkin 560–77, 591–613). Finally, such films significantly upped the ante on violence and sexuality while employing art-cinema-influenced and period-specific narrative structures and stylistic choices. In particular, *The Wild Bunch* was a landmark example of "visceral screen effects" such as graphically depicted blood spatter and skin-piercing wounds, rendered in slow motion, which Paul Monaco refers to as part of an emergent "cinema of sensation" (Monaco 2, 181). The film's female nudity was almost unnoticed, although impossible only two years earlier. Peckinpah also employed noticeable use of the zoom lens and rapid, innovative editing such as "cutting directly into slow-motion shots," which also "set a record for the number of separate shots in a feature film with 3,624" (Monaco 200–1). The potential anti-imperialist discourse aside (Peckinpah clearly sympathizes with Mexican revolutionaries, readable within the framework of the 1960s leftist guerilla movements), the film features many older actors and, per David Cook citing Dana Polan, has the same focus on aging as what he refers to as "traditional" Westerns (Cook 180).

In partial contrast are a late effulgence of films viewed as traditionalist Westerns, which often performed well at the box-office. For instance, *Bandolero!* (Andrew V. McLaglen, 1968), grossed $5.5 million, *True Grit* returned $14.5 million (1969), *Chisum* (McLaglen, 1970) made $6 million, and *Big Jake* (George Sherman, 1971) $7.5 million ("Big Rental Films of 1968, 1969, 1970, and 1971"). These productions featured many of Hollywood's most iconic, dependable stars (James Stewart, Henry Fonda, Robert Mitchum, Glenn Ford, Dean Martin, and of course John Wayne), were directed by legendary filmmakers (Howard Hawks, Henry Hathaway), well-traveled journeymen (George Sherman, Richard Thorpe), and their own auteurs such as former Budd Boetticher scenarist Burt Kennedy, Hollywood-spawned Andrew V. McLaglen, and even Sydney Pollack.

Furthermore, these films were spared the critical savaging visited on the other three traditionalist groups of movies. In fact, some critical accounts were surprisingly favorable. The most famous and financially successful traditionalist Western of the period, *True Grit*, received raves, including from Vincent Canby, who had been highly deprecating vis-à-vis the era's musical spectacles, in the *New York Times*. His glowing review begins "True Grit . . . comes very close to being as good as we remember certain movies of our childhood to have been (but seldom are when we revisit them)" (Canby, Movie Review: *True Grit*). Even a Glenn Ford vehicle such as *The Last Challenge* (Richard Thorpe, 1967)receives praise in *Variety* as "good entertainment" ("Film Review: *The Last Challenge*"). Meanwhile, one critic was inspired enough by the film's narrative, whose full "elucidation" he judged as "precluded by the demands of the screenplay which the novelist could perfectly well describe" that he expressed interest in seeking out its literary source ("The Pistolero of Red River" 24). Considering the dismissive tone toward noncanonical or insufficiently innovative movies evinced by many historians and critics, it is positively touching that someone took their job seriously enough to thoughtfully consider a seemingly routine programmer. In contrast, certain films were poorly received, such as *Bandolero!*, which *Variety* deemed "dull" and characterized by "distended scripting, routine direction and overlength" ("Film Review: *Bandolero!*"). *Playboy* found the same film "sleazy" and hoped it might lead to a "moratorium on gratuitous violence and implicit racism" (Untitled review). The moralizing about violence is odd considering the film's M rating and gore-free mayhem, which has none of the visceral power of the brutality in *Bonnie and Clyde* or *The Wild Bunch*.

Because of their number—and the mode's multiple intersections with sociocultural issues and the era's aesthetic tendencies—close readings and mention of basically every film proves impractical when discussing Westerns. Instead, briefer consideration of a large, exemplary, but incomplete, group of titles details the genre's negotiation of various concerns. The period's so-called maverick Westerns, which share many common interests and aesthetic similarities, function as a shadow to these more old-fashioned movies,

First, and perhaps most characteristically, a morbid, melancholic fascination with their protagonists' advancing age and infirmity, and the frontier's concomitant closing and transformation, consistently haunts these narratives. Certain aging characters, and perhaps by proxy golden-age directors and actors, almost serve as embodied classical-era residua within an era synchronically marked by its valorization of youth. In particular, technology and "progress" are presented as usurping forces. Similarly, youth are sometimes depicted as threats to older protagonists and an increasingly ordered society, yet also represent a newer generation who occasionally emulate their heroic predecessors.

This rapidly civilizing frontier may hasten the cowboy's obsolescence, but the need for such men to keep its peace remains, although ambivalence surrounds both representations of the lawman's methods and the worth of the society he protects. Nevertheless, the question of maintaining order proves crucial to the budding action movies that are the genre's intertextual spawn.

Questions of taming of the wilderness extend to narratives about American expansion and influence, and are relevant to films set in Mexico that serve as allegorical vehicles for discussing then-current situations such as the Vietnam War, and Third World liberation. Furthermore, beyond depicting the United States as a world power, the era's Westerns also reflected the struggles by the internally colonized (people of color, women) for empowerment and recognition.

Finally, as with the discussion of musical extravaganzas, issues of narrative structure and style require consideration to round out this account of traditionalist movies and their relation to the period's ground-breaking productions. This comparative analysis perfectly applies to the maverick classic *The Wild Bunch*. Peckinpah's film narrativizes many of genre's key thematic concerns from an iconoclastic, yet deeply nostalgic, position while exemplifying the Hollywood Renaissance's formal innovations.

No Country for Old Men?

The quintessential signifier of the period's traditionalist (and progressive) Westerns is the nostalgic, crepuscular tone they share with maverick entries. In particular, and appropriate to a genre itself winding down, the aging actors portraying middle-aged cowboys, sheriffs, or outlaws exude a feeling of weariness; they are often depicted as coming out of retirement or jail, or embarking on a final mission. Even when the characters are oblivious to the oncoming twilight, this reality is blatantly presented through titles such as *The Last Challenge* that imply finality or *El Dorado*, whose title symbolizes Hollywood's partly quixotic attempts to continue releasing classical productions and also references Edgar Allan Poe's poem promising an imaginary, utopian trail's end following the hero's final ordeal.

Nevertheless, these elder statesmen are still the films' protagonists, while younger talent are sidelined as love interests, sidekicks, or villains. For instance, the misleadingly titled *Young Billy Young* (Burt Kennedy, 1969) actually focuses on Marshall Kane (Robert Mitchum), who has buried a teenage son. In the 1950s, Westerns certainly provided aging talents such as James Stewart, Randolph Scott, Joel McCrea, Robert Taylor, and Gary Cooper with leading roles, but they usually shared narrative agency with younger performers such as Burt Lancaster in *Vera Cruz* (Robert Aldrich, 1954) or John Cassavettes in *Saddle the Wind* (Robert Parrish, 1958).

The mere narrative inclusion of middle-aged heroes in both traditionalist (and progressive) Westerns is unremarkable in the context of the American film industry. More significant are these productions' consistently autumnal, weary tone, which these performers' mere presence perfectly connotes.

The physical ailments plaguing these middle-aged cowboys consistently establishes a mood of decay. Most notable is the eye patch worn by Rooster Cogburn (John Wayne) in *True Grit*, which, combined with Wayne revealing his paunch and actually playing a character affected by hard drinking (in a Hawks film he would never fall off his horse while intoxicated). He even suffers disparaging, puritanical remarks from a teenage girl, Mattie Ross (Kim Darby), who paradoxically seems more interested than this elder statesman in upholding traditional values; this makes the film's philosophy more ambiguous than one might expect from a John Wayne vehicle. Similarly, Colonel McNally (Wayne again) is constantly described as "comfortable" in Hawks's *Rio Lobo* (1970), while Robert Mitchum's character, Summers ("Winters" or "Fall" might be more apt), is losing his eyesight in *The Way West* (Andrew V. McLaglen, 1967); McCandles (Wayne) in *Big Jake* requires spectacles to read a note.

As Hawks's oeuvre often includes infirm characters and a philosophical tone that valorizes his heroes' stoic dignity and professionalism despite their physical ailments, *El Dorado* is the most detailed depiction of the effects of age and injury. Both Sheriff J. P. Harrah (Mitchum), who is shot in the leg and recovering from alcohol-induced decrepitude, and gunfighter Cole Thornton (Wayne), who carries a bullet in his side that causes increasingly frequent and painful attacks of paralysis, suffer throughout the film. Per this auteur's dictates about the paramount nature of one's responsibilities, only after removing the threat to Harrah and the community does Thornton meet a doctor who, in typical Hawksian parlance, is "good enough" to remove the bullet without risking severe spinal damage. The film's last image shows both Wayne and Mitchum on crutches patrolling the town's main street. The director may have only unwittingly invoked Greek myth, yet this image recalls the Sphinx's riddle of the man walking on four legs in the morning (childhood), two in the afternoon (adulthood), and three (i.e., with a crutch or cane) in the evening (old age). The two also resemble an aged married couple as Harrah sarcastically/affectionately states the town would be better without Cole, because "we don't need your kind around here," which, in typical Hawksian fashion, is how male characters express affection by stating the opposite of their actual feelings. In keeping with the film's title, theme song, and narrative, their future will presumably also involve dangerous adventure, because despite infirmity or aging these men will

Figure 4.1. Infirmity and camaraderie between Cole Thorton (John Wayne) and J. P. Harrah (Robert Mitchum) in the autumnal *El Dorado* (Howard Hawks, 1967).

continue their bickering, manly camaraderie, and virtuous achievements. This undoubtedly tempers notions of decline by suggesting continuity and grants Hawks's penultimate film a conservative tone indicating the genre's hoped-for permanence.

Beyond infirmity, death haunts many of these films in a manner unusual for classical Westerns but similar to the morbid, apocalyptic tone of *The Wild Bunch*, *Once Upon a Time in the West*, or even the lighthearted, newfangled *Butch Cassidy and the Sundance Kid* whose titular heroes are ultimately killed. This mood may reflect the aging of the genre's legendary actors and directors, and even the mode's own temporary extinction. Interestingly, the doomed characters in films made near the beginning of this period are usually either likeable outlaws such as Dee and Mace Bishop (James Stewart and Dean Martin) in *Bandolero!* and Bob Larkin (Henry Fonda) in *Firecreek* (Vincent V. McEveety, 1968), or ambivalently depicted heroes such as the slave-driving Tadlock (Kirk Douglas) in *The Way West*, who dies at the hands of a widow who blames him for her husband's death.

By 1972, even the unambiguously sympathetic protagonist, the archetypical character whose very longevity seems to symbolize the genre's hardiness, is killed off in *The Cowboys* (Mark Rydell). This development clearly possesses extra-narrative significance, since the ultimate Western icon, John Wayne (who had never before died onscreen in an

"A" Western), bites the dust. The part of Wil Andersen, a hard-driving yet aging rancher, furthers the identification of star and character since it is reminiscent of Wayne's persona-creating performance as Tom Dunson in Hawks's *Red River* (1948). That character also undertakes an arduous cattle drive in his later years because of economic necessity. The earlier film, though, dealt with a period of expansion and involves the pioneering of the Chisholm trail, while in the later production Andersen notes that his hired hands, who have proved unreliable and been fired, differ from past help who made a deal based on a handshake. His wife responds that "Times have changed" in response to the men's desire to leave the drive and pursue a gold strike—a more individualistic (or selfish) and rapacious career path indicative of the West's economic development. He considers asking his neighbor for help, and she replies that the man is sixty years old. "So am I" declares Andersen/Wayne in an epochal moment.

Dunson led a group of experienced cowhands while Andersen must hire literal cow*boys* from the local school. Slowly the torch of heroism passes to these novices, which mirrors Wayne's eclipsing star allowing the rise of newer generic luminaries such as Clint Eastwood. The film becomes a group bildungsroman detailing their initiation into adulthood, acceptance of responsibility, and overcoming of adversity. For instance, one boy's stutter is cured when Andersen's taunts prompt him to clearly, quickly call his elder a "son of a bitch," while in another scene they successfully cross a difficult river. The depiction of Andersen's decline and the "cowboys" rise climaxes when a nasty group of outlaws led by an archetypical sneering psychopath, "Long Hair" (played by Bruce Dern, a specialist in such roles), attacks the party. Andersen gives the villain a deserved thrashing (which provides brief spectatorial pleasure in witnessing the aging star's strength), but is brutally and repeatedly shot in a manner calculated to prolong his death. He lingers until morning, which could be read as symbolic of the Western genre itself unwillingly but slowly shuffling into oblivion. At this point, under a new patriarch, Nightlinger, the kids plot an elaborate, gruesome ambush that involves bashing in heads with gun butts and stabbing sleeping villains. After Long Hair's leg is broken, he lies prone, and begs for mercy. In the stoic, sadistic fashion of an Eastwood or Bronson, they simultaneously fire their guns and he is dragged to an undoubtedly painful death. The camera records their impassive gaze during the moment's aftermath until they solemnly exit the battleground.

Andersen's empty horse accompanies the herd to the cattle market, which reminds the audience of his invisible, guiding presence. Furthermore, the film's final line, spoken by Hunnicutt (Robert Carradine), is the fallen legend's catchphrase: "We're burning daylight." The fiery metaphor also could suggest a torch passed from age to youth; from Wayne to cruel, youthful stars such as Eastwood or, at present, to John Carradine's son. As noted below, other films prove less sanguine about this handoff.

Another late star vehicle for the screen legend, *Big Jake*, represents youth more ambivalently, unlike titles noted below that pose an active threat from the next generation, and also confronts its aging hero with modernization and technological change. These latter forces, represented in many of the period's allegedly traditionalist (and maverick) Westerns, are the logical outcome of pioneering and Western expansion. They hastened both the cowboy hero's irrelevance—and the actual frontier's end—and are narrativized in the genre's declining years, often via advances in weaponry.

Big Jake begins with a series of stills, accompanied by ragtime music, depicting an America circa 1909 in which each photograph literally slides over to reveal the next in imitation of silent film exhibition practice. Change is already under way. Images of New York City, Einstein, Toscanini, and the Barrymores present a "genteel civilization" of "culture and refinement" on the East Coast juxtaposed with shots of the "wild" West, which include Indians in captivity and a public hanging, that depict the cost of "taming" the frontier. The next set of photos contrasts the three-hundred-pound President Taft, whose body suggests luxury and comfort, with the hard life of range wars and cattle drives. Following this, city women who "lived in style" are opposed to females out west who "didn't think about style, just living." The viewer knows that this frontier ethos will transform into sophisticated urbanity. The pattern continues, yet East and West are also inextricably connected through this lengthy series of comparisons while each is described as having its own "empire builders" such as Morgan and Carnegie, or the fictional McCandles, whose ranch, unlike an industrial fortune, is "held together by having enough men and guns." Mentioning this imaginary character in the same sentence with real moguls continues an attempt to grant the narrative greater significance through its inscription in history.

The narrator then notes a technological development: by 1909, "still photographs had come to life, motion pictures had been born with *The Great Train Robbery*" (Edwin S. Porter, 1903), an account that ignores the contributions of Lumiere, Melies, and others. Following his words, the visual register suddenly changes—mirroring advances in cinematic technology—as stills give way to a clip from this early film. The stylistic "progression" continues as the square frame surrounding the slide show then "widens" to the movie's 'scope ratio before, a few shots later, turning from sepia to full color. Paradoxically, these more "modern" techniques are used to present the narrative's atavistic villains, not urban or mediated images. The voice-over continues over these stylistic shifts and then replaces the meta-cinematic tone with a "reality effect," as with documentary narration, to describe what is still clearly fiction by stating, in reference to *The Great Train Robbery*, "while that make-believe drama was on the movie screens, nine men crossed the Rio Bravo into Texas."

Linking the narrative world of *Big Jake* to actual historical photographs and thus the "real West" by contrasting it with Porter's fiction may seem disingenuous since both are cinematic representations and thus linked to one of the many technologies that actually tamed the actual frontier. Nevertheless, the movie's layering of media and temporalities also provides a palimpsest of the entire process by which the pioneering era gave way to modernity and survived only in changing filmic representations (whether silent, monochrome, and 1.33:1, or sound, color, and Panavision) within a narrative mode itself fading out by 1971. Per David Bordwell, this self-consciousness (paradoxically blended with invocations of "reality") is contained under the opening credits (Bordwell, "Classical Hollywood Cinema," 22). Further reflexivity emerges, though, when the narration describes these nine villains and identifies the final man, played by archetypical heavy Richard Boone, as "John Fain," a moniker close enough to the star's name that the fictive is reinvoked.

These villains soon kidnap "little" Jake McCandles, first shown practicing the piano but soon revealed to be tough and courageous, a successful synthesis of Western and civilized values. His grandfather, "Big" Jake (Wayne), is summoned to retrieve the boy with the assistance of a middle generation—his sons, James (Patrick Wayne, the star's actual offspring) and Michael (Chris Mitchum, son of Wayne's *El Dorado* co-star). Similar to both *The Cowboys* and *The Wild Bunch*, the elderly and the young prove more likeable than the generation in between.

Jake's ex-wife (Maureen O' Hara) states "You haven't changed," and he replies "Not one bit." He requires reading glasses, and many characters greet him with the words "I thought you were dead," to which, intertextually invoking Ethan's famous comment in *The Searchers*, Jake replies "That'll be the day." Soon, though, his traditional, often brutal, methods are revealed as clever and successful in "getting the job done." Unlike some conventional Westerns, and despite its highly modernist opening, the elder statesman in *Big Jake* still maintains his time-worn habits, yet proves efficient and commands respect.

Beyond agedness, Jake is also vulnerable since he is only asked to deliver ransom, a more civilized means of restoring order than vengeful killing. In another 1971 film from the same screenwriting team of Harry and Rita Fink, Don Siegel's *Dirty Harry*, Inspector Callahan (Clint Eastwood) is given this seemingly nonviolent chore but soon reverts to his brutal methods. He aids an effeminate city government, while Jake—who also seems an odd choice for this task—does a woman's bidding. Since cinematic kidnappings inevitably involve treacherous ruses, the "ransom" is ultimately revealed to be cut-up newspapers, allowing Jake's violent approach to reign just as he overcomes age and infirmity.

The next challenge involves an automobile, a classic symbol of usurping technology in the era's maverick Westerns such as Peckinpah's *The Wild Bunch* and *The Ballad of Cable Hogue* (1970), where a car literally kills the protagonist. His sons wish to drive to their rendezvous with the kidnappers, while Jake stubbornly insists on riding a horse. Immediately following this conflict, Michael's motorcycle startles his father into falling out of the saddle. The motorcycle enjoyed an outlaw mystique in the early 1970s, and perhaps because of these rugged associations proves useful within the narrative by terrifying some of the kidnappers. In contrast, the automobile ends up driven off a cliff, resulting in its passengers' deaths, and exploding in a manner reminiscent of a modern action film. Nevertheless, a certain mellowing in the protagonist's attitude occurs at this point, when Jake mentions that fifteen years earlier he would have killed the men who drove a car into the kidnapper's ambush. This statement indicates a civilizing influence on his behavior and may even constitute a paper threat solely intended as a reminder of his authority, since these incompetent rescuers are already dead. The discourse on change and infirmity then continues as he again mentions the scare from Michael's motorcycle. In the next scene, Jake is again shown with reading glasses.

Figure 4.2. Michael McCandles's (Chris Mitchum) new mode of transportation lies in wreckage behind him after his father has twice knocked him to the ground in *Big Jake* (George Sherman, 1971).

Big Jake mounts a sustained challenge to its hero, with each obstacle followed by another. Following the aforementioned difficulties with technology, a scene occurs where Jake's sexual identity is itself doubted, which seems the most radical possible interrogation of such a figure. He asks James to drop his pants to facilitate removing some buckshot and is asked "Are you on the level?" This comment seems to almost accuse the hero of homosexual tendencies, especially when, in the next scene, the same character questions whether Jake's reputation as a "ladies' man" was the actual cause of his parents' divorce. This is a surprising question to direct at a character played by this paradigmatically macho and heterosexual icon.

Later his identity is again questioned through his further doubling with Fain, beyond the villain's name resembling Wayne's, when both make identical statements prior to their showdown. The bad guy promises that any double-crosses or trouble will result in Little Jake dying "no matter what," while McCandles replies that "no matter what" he will kill Fain. Jake triumphs, but his nemesis' last words are, predictably, "I thought you were dead." The hero's response is "Not hardly"; yet again the uneasy suggestion of age and mortality has occurred. Jake's image, similar to that of McIntosh in *Ulzana's Raid* (Robert Aldrich, 1972), is frozen into a still as he rides off, which again commemorates this avatar of archaic manliness and traditional star power. The title song to another Wayne film, *Chisum*, whose lyrics state "and he still keeps goin' on" could be unnoticeably inserted at this moment.

One scene in *Big Jake* features another technological innovation: a rifle with a telescopic sight. The machine gun and other new, more-lethal automatic or semiautomatic weapons brought images of mechanized slaughter to the genre during the Hollywood Renaissance and, in tandem with World War I where their horrific use was first widely demonstrated, also signify the frontier era's (and thus the mode's) endpoint. They threaten the hero indirectly, not so much with his own bodily harm, but through suggesting that traditional means of settling disputes are becoming obsolete. The cowboy's classic gun and rifle are primitive, manual devices whose successful use demands intuition, speed, and skill. During the Hollywood Renaissance, few Westerns feature the classic showdown in which rival gunfighters—following notions of honor and fair play derived from the medieval duel—meet on the town's main street armed with six-shooters or perhaps rifles; exceptions include such films as *The Last Challenge, Firecreek*, and *The Day of the Evil Gun* (Jerry Thorpe, 1968), all released early in the period. A different talent, seemingly of little interest to the aging cowboy hero, is required with these newer weapons, or mayhem can ensue, as in the classic moment from *The Wild*

Bunch where a machine gun randomly and berserkly destroys flesh, food, and furniture but later the film's heroes use it more appropriately—to kill many bad men. In *Big Jake*, Michael loses control of his semiautomatic gun amid a narrative that equates technology with egomaniacal performance (as with this character's motorcycle tricks), incompetence (the ambushed car hurtling off a cliff), and villainy (the bad guys' telescopic rifles make it easy to destroy the automobile).

In another seemingly traditionalist Wayne vehicle, *The War Wagon* (Burt Kennedy, 1967), the actual title references the most complex technology depicted in the period's Westerns—a metal-covered, proto–armored car freighted with metaphorical significance. The film's aging, outlaw "heroes"—Taw Jackson (John Wayne) and Lomax (Kirk Douglas)—plan its robbery as an act of vengeance, but may also strike a blow against this skill-usurping invention symbolic of a closing frontier. Furthermore, a lyric in the title song states "All men are fighting for a wagon full of gold," which invokes the competitive and mercenary end result of pioneering rather than the idealistic dream of bringing law and order to a wilderness. Instead, wealth and "civilization," and hence the end of the Wild West, have arrived via exploitation of natural resources, such as mining, enabled by technology. Other inventions are then needed to protect this gain and hinder the outlaw's more atavistic attempts at robbery just as automated weaponry diminished the cowboy gunman's personal skills as a factor in combat. Regardless, the film still grants power to its criminal heroes, who successfully commandeer the wagon and, following a series of complications, retain some of its contents in an ending that suggests their mastery and skill are still viable.

As noted previously, youthful characters, by their mere presence, also pose a challenge to aging protagonists. This potential threat clearly mirrors the replacement of the cowboy who tamed the increasingly civilized West by his symbolic (or literal) offspring, the genre's recruiting of new talent to fill the shoes of aging actors, and unwittingly invokes the mode's own near-extinction during the early 1970s. In addition, the burgeoning and rebellious youth culture of the period also finds itself allegorized in various fashions by the era's Westerns.

The Cowboys proves optimistic by showing its teenage heroes as worthy heirs to Andersen/Wayne. Other films both admit *and* assuage a potential threat by ridiculing youthful characters, as in *Big Jake* where the father constantly rescues his kin. In *The War Wagon*, when two hoods—one played by Bruce Dern—try to kill Jackson and Lomax, they are easily gunned down and become the subject of the protagonist's amused argument. Lomax states that his corpse hit the ground first while Jackson claims "Mine was taller"—the type of cynical joking that the James

Bond cycle popularized. Some movies betray greater anxiety about the next generation.

Four Westerns—*True Grit*, *Young Billy Young*, *The Last Challenge*, and *Shootout* (Henry Hathaway, 1971)—attempt a detailed representation of youth, and fall along a continuum from positive to negative.

True Grit is interesting for its conservative yet rational attitude. Rather than bemoan the condition of "kids today," the film presents a teenage heroine, Mattie Ross, who functions as a counter-myth to hippie culture. She is pious, sober (and contemptuous of drunkenness), brave, astonishingly determined, and a hard bargainer who manages her family's accounts and terrifies opponents by invoking her litigious lawyer "J. Noble Daggett," while in another scene outmaneuvering an experienced horse-trader (Peckinpah regular Strother Martin). The attributes spectators expect from John Wayne are transferred to a teenage girl seeking vengeance for her father's murder. This switch necessitates the legendary actor playing a less upright character, since as elder statesman Wayne is textually required to evince some antagonism toward and difference from any youthful character. Unlike the transposition of these attributes to the periods' urban heroes, Mattie's attainment of these characteristics possesses a progressive valence since a young woman benefits, not a masculine authority figure, which suggests feminist empowerment within a tale whose heroine rides besides lawmen on a dangerous mission. She does require rescuing at the film's end, but survives, unlike La Boeuf (Glen Campbell), the other party member. Furthermore, after avenging her father's murder (a mythical prerogative of men) she will presumably head her family.

Young Billy Young features Robert Walker, Jr. (the spawn of Jennifer Jones and Robert Walker) in the title role, although the film stars Robert Mitchum as his mentor Marshall Kane. Billy's representation combines period-specific youth culture associations with Mattie's skill and ultimate integrity. In fact, Walker himself appeared in both the traditionalist Western *The War Wagon* and the maverick classic *Easy Rider*. He sports long hair, looks disheveled, and first appears as a train robber named Billy—the same name as Dennis Hopper's character in *Easy Rider* and also invoking the archetypical teenage Western outlaw. In the film's opening he and a comrade (David Carradine, also industry offspring) daringly assassinate a posse of Mexican soldiers. Following this, Billy kills a sheriff for cheating at cards. Kane initially intends to arrest him, but when he hears the youth's story he merely takes down a statement. The old sheriff then begins mentoring Billy by the "trial and error" method. Eventually the former outlaw helps Kane protect a stagecoach from his old comrades and ultimately decides to become a deputy.

In contrast, *The Last Challenge* presents irreconcilable conflict between an impulsive youth, Lot McGuire (Chad Everett), and a middle-aged patriarch, Sheriff Dan Blane (Glenn Ford), who is repeatedly referred to as the fastest draw in the territory. Blane views the younger man as unformed, states that "he hasn't even been born," and sees him as a potential protégé. Despite McGuire's announcement that he will eventually seek a showdown, the sheriff repeatedly attempts reason, gives fatherly advice, and tries to avoid combat. In the film's conservative vision, talk is wasted on such crazy kids, and ultimately the lawman unblinkingly kills his rival in a classic duel employing primitive technology. Nevertheless, the haunted, weary expression on Blane's face denies viewers a cheerful final image. Even when upholding the status quo by necessary violence, weariness has seeped into the genre's bones.

Shootout also betrays less optimism by presenting a hysterical and nightmarish vision of renegade youth seemingly sprung from the "silent majority's" unconscious: the villainous Bobby Jay (Robert F. Lyons). The character first appears in a saloon opining—with the intention that the protagonist, Clay (Gregory Peck), overhear—that the aged should be killed. He then mocks the bartender, Trooper (Jeff Corey), for being old. This tirade presumably creates spectatorial enmity toward this monster, which Trooper directly expresses by advocating the elderly murder the young. The more moderate Clay quietly states that every man ages if he lives long enough, suggesting Bobby's imminent death. This exchange occurs in a film directed by a seventy-three-year-old Hollywood veteran and featuring a middle-aged star that reflects the era's generational antagonism and polarization. Furthermore, the unshaven, grimy, and long-haired Bobby Jay contrasts with Peck's clean-shaven, short-haired, square-jawed rectitude.

Interestingly, the two seeming antagonists are doubled at this point since each retires to bed with one of the tavern's prostitutes. Inevitably, their enmity resumes as Bobby's noisy lovemaking angers Clay into a confrontation, which results in the villain receiving a deserved, albeit mild and controlled, beating. Following this, he and his gang brutally gun down Trooper—a helpless paraplegic. In a moment of excessive spectacle, they riddle the old man's body with bullets, causing his wheelchair to spin around the empty saloon in a gothic flourish. His appearance, sexual appetite, noisiness, and cruelty combine into a caricatured, horrifying figuration of American youth. He continues to behave monstrously throughout the film, until Clay achieves vengeance in an unfair manner. Such treachery, at odds with the typical Western hero's ethos, might have aggrieved many spectators' sense of fair play if Bobby Jay's barbarity had not been consistently depicted. Clay's solution echoes the vigilantism of the period's action films, which furthered the Western's concerns about protecting society from deviant scum.

Shootout and *True Grit* were both written by Marguerite Roberts and directed by Hathaway. The latter partially achieves representational balance through creating a sympathetic representative of youth in Decky (Dawn Lynn), who functions similarly to Mattie in the former film. She is presumably Clay's child by a deceased Mexican prostitute. Her character is only minimally developed, but evinces bravery and resolve, and, through some carefully engineered bits of cuteness, softens Peck's saturninity.

Nevertheless, small victories aside, during this period the genre's heroes are portrayed as aging and weakening or rendered obsolete by technology and progress while ambivalently depicted youthful figures stand ready as their replacements. These concerns were also germane to the society that produced these films and reflect its rapid technological progress, concomitant doubts about the merits of industrialized "civilization," and the uneasy relation between a budding youth culture and the older generation. The older values associated with classical Hollywood and the genre were revalorized, albeit as noble and faltering rather than robust, with the synchronically relevant portrait of youth equally ambivalent.

Keeping the Peace

A hardy genre may have been fading out and its heroes challenged. Nevertheless, the mode's protagonists still kept the peace within narratives reflecting an eventful period in American history where many were simply concerned with maintaining order amid riots, protests, assassinations, and a supposedly rising crime rate. Representations of the frontier lawman's duty are also relevant since they beg the question, "Is this (American) society he protects a good, decent, functional place?" These films' depictions of two status-quo institutions and key forces of civilization—family and religion—are less detailed than their protagonist's complex figuration, but require mention since these pillars of order are presumably what the frontier lawman defends. Once again questions of residual discourses/ideologies and their dialectical relation to more progressive notions are germane.

The portrayal of the frontier lawman and the legal institutions he serves are also significant as reflections of overall societal polarization. Many of the era's spectators felt the police were overwhelmed by chaos and violence; others viewed them as similar to the army, the CIA, or the government itself—oppressive symbols of the United States's corrupt, brutal power structure. This cynicism would culminate, with the period itself, in 1972 with the Watergate break-in and subsequent resignation of President Nixon. Typically, Westerns valorized this figure as a guarantor of justice and the public's safety. For instance, the noble sheriffs of John Ford's *My Darling Clementine* (1946) or Hawks's ultraheroic John T. Chance in *Rio Bravo* (1959) were likable, skilled, moral, and basically infallible. During the Hollywood Renaissance, though, even conventional texts eschewed this approach. The closest analogue—Blane in *The Last Challenge*—is weary, troubled, and ultimately quits his post after a legally (and perhaps morally) justified killing hardly likely to ruffle Wyatt Earp (Henry Fonda) in Ford's film. Even *El Dorado*, Hawks's semi-remake of *Rio Bravo*, proves revisionist as John Wayne plays an upright hired gun, Cole Thornton, whereas the sheriff, J. P. Harrah (Robert Mitchum), fills the role of lovesick drunkard held by an ex-deputy (Dean Martin) in the earlier film. Harrah was a first-rate peacekeeper and is rehabilitated, but much of the narrative depicts a bedraggled, grimy, unshaven Mitchum lurching around his office. In one scene, he even resembles a cartoon character, not a brave lawman, when Thornton hits him with a frying pan and Harrah falls backward in an exaggerated straight line with eyes bugged out like Sylvester the Cat. Nevertheless, his character defects are personal and not presented as an institutional critique.

In contrast, two films—*True Grit* and *Valdez Is Coming* (Edwin Sherin, 1971)—provide aberrant representations. The protagonist, Rooster Cogburn (Wayne), of the former wears an eye patch, sports a potbelly, lives with a Chinese launderer and a cat, and drinks more excessively than is typical for the genre. Nevertheless, John Wayne plays this role. Rooster also succeeds in his mission and is presented as funny, charismatic, and heroic. In fact, these flaws even make the character interesting, and to acknowledge this acting "stretch," Wayne was rewarded with his sole Best Actor Oscar.

Furthermore, the film's ideological stance is traditional, even reactionary. Rooster is introduced kicking a prisoner in the back to hurry him into jail, and is next viewed testifying in court, which results in a conviction leading to the following day's public hanging/Foucauldian spectacle. Furthermore, reminiscent of Harry Callahan in *Dirty Harry*—who ignores a suspect's Fourth Amendment and Miranda rights—Cogburn willingly breaks the law when Mattie requests that he enter Indian territory to pursue her father's killer. Finally, in high conservative dudgeon, he drunkenly rants about "pettifogging lawyers" just as many reactionaries declaim against "big government." Rooster employs homonyms to mock their demands that he serve a "writ" when arresting a "rat." This speech is delivered to an actual rodent, which he then shoots dead,

Figure 4.3. Age and youth: "Rooster" Cogburn (John Wayne) and Mattie Ross (Kim Darby) as he discusses serving a "writ for a rat" in mockery of the legal system in *True Grit* (Henry Hathaway, 1969).

foreshadowing later actions. Clearly this character is the prototype of later action film heroes who gleefully flaunt "bureaucracy" and legal fine points.

Bob Valdez (Burt Lancaster) proves a less traditional figure: half-Mexican, and somewhat ineffectual as a lawman since he is beholden to moneyed interests. His character is first represented as neither a reactionary nor vigilante, and the film seems progressive in detailing a competent, kind, moral ethnic minority that is in keeping with its star's liberal public image. Nevertheless, *Valdez Is Coming* soon surpasses the slight revisionism of *True Grit*. He is tied to a makeshift log cross by the villainous Tanner (John Cypher) and forced to walk home under this heavy, humiliating weight. Clearly the Christian or even liberal notions of turning the other cheek and carrying another's burden are pointless out west or, by association, in the contemporary lawman's world, since Valdez hardly regards this task as ennobling but instead seeks vengeance in a manner suggestive of the period's conservative revenge narratives, such as *Death Wish* (Michael Winner, 1974). He responds with previously unseen fury by taking matters into his own hands and kidnapping Tanner's wife, who is revealed as a murderer. This revelation may potentially justify Valdez's vigilantism, yet Tanner's equally extralegal behavior caused an innocent African American's death and started this bloody saga.

Many die at the half-breed's competent hands since he is hiding in familiar mountainous terrain, which invokes the methods of Third World guerrilla fighters conversant with using natural cover for their actions. Ultimately, a stalemate is reached and Valdez rides away, but without compensation or his job. Unlike in many right-wing vigilante fantasies, the hero's actions are fruitless, which is reminiscent of the failure-oriented narratives of alienated maverick texts of the Hollywood Renaissance. Furthermore, in accordance with the character's already "othered" status as half-Mexican, he more resembles a left-wing Clyde Barrow–style outlaw than an auxiliary lawman like Charles Bronson in *Death Wish*.

In terms of the institutions putatively defended by frontier lawmen, the era's progressive Westerns certainly betray scant interest in the familial. Their protagonists are usually outlaws oblivious, if not actively hostile, to domesticity beyond producing children out of wedlock or experiencing carnal love with a whore. The Man with a Harmonica (Charles Bronson) in Leone's *Once Upon a Time in the West*, who seeks vengeance for his father's murder, is a relatively rare figure within that corpus. Following generic pattern, family proves more figurative than literal in the period's traditionalist Westerns, symbolized through the bond between townsfolk and their sheriff, in the often-patriarchal organizational structure of outlaw bands, or where a makeshift domestic unit forms on the trail and during moments of crisis. Occasionally, the institution is narratively important and portrayed positively.

For instance, Mace Bishop (James Stewart), the protagonist of *Bandolero!*, willingly takes risks and even sacrifices his life to save his brother, Dee (Dean Martin). Their mere kinship is the only reason he requires, although the latter's inherent decency, albeit tarnished by association with his trashy outlaw cohort, is also mentioned. Dee's "partners" provide a ghastly alternative conception of family reminiscent of the Clantons in *My Darling Clementine*. A degenerate father (Will Geer), and rape-minded son contrast with the Bishops' background as the spawn of pious, impoverished farmers. Dee may have chosen crime, but he understands the concept of decency and protects Maria (Raquel Welch) from the younger Chaney's sexual advances thanks to good parenting and his brother's (relatively) positive influence.

Another example of representation of the familial, the initiatory narrative where an experienced pro helps a young gun or child or a paternalistic military officer (as in Ford's Cavalry Trilogy) guides recruits usually replaces stories of biological fathers and sons. *The Last Challenge* flirts with this relationship but in keeping with the period's fixation on rebellious youth ends with mentor (justifiably) killing pupil. In *Young Billy Young*, Marshall Kane (Robert Mitchum) both instructs the title character and mourns his real son's untimely death. This lawman's grief is exacerbated since, in a revisionist twist, his offspring was minding the jail while the marshall enjoyed nonmarital sexual relations. The elder generation contaminates here, so Kane seeks retribution by helping Billy.

Marriage receives far less attention than in most of the period's supposedly traditionalist genre films (war narratives proving the other exception). In a novel touch reflecting the era's actual demographic trends, the protagonist of *Big Jake* is divorced, while the bachelor hero of *Chisum* views marriage as incompatible with frontier life. Sometimes a wife appears in the background as in *The Cowboys* or an obligatory romantic interest presumably leading to wedlock fulfills convention as with *5 Card Stud* (Henry Hathaway, 1968). Two films—*The Way West* and *Firecreek*—depict marriage, and the nuclear family in the latter, in more detail and with surprising results.

The Way West—a story of the Oregon Trail—presents marriage peculiarly as an impediment to the civilizing process. Typically, female characters in Westerns require protection, but this film both tiresomely, conservatively invokes the clichéd representation of the worrying wife as an actual hindrance to male ambition, yet at least also allows women rare narrative agency within a highly masculine genre. Their influence even predates the mission's commencement as Summers (Robert Mitchum), haunted by his wife's death, proves initially reluctant to embark while Tadlock (Kirk Douglas), freed by his spouse's suicide, quits the Senate to lead the expedition. In other words, a dead wife can still dampen the adventurous spirit, yet her absence at least allows for the possibility of male achievement.

Live women cause more trouble. After the journey begins, new problems arise when the Macks, a newlywed couple, experience marital discord, since according to another female settler, Mercy (Sally Field), the wife is stiff as "a pine board plank." Mr. Mack first tries to rape his unwilling spouse but soon seduces Mercy and accidentally kills an Indian chief's son. Tadlock hangs him to preempt a retaliatory native attack. A whole host of related difficulties ensue, such as Evans's (Richard Widmark) wife suggesting rebellion against Tadlock, after he forces each family to relinquish even cherished possessions—key signifiers of feminized domesticity—to cross a treacherous mountain range. In fact, he is ultimately killed by Mack's bereft widow, and the eroto-thanatogenic circle closes. Whether deceased, antagonistic, or representing material comfort, women hinder progress in this film. Their representation is innovative within a genre where female characters either unquestioningly support male ambition or are rendered ineffectual, yet also reactionary through expressing a backlash against female agency.

Firecreek actually features an active parent and husband, Johnny Cobb (James Stewart), a poor farmer and head of a large, happy family who might have sired the Bishops in *Bandolero!* Once again, domesticity causes timidity and could allow lawlessness free reign. Johnny holds the (largely ceremonial) position of sheriff to the community of Firecreek, but fears leaving his family unprotected in case of his death in the line of duty. Johnny also lacks experience, since farming is his primary vocation, the town is normally quiet, and its citizens actively avoid conflict. The reason men of action are traditionally unattached informs the film, since his concern for family conflicts with a commitment to maintaining order. An ideal sheriff requires both bravery and the willingness to risk his life protecting a community he can only truly join at the expense of his effectiveness.

The town of Firecreek, which Johnny describes as inhabited by "losers," mirrors his reticence. Founded by pioneers who had fearfully abandoned their wagon train, the community's later arrivals include misfits such as a half-wit apprentice blacksmith and a storekeeper and ex-lawyer, Whittaker (Dean Jagger), fleeing the big city. Firecreek almost resembles a gated or retirement community, especially considering its members' ages and timorousness, but it could also metaphorize a 1960s-style rural commune where, in the Thoreauvian tradition, people avoid urban tensions. The town's representation also invokes a significant discourse of the period about the terror and impotence of average American citizens victimized by supposedly increasing crime rates. Particularly relevant is the film's (possibly unwitting) invocation of the notorious Kitty Genovese case, where a group of New Yorkers allegedly failed to lift a finger to aid a murder victim, just as Firecreek's citizens prove unwilling to help their (already cautious) sheriff. After a group of hired guns led by Bob Larkin (Henry Fonda) arrive in town, they easily establish dominance until one is killed by a citizen while attempting rape. In vengeance, the outlaws lynch the Samaritan.

Johnny finally acts, after having earlier stated "often one has to step back and wait." This caps his indecision and ambivalence, in keeping with film's "examining questions of good and evil moral imperatives," as noted by a perceptive, sympathetic reviewer for the *Film Daily* ("Firecreek: Conflict of Good and Evil in a Little Frontier Town"). Conveniently absent the night of the lynching, through impotently "aiding" his wife's delivery, Johnny was initially able to avoid a life-threatening situation. Presumably the film's screenwriters saved his ultimate rebellion for last to produce a dramatic climax and render realistic his slow regeneration and ultimate triumph. Similar to subsequent vigilante texts, such as *Death Wish*, he enters combat untarnished and possessed of righteous vengeance, which allows the spectator to enjoy some sanctioned violence. After Johnny hectors the townsfolk, and also acknowledges his responsibility, he forgets the risk involved, takes action, and kills all the marauders single-handedly without even the assistance of a Quaker wife, although the town prostitute helps him out. The climax resembles that of Peckinpah's *Straw Dogs* (1971), where another meek refugee from societal turmoil (Dustin Hoffman) shouts "This is my house" and commits mass slaughter. Ironically, the allegedly traditionalist *Firecreek* has a more liberal tone than Peckinpah's seemingly maverick production—its hero hardly seems to enjoy the mayhem, as a shot of an exhausted, aging Stewart (himself a specialist in frayed hysteria) with mussed hair makes clear.

Familial constraints hamper male resolve, but Johnny still becomes a new father, symbolizing his newfound potency, and a competent sheriff who has symbolically birthed a self-respecting town through taking action. In an unusual move for the genre, he successfully synthesizes the two crucial roles of lawman and patriarch that foster a stable society.

Family remains in the background, as a signifier of progress and order, or is presented ambivalently in the period's Westerns. In contrast, a markedly dim view of spirituality diverges from the genre's typical, albeit again usually tangential, representation of religion as a relevant institution and symbol of civility (as in *My Darling Clementine*) often invoked during graveside ceremonies. Peckinpah's maverick classic, *The Wild Bunch*, represents a hysterical, foolish temperance preacher railing against alcoholism—a minor vice compared to the film's catalog of violence—who unwittingly leads his parishioners into a melee between outlaws and bounty hunters. Both sides unflinchingly shoot through these

Figure 4.4. James Stewart in frayed hysteric mode as Johnny Cobb desperately crawling for his gun at the climax of *Firecreek* (Vincent V. McEveety, 1968).

churchgoers and deliver many to a better place. The depiction of religion in the period's putatively traditionalist texts proves less violent or overt in ridiculing the church, yet it is often negative. For instance, a scene in *Firecreek* shows Johnny's bored children presciently disdaining a thundering preacher (Ed Begley), who soon behaves in a cowardly fashion when Larkin's outlaw band enter his makeshift church.

One film even evinces previously unthinkable sacrilegious attitudes. In *5 Card Stud*, George (Yaphet Kotto) is known by his friends as an atheist. This awareness allows them to understand a clue he leaves revealing his murderer when Van (Dean Martin) sees the dead man's hands folded in a gesture of prayer. Realizing George's lack of belief, he interprets the gesture as blaming the film's major representative of religion, the gun-toting Jonathan Rudd (Robert Mitchum)—a phony holy man who intertextually invokes the psychopathic con artist posing as a clergyman famously played by Mitchum in *The Night of the Hunter* (Charles Laughton, 1955). Van's blasé acknowledgment of atheism, amplified by Dean Martin's relaxed delivery, is noted with the same degree of affect he might use to state that George was a stamp collector or expert shot. The film's dim view of religion continues through Rudd's characterization as an old-testament-style vengeance-seeker whose hollowed-out Bible holds a pistol, which visually associates faith with violence. Defacing the good book is also a scandalous act, which indicates that the representational boundaries of traditionalist Westerns have weakened, although it is performed here by a villain who is eventually punished, which helps restore the community's social order. Nevertheless, in a reversal of the genre's typical presentation of religion, a man of the cloth threatens rather than protects the status quo.

Think Global, Portray Local

The Hollywood Renaissance's ostensibly maverick and traditionalist Westerns reflected then-contemporary domestic concerns through their ambivalent depictions of frontier lawmen protecting a fundamentally problematic society. Extending the genre's scope to the global raises questions about the cinematic representation of the United States as international peacekeeper in an increasingly postcolonial world. The American film industry traditionally lent ideological support to the nation's foreign-policy positions but grew quiet, with the exception of *The Green Berets*, during the Vietnam era, and only indirectly broached the subject. World War II films, as previously noted, often presented Cold War anxieties metaphorically, but the period's Westerns also aptly negotiated this terrain, as discussed in Richard Slotkin's seminal *Gunfighter Nation*, which analyzes classics such as *The Wild Bunch* and *The Professionals* (Richard Brooks, 1966) but elides lesser-known traditionalist films (Slotkin 560–77, 591–613). Since Westerns directly show America's earlier imperialist expansion and extension of influence, they are suitable allegorical vehicles.

The privileged site for such indirect narratives was Mexico—a former Spanish colony that then lost half its territory to the United States and subsequently suffered French invasion in 1861. *Bandolero!* and *The Undefeated* employ this setting.

The first focuses on the fugitive Bishops (James Stewart and Dean Martin), who flee to Mexico pursued by the local sheriff (George Kennedy). They travel deeper into the desert and enter territory where Bandoleros—practicing guerilla warfare based on thorough knowledge of their terrain—silently ambush and slaughter all intruders. This representation clearly invokes contemporary notions about the military tactics used by Third World anti-imperialist movements in Cuba, Bolivia, Algeria, and, most relevantly, Vietnam. On the surface, *Bandolero!* simply uses their vicious presence as a mechanism for suspense hardly different from an earthquake, blizzard, or animal attack in its effect on the protagonists and their pursuers, the narrative's seemingly main conflict. In fact, a tight closeup of their pock-marked bandit leader might as well represent a monster or wild beast. In some ways, they are even worse, since animals do not try to rape women, as almost happens with Maria. Nevertheless, the film betrays a conservative political stance and climaxes with a bandit attack on an abandoned village in which outlaw and lawman fight this common dark-skinned foe and both protagonists die. In other words, even enemies can unite when combating the malevolent other. This representation of revolutionaries as simple autochthonous menace to civilization, lacking any ideological justification or reason for their aggression, also tacitly encourages Americans to work together against rising Third World insurgency. Considering that U.S. involvement in Indochina peaked the year *Bandolero!* was released, the message is unsurprising from a so-called traditionalist production.

The Undefeated constructs a more complex allegory. The film commences immediately following the American Civil War and depicts a divided nation, which suggests the severe polarization over foreign policy between conservatives and progressives in 1969. In an early scene, Colonel Thomas (John Wayne) asks a Confederate (Royal Dano) why his men continued fighting knowing the conflict had officially ended; he is told "you're on our land." The officer replies "We're all Americans" and the Confederate responds "That's the saddest part of it."

The narrative proper concerns two groups heading for Mexico to support the French-backed Emperor Maximilian's forces. Thomas and his men intend to sell them horses. A band of southerners, led by Colonel Langdon (Rock Hudson), have similar plans. This group lowers the Confederate flag at sunset and refuses to admit defeat. In *The Green Berets*, set in contemporary Vietnam, Wayne's character, Colonel Kirby, claims to aid a democratic regime. Here Thomas can openly acknowledge assisting an "unpopular government" led by a puppet installed by Napoleon III.

The two groups soon band together against common enemies, but they also argue. Since the film is determined to resolve the two groups' schism, and by implication contemporary ideological debates, similarities between the parties are highlighted in *The Undefeated*. Both are led by ethical, charismatic, military figures, while the obviously polarizing issue of slavery is elided—and any concern about racism negated—since Thomas relates peaceably with natives while Langdon, implicitly a former slave owner, has adopted Blue Boy (Roman Gabriel), whom he defends from attack by another less-tolerant party member.

The parallels to Vietnam fully develop when Langdon's party reach Maximilian's encampment. The film clearly reveals French support for his campaign, which potentially functions as an allegory of that nation's later involvement in other colonial wars in Algeria and, of course, Indochina. Suddenly, Juarista insurgents appear and surround both the French and the Americans. The rebel leader then proceeds to list abuses committed by the French and also condemns the Confederates' assistance. This speech is easily transposed into a lecture about European colonial dominance over Indochina and American support of an unpopular and corrupt South Vietnamese government. The Juaristas then assassinate a group of French soldiers who, similar to American military personnel in Vietnam, have burnt down an indigenous village. This leads to a later battle between Maximilian's forces and the suddenly united, Juarista-sympathizing northerners and southerners. Does this situation wishfully suggest that Americans unite to destroy the corrupt South Vietnamese government, aid the Viet Cong, and eliminate the stain of French colonialism? Perhaps, but this alliance against the emperor *definitely* cements solidarity between North and South as, after victory, they toast the Union, the Confederacy, and the Juaristas. Another reading might even show this reunion as symbolizing a healing of northern-southern tensions related to the period's civil-rights struggles. While the group rides back to the United States, where Langdon intends to run for Congress, the rebs start singing "Dixie," which Thomas's men drown out with "The Battle Hymn of the Republic" until both sides join in "Yankee Doodle," which, northern-associated title aside, is a tune that provides dialectical synthesis by stressing the common Americanism of both sides; a cheery coda to the mournful words spoken at the film's beginning by Royal Dano.

Related to America's Cold War–era participation in conflicts raging throughout formerly colonized nations such as Vietnam are narratives of the United States own imperialist legacy. European nations' expansionist efforts eventually failed since the "mother country" retained geographical and cultural distance from the peoples they subjugated, whereas the pioneers who "tamed" the frontier wholly occupied the territory and killed or marginalized the indigenous population. Reflecting the increased sensitivity during this period toward the plight of Native Americans, though, maverick or traditionalist Westerns rarely depicted westward expansion, unlike many classic titles such as Ford's cavalry trilogy, *Wagonmaster* (1950), and *The Searchers*; Hawks's *Red River*; DeMille's *Union Pacific* (1939); and Anthony Mann's *Bend of the River* (1952). In fact, most of the era's Westerns represent a closing, relatively settled frontier only requiring policing to maintain order.

The Undefeated starts with settlers heading to the new frontier of Mexico but ends with their return east. *The Way West*, though, is a genuine, old-fashioned covered-wagon epic. The summer of 1967's other supposedly traditionalist Westerns—*El Dorado* and *The War Wagon*—proved successful, but this film, a long-nourished dream project of Burt Lancaster's producing associate Harold Hecht, was a financial failure, returning only $1.6 million, perhaps a victim of shifting popular attitudes toward the American Indian and awareness of (overt) colonialism's worldwide decline during the Cold War ("Big Rental Films of 1967"). In contrast, more routine or elegiac genre items possibly provided comfort and familiarity to weary spectators. Nevertheless, *The Way West* depicts expansion with pessimism and fully presents its harsh realities.

The narrative commences conventionally with grand ambitions of finding paradise in Oregon, where Tadlock (Kirk Douglas) intends to create a "new Jerusalem," including a park covered by a crystal roof! He is also an obsessed megalomaniac. In contrast, a more sympathetic character, Lodge (Richard Widmark), in typically American fashion, simply wishes to travel. A revisionist tone soon develops when the inevitable hardships and deaths occur, with many blaming the grueling pace set by Tadlock. The group encounters Native Americans and must sacrifice the adulterous Mack, who had accidentally shot an Indian boy he overheard spying on his tryst with Mercy (Sally Field). A more conservative text might instead present a devout and unified party—similar to the Mormons in *Wagonmaster*—and include a scene where they band together in ethnic solidarity with Mack and rebuff an attack. This cohort pragmatically sacrifices an adulterer.

They reach the Hudson's Bay Company, where many wish to stay. This results in Tadlock telling their temporary hosts a female settler has smallpox, knowing that this will cause their forced departure. This deceptive and tyrannical decision suggests an invidious nation with a martinet leader, not Ford's brotherly utopia. The dissension peaks when he forces the settlers to relinquish prized possessions to cross a treacherous mountain pass. When one member refuses, Tadlock tries to shoot him and is almost lynched. This strong, authoritarian leader incurs relentless criticism, which further distinguishes the film from other exploration narratives. Tadlock is even abandoned and eventually killed by Mack's widow. Since he is beyond redemption, only death can resolve the contradiction between this tyrant and the group, a defeatist position contrary to notions expressed in many films of the individual's gradual improvement.

The party ultimately reaches Oregon, but the expected flash forward to the community's future as an outpost of civilization or even some vague suggestion of its utopian promise is avoided. The refusal to sanction the conquest of native lands by showing a positive end result is a liberal position, yet cynical and defeatist about the likelihood of progress. In fact, Summers returns east like the party in *The Undefeated*, which differs from the optimistic growth of civilization visualized in classical Westerns such as *My Darling Clementine*.

The Internal Colonized

Narratives of the United States as imperialist peacekeeper during the Cold War or of America's fractious early expansion, inevitably lead to the question of the nation's internally colonized. Cinematic representations of the American Indians displaced by settlement often directly deal with the genocide of this persecuted group, or serve as metaphors for the lot of other minorities such as blacks, Hispanics, and women. For instance, *The Searchers* has been discussed in relation to the 1954 *Brown v. The Board of Education* decision allowing school integration (Henderson 19–23). By the late 1960s, direct, nonallegorical representation of America's internal others also inflects the era's Westerns. The genre's checkered history renders it particularly suitable to present various interest-group struggles raging during the Hollywood Renaissance. Sympathy for Indians had generic precedents while the black civil rights movement's success inevitably led to retooling of their cinematic image. The figuration of Hispanics, whose empowerment struggles were fairly recent, and women—a newly active group despite their earlier wave of political gains—reveals either less generic interest, with the former, or greater ambivalence, in terms of the latter, toward the internally colonized. The genre's synchronic relation to progressive ideas is most apparent here.

Classical titles such as *Stagecoach* (1939) and Ford's Cavalry Trilogy once proved especially egregious in portraying natives as irrational, murderous, cruel savages requiring extermination in the name of civilization. Subsequently, relatively tolerant films such as *Broken Arrow* (Delmer Daves, 1950), *Run of the Arrow* (Sam Fuller, 1956), and Ford's *Cheyenne Autumn* depicted decent, reasonable, ecologically sensitive, honorable Indians and treacherous, treaty-breaking white settlers.

The period's maverick Westerns, such as Abraham Polonsky's *Tell Them Willie Boy Is Here* (1969), and traditionalist vehicles include nuanced, sympathetic representations of natives. For instance, in Arthur Penn's remarkable *Little Big Man*, Indians are neither savage or noble but diverse and individualized. Similarly, in *Chisum*, the titular protagonist discusses his respect for Indian chief White Buffalo and describes their relationship as one of brotherhood. Ironically, this remark follows his acknowledgment of having forced Indians off "his" land. He mournfully describes this defeated people's pitiful existence on a reservation bereft of their traditional lifestyle, which Chisum calls "a good way." Interestingly, only seven years earlier, Wayne refused to work on Ford's pro-Indian *Cheyenne Autumn*. The star's other vehicles during the era, such as *Big Jake*, *The Undefeated*, and *The War Wagon*, contain similar moments. *The Last Challenge*, a Glenn Ford programmer, is the only allegedly traditionalist Western discussed here that includes overtly racist stereotyping, as when Sheriff Blane subdues revolt by intoxicating a hostile Indian, which reinforces clichés concerning drunken natives. A liberal yet old-fashioned film, *The Scalphunters* (Sydney Pollack, 1968) even attempts to represent natives with relative complexity.

The film's narrative manifestly and sympathetically portrays the plight of African Americans on the frontier. A runaway slave, Joseph Lee (Ossie Davis), is initially captured by Indians and then "sold" to an unwilling trapper, Jim Bass (Burt Lancaster), for his entire winter's bounty. Blacks were considered property, and Bass even refers to Lee as "the converted image of my pack horse and fur pelts." *The Scalphunters* does not substitute the tribulations of Indians for those of African Americans like older Westerns, but shows their equivalence while reversing the representational focus of classical titles by instead depicting the black man's experience in more detail than the situation of any Native American character and even giving Davis a costarring role with the legendary Lancaster. Lee's stated desire to live with the Comanches invokes this parallel between the two oppressed peoples. Furthermore, Bass conflates the two races by claiming this arrangement would make Lee an "African Comanche."

Indian matters, per the film's titles, soon move to the narrative foreground when a loathsome band of whites led by Jim Howie (Telly Savalas) mercilessly slaughters a group of natives in hopes of receiving twenty-five dollars a scalp. The metaphor of humans as property, inherently invoked by the presence of an ex-slave, reaches its grotesque extreme. Furthering this discourse, Howie later captures Lee and plans his auction at a slave market. In other words, forms of exploitation by white pioneers such as hunting, scalping, and trading human flesh are interchangeable and function as means of barter that link and create the frontier's economy. This notion is undeniably revisionist in refusing to portray exploration as idealistic or noble, and expands into a general critique of the white man, who alone is shown committing massacres or instigating violence, unlike many films in which only Indians senselessly rampage.

The ecologically sensitive language Bass uses also echoes the rise of environmentalism and respect for natives in the era's counterculture. At one point he describes the Indians' ingenious use of endemic flora and fauna as sources of food and clothing, and refers to the landscape through which he rides as a "Garden of Eden," yet also cites the naturalness of slavery by quoting the Bible, which per Barthesean notions, makes the institution seem inevitable and preordained. A further incoherence in his position occurs when, after refusing to drink with Lee since he is a "slave," Bass expresses admiration for Indians and contempt for scalp hunters, which muddies his ideological position and the film's conflation of the two oppressed peoples.

This dilemma, concerning his and the text's exact position on racial matters, never resolves clearly. Basically, bigotry is criticized, with Howie ultimately punished when killed by Lee. The ex-slave then gives Bass a beating, which adds to the trapper's injury of losing his pelts to the Indians for a second time in a final permutation of the narrative's system of exchanges. Nevertheless, the two friendly rivals ride off together, yet they still feign animosity, since even a liberal (yet traditionalist) Western stops short of directly presenting unambiguous interracial comradeship. Viewers knew that slavery would end, putatively putting the two men on equal footing, but that blacks would not achieve true freedom (and that natives eventually suffered near-extinction), which makes Lee and Bass's continued feuding a more accurate metaphor for race relations.

The cinematic representation of two other ethnicities—African-Americans and Hispanics—inherently evokes internal colonization. One group was forcibly brought to the United States in chains; the other, a product of racial mixing between Spanish conquerors and indigenous peoples, lost territory to an expanding American empire and became a minority.

The Scalphunters engages in a metaphorical mirroring between African Americans and Indians, but blackness qua blackness requires discussion. In particular, two films—*5 Card Stud* and *The Cowboys*—develop nonstereotypical characterizations of African Americans.

In the former, itself an intriguing synthesis of murder mystery/whodunit and Western, George, a bartender, witnesses a lynching. The men responsible are soon systematically murdered. One of the vigilantes, the vaguely psychotic and prototypical wastrel/bad seed, Nick (Roddy McDowell), accuses George of the killings. His suspicions implicitly stem from racism, although in an early example of color-blind casting, the character's blackness is never directly mentioned. More astute detective than dimwitted Negro servant, George dies at the psychotic minister Rudd's hands, but proves semiotically adept by leaving a clue exposing the killer. Beyond the textually unique presentation of impiety, its attitude toward his irreligious status, noted above, once again proves to be ambivalent. On one hand, George's disbelief suggests African Americans' capacity for a logical, scientific worldview, which contradicts stereotypes of unwaveringly God-fearing Negroes. In contrast, conservative spectators might view an atheist as a hell-bound sinner rather than a sympathetic realist.

In *The Cowboys*, the characterization of Nightlinger (Roscoe Lee Browne) also avoids stereotyping in a manner reminiscent of Sidney Poitier's roles as a sanctified, multitalented, ultradignified spokesman for black pride such as John Prentice in *Guess Who's Coming to Dinner?* Nightlinger, a Renaissance man, cooks skillfully, shrewdly bargains for his salary, speaks with lofty diction, provides sage advice, and expertly plans the boys' vengeance. He even strategically acts as a decoy and seemingly allows the villains to almost lynch him, which daringly invokes the real-life vigilante "justice" suffered by many freed blacks. In contrast to George, his race is definitely noted when the bad guys reveal their perfidy by calling him "Nigger." The kids also discuss his otherness when he first enters their bunkhouse. They ask if he is "black all over" even on "your . . . ," at which point they, and perhaps the film's script, are tongue-tied, yet they are obviously expressing curiosity about Nightlinger's penis, which also invokes myths of the well-endowed Negro. Most significantly, he assumes Andersen's command of the cattle drive, suggesting innovative racial politics even within a John Wayne vehicle.

The so-called traditionalist Western's depictions of Hispanics basically provide a coda to the previous analysis of postcoloniality's allegorical representation. This particular minority's place in American society was still marginal in the popular imaginary during the Hollywood Renaissance, while their civil rights movement had just commenced. Therefore,

Figure 4.5. Nightlinger (Roscoe Lee Browne), a black Renaissance man out west in a racially charged image of lynching, along with psychopath supreme Bruce Dern, in *The Cowboys* (Mark Rydell, 1972).

Mexican nationals' depiction as bandits or revolutionaries usually functions metaphorically to narrativize then-contemporary global issues. In contrast, Hispanic characters living in the United States, since they lack this allegorical potential, are usually relegated to bit parts such as bartenders (*El Dorado*) or background extras.

Only *Valdez Is Coming* includes a full-fledged Mexican American protagonist. Nevertheless, Lancaster's charm and acting talent fill out a character who first resembles the humble Mexican, sombrero in hand, gazing imploringly with moist brown eyes at *el jefe* until he quickly transforms into an avenging bandit, similar to antagonists in *Bandolero!* and *The Undefeated*, who successfully employs guerrilla methods. Valdez's characterization gains depth when he kidnaps a white woman without attempting to seduce her, contrary to racist notions concerning the lustful and envious minority, but this may also reflect his earlier figuration as castrated Christ figure, both an ennobling and a humiliating mantle for a lawman. Nevertheless, the only Mexican American character granted protagonist status in the genre's traditionalist entries is played by the Euro-American star Burt Lancaster.

The rise of feminism during the 1960s created another significant interest-group discourse. The era's big musicals dealt with changing gender roles and shifting relations between the sexes, but an emancipatory strain also permeates the Western. The role of women within the family required discussion in terms of status quo institutions protected by the lawman, but questions of their position within the workplace also directly reflected current social issues. Female employment usually occurs in the saloon, often a euphemized bordello, where a sexy "entertainer" in the Marlene Dietrich tradition captivates and is objectified by male characters and the camera's gaze.

Angie Dickinson, who achieved stardom in *Rio Bravo* as a gambler turned singer, played saloon girls in *The Last Challenge* and *Young Billy Young*. In the latter, her character, Lily Beloit, basically functions unproblematically. She initially performs on stage, but Marshall Kane, who ignores her self-description as "rotten straight through," bestows a symbolic cleansing while engaging in some ogling: he makes her bathe in his presence to remove the makeup she wears while singing in the villainous Behan's saloon. The scene functions purely ideologically, since she is not actually dirty. Eventually, Kane proposes marriage and states that her clothes will be unnecessary on their honeymoon. Aside from suggesting nakedness, which reflects the increasingly honest tone of the period's films, his command facilitates her shift from gaudily dressed career girl to sexually available wife, and furthers a patriarchal discourse that counterbalances any "permissive" tone.

In the otherwise more traditionalist *The Last Challenge*, Dickinson plays Lisa Denton, a hostess who has "risen" from whore to Sheriff Blane's girlfriend, although the local merchants still viciously gossip about her "low-class" status. This "progression" invokes the same process of domestication as in *Young Billy Young*, but this film is more daring because she and the lawman have no plans of marriage yet share a bed, a situation that the dying Production Code would clearly forbid. Lisa and Blane are also directly presented as sexually active and in one barely veiled exchange debate whether to have sex.

This "permissiveness" mildly subverts genre paradigms, but her actions undermine the lawman's authority and pose a challenge to gender roles. Lisa, despite good intentions, commits a treacherous act at odds with the direct violence of the cowboy, which involves warning one's foe and following chivalric rules of combat. She hires an assassin, Ernie Scarnes (Jack Elam), to kill the film's antagonist, McGuire, before he challenges Blane to a duel. Contracting out murder is typically the province of villains such as Bart Jason (Ed Asner) in *El Dorado* or Sam Foley (James Gregory) in *Shootout*. Furthering this narrative's aberrance is that Lisa, contrary to stereotypical female fearfulness, is not worried Blane will lose the fight, but that his victory will take a devastating psychological toll since he identifies with McGuire. Her concern reveals an unusual sensitivity to mental frailty, hardly a hallmark of the Western genre's worldview, while she even usurps the male role of protector by attempting to shield her love interest from pain and guilt. Beyond challenging male authority, her plan also suggests the genre's contamination by a scheming female character from the film noir's imaginary, an influence also present in *5 Card Stud*. Furthermore, Blane discovers her perfidy and, like a hard-boiled detective after his investigation, walks out on this tainted woman. Lisa will presumably continue managing the saloon. Therefore, a "progressive" outcome, representing this female character as not only gainfully employed but even as a small business owner, coexists with a traditional, punitive morality in which her actions, perhaps predictable in a woman willing to "live in sin" with a man, result in spinsterhood. In *The Last Challenge*, the lawman still proves victorious over the forces of youth but can only turn his back on dangerous femininity.

By the late 1960s, prostitution could also be represented directly, and fewer "saloon girls" appear. Nevertheless, some films still coyly hinted at the professions' reality, as in *5 Card Stud*, where Van enters a "barber shop" and notes the low prices (below fifty cents) of haircuts and baths before inquiring with the madam (Inger Stevens) about an item entitled "extra," which costs ten dollars. At the film's end, he moves on to Denver and suggests she visit. Since Van is hardly the marrying type, the film's potential resolution—a fling in the territory's most luxurious city—differs greatly from the chaste yet romantic denouements of many previous Westerns.

Two subsequent films—*The Cowboys* and *Shootout*—offer realistic views of prostitution, in keeping with the period's increasingly frank representations.

In *The Cowboys*, a group of prostitutes encounter the boys, who express interest in a "tumble" with the ladies. Nightlinger gently asks them to demur so his charges can first experience erotic activity with a girl "they think they're in love with." The film valorizes risky initiatory behavior such as intoxication and even killing but looks askance at using a whore's services for sexual awakening. Nevertheless, the situation is directly presented in a manner previously unimaginable within the genre.

Shootout ups the ante and shows prostitutes charging money for their services and unambiguously shows lovemaking, but eschews nudity. Alma, a figure of disturbing contagion, played by the highly stylized actress Susan Tyrell, even enjoys sex and her characterization, perhaps not coincidentally, opens a Pandora's box of perversion within a relatively chaste genre. She immediately asks Bobby Jay, the film's villain, to "snoggle" (an odd euphemism) and their loud revelry disturbs Clay, the aged protagonist, and trouble begins. The narrative then introduces risqué content previously unimaginable in a traditionalist Western, while her attitude toward sex, perhaps to counter the text's increasingly libidinal tone, becomes relatively traditional.

Bobby forces Alma to accompany his gang, and then starts slapping her around, which begins a narrative pattern of equating sex and violence that develops when he decides she needs "punishment" after making an inedible dinner. This linkage of patriarchal discipline with her unsuccessful performance of traditional feminine duties typifies the sexual politics of a 1950s sitcom like *I Love Lucy* when shown lightheartedly, but raises more transgressive possibilities in *Shootout*. Granted, Bobby's sadism has certainly been shown as nonsexual when he gleefully anticipates torturing Clay, but when he claims Alma lacks imagination "in or out of bed" and then smacks her ass (which has literally burst through her tight pants to suggest femininity as excess) and states "this is what happens to bad girls," a clearly sadomasochistic tone develops, unusual even in a supposedly maverick Western. Applying psychoanalytic theory connects this "perversion" and the Western; both share a nostalgic impulse. Sadomasochism allegedly expresses the desire to reclaim a pre-Oedipal state of lost plenitude, whereas the frontier myth, as enjoyed by twentieth-century movie audiences, feeds on similar cultural yearnings to revisit a pristine, prelapsarian America (Benjamin 285; Studlar 606). Nevertheless, the genre and this sexual practice blend uneasily. Imagine John Wayne making lewd jokes about spanking rather than, at worst, simply threatening an unruly cowhand with a whipping. Similarly, Tyrell's somewhat revealed rear differs in representational explicitness from the suggestion of exposure in classical era narrative situations—such as the back of Katharine Hepburn's skirt tearing in Hawks's *Bringing Up Baby* (1938) to reveal her underwear. Furthermore, this earlier scene, which certainly suggests (yet disavows) sexuality through its comic manner, lacks the serious, literal fetishistic depiction of its counterpart in *Shootout*.

This textual prurience continues when Alma, now basically a hostage, is forced to strip before Clay, Bobby's gang, and a captive mother and child. This humiliation resembles the "innocent" genre's contamination—although Julie London's striptease in *Man of the West* (Anthony Mann, 1958) set a precedent—via a child's involuntary confrontation with sexuality. This spectacle is juxtaposed with another moment of voyeurism: Bobby watching Clay and the mother tenderly embracing before he enters her cabin and takes them hostage. The hero eventually enjoys cruel revenge, yet despite restoring order and allowing an elder character's triumph, his unfair method mimics the villains' vile practices. Eroticism, consistently intertwined with sadism, has been frankly depicted, in keeping with the honesty of maverick Westerns, yet portrayed as contaminating. This contradiction exemplifies a supposedly traditionalist genre's ambivalent, dialectical presentation of contemporary realities such as increased sexual expression.

Therefore, the period's many dramatic societal changes were negotiated by these Westerns, which alternately disputed, ignored, contained, addressed, and even supported cultural shifts. Only the musical spectacular tackled so many contemporarily relevant topics. On the formal level, the genre's basic conservatism proved more obdurate, although occasional incorporation of innovation on the levels of narrative structure and cinematic style also suggest a (limited) awareness of changing (aesthetic) paradigms.

Matters of Form

In general, classical narrational principles that make a film easy to follow, such as causality, spatiotemporal clarity, and psychological motivation, are immutable even in seemingly maverick Westerns. For instance, *Once Upon a Time in the West*, despite a long and often digressive emplotment, still clearly establishes the reasons for character's actions, while any incoherencies in *The Wild Bunch* disappeared once Peckinpah's original cut resurfaced in the 1980s. In contrast, a few traditionalist titles employ narrative structure unconventionally.

The Scalphunters, similar to *How to Succeed in Business Without Really Trying*, relentlessly foregrounds causality rather than simply using it to foster spectatorial comprehension. The film is obsessively structured around Bass's attempts to retrieve his winter's trappings and horse. These possessions pass from a native tribe to the "scalphunters" to Bass to the Indians again, and are such a clear motivational device that the film's mechanics are, in defiance of classical principles, reflexively exposed in a frontier version of Ophüls's famous transactional narrative structure in *The Earrings of Madame De* . . . (1953).

Temporal gaps potentially undermine classical principles and the period's traditionalist texts feature a few examples, although strong causal relations remain. Two Hawks films have major ellipses. Andrew Sarris describes this pattern as typical when this director tackles epic stories, which he makes less daunting by creating a two-part narrative structure as in *Red River* or *Land of the Pharaohs* (1955) (Sarris 54). Nevertheless, in the former, title cards or narration (depending on the version seen) clearly present time passing (plus makeup visibly ages the actors), while the latter has an explanatory voice-over. In *El Dorado*, though, the viewer may not instantly register his use of a temporal ellipsis. The film's first twenty minutes depict Cole Thornton deciding, on Sheriff Harrah's advice, to refuse Bart Jason's offer of employment. Following a dissolve, an optical effect often indicating some temporal shift, Cole rides into an unidentified town, without the narration immediately cueing the audience that six months have gone by, and his friend Harrah has become a drunk. This sudden surprise startles spectators who witnessed the sheriff's upright demeanor in the first scene. Nevertheless, this new information is soon assimilated and the temporal jump smoothed by a comment that a bullet in Cole's side, fired during the opening sequence, has become increasingly painful, which indicates time has passed. Similarly, in *Rio Lobo* an unmarked narrative gap occurs until, once again, temporal and narrative matters are clarified.

In contrast to gapping, excessive selection of detail or repetition appear in two seemingly traditionalist Westerns through use of flashbacks. This generically atypical device, associated with films noir, highlights key narrative events.

In *Shootout*, only one flashback sequence occurs, but it crucially motivates the protagonist's behavior through depicting Clay's betrayal by his former bank-robbing partner, Foley, who shoots him in the back after a successful heist. Therefore, his willingness to pay two hundred dollars for this man's address, and his dogged pursuit of Foley, are clearly comprehensible. Interestingly, and either unclassically uncommunicative or simply providing an enigma to spur spectatorial interest, his obsessive behavior's exact cause remains unrevealed until halfway through the film.

Young Billy Young also withholds explanation of Marshall Kane's quest. In fact, despite Mitchum's star billing, his status as the film's protagonist is not immediately apparent, as the film bears Billy's name and this young outlaw's actions provide the narrative's initial focus. Eventually, the revelation of his son's murder provides motivation and explains his psychologically displaced paternal feeling toward Billy. Two flashbacks depict the killing. In each, a shot of Kane's eyes triggers the sequences and his gaze is then superimposed, as if his thoughts cause the image's existence. The Marshall symbolically commandeers the narrational function usually attributed to a motion picture's creative personnel and technical apparatus. A series of dissolves show Kane's eyes, an unidentified man being shot, his superimposed gaze, an image of him running, a shot of the dead man, and then a final dissolve to the sheriff's eyes.

His memory's obsessive recurrence is explained in the second flashback, where new information reveals that his son, not simply an anonymous deputy sheriff, died that night while Kane was engaged in sexual intercourse instead of at the jail guarding his prisoner. The first flashback simply depicts an unidentified murder and a distraught sheriff. Repetition allows the repressed to return and explain his persistent vision. This sequence also begins with a close-up of Kane's eyes. After a quick cut, rather than a slow dissolve, two people—presumably the sheriff and his girlfriend—are revealed making love (with her on top!) until a violent gunshot causes them to abruptly separate and another cut reveals the sheriff running in the rain toward his son's body. Such content, previously forbidden by the Production Code, explains the main character's guilt and exemplifies the newly allowed cinematic representation of sexuality in an allegedly more permissive era. This buried content bursts into the open only during this second telling, as if the first flashback was a censored/repressed version while the latter one presents unadorned reality.

~

Stylistic parameters provide relatively fertile analytic terrain, although once again, by definition, the era's maverick Westerns—or even traditionalist musicals, which generically tend toward excess—furnish more examples of the consistent formal hyperbole that characterizes the Hollywood Renaissance. Nevertheless, the often functionally directed, classical, allegedly traditionalist Westerns include occasionally excessive or interesting stylistic qualities. Cinematography, optical effects, editing, and even credit sequences provide interesting examples of both normative and unusual formal decisions.

In terms of camera work, the zoom lens, easily the era's key stylistic signifier, requires note. Peckinpah's virtuosic use of this device in *The Wild Bunch* parallels traditionalist Westerns' more reserved employment. For instance, in *The Day of the Evil Gun*, a sole zoom shot is needed to economically depict a character's point of view when Warfield (Glenn Ford) notices Forbes (Arthur Kennedy) following him, or to reveal his family tied to a stake about to be burned alive by Indians. The latter scene uses this lens to economically reveal information. Similar examples occur in *Young Billy Young* and *The Scalphunters*.

Slightly aberrant zooming also surfaces, as in *The Scalphunters*, where an odd combination of zooms and dissolves ambiguously marks scene changes when a shot of a stream is replaced, through a match cut, by an almost identical space. This creates a fluid transition, yet the zoom lens produces an excess of stylistic interest. Nevertheless, the film hardly equals Robert Altman's formal experiments with the same lens.

Hand-held camera, quite prominent in many maverick texts, appears sparingly except in *The Undefeated*. This device typically simulates documentary-style objectivity or character subjectivity. The opening scene of *The Undefeated* uses hand-held camera to place viewers within a Civil War battle, but avoids suggesting any specific character's point-of-view to instead resemble a newsreel photographer's perspective amid the melee. This scene also uses zoom lensing to propel the spectator into the fray. These overt devices still foster spectatorial involvement and provide vivid mimesis, which suggests their basically classical employment.

Pronounced camera angles may potentially disrupt narrative flow and create awareness of the technical apparatus or simply provide dramatic emphasis. Interestingly enough, the traditionalist Western frequently used this stylistic choice while only sparingly sampling many of the era's other excessive techniques. The aforementioned influence of film noir could partially explain this development.

Surprisingly, even Hawks, well known for his visual austerity and level camera, includes an ostentatious shot in *El Dorado* of a man falling from a church bell tower seemingly onto the camera, since it obviated "another day's shooting and building a new set" (Bogdanovich 359). A younger filmmaker such as Burt Kennedy employs a similar angle in *Young Billy Young*, where a low camera position shows a body crashing through a wooden canopy. This angle is less dramatic than Hawks's, which is directly below pointing straight upward, and a logical choice when shooting from the vantage point of a town's main street. These two directors' choices economically present an entire action in a single take and also emphasize inherently dramatic moments when the audience, presumably on the edge of their seats, fails to notice these compositions' baroque or distracting qualities. During a dialogue-based sequence, such angles would seem aberrant and overt.

Nevertheless, Kennedy also shoots a poker game—a quotidian event within the Western genre and hardly requiring dramatic emphasis—in *Young Billy Young* from a unique angle, placing the camera above the table. The shot thriftily avoids cutting but also attracts attention while suggesting the influence of noir, another genre fond of card-playing as determinist metaphor. Kennedy also stages a heist—another classic noir event—in *The War Wagon* with low angles, which are motivated by heightening suspense through emphasizing the seeming impregnability and magnitude of this titular and fabulous conveyance. *5 Card Stud*, a true noir-Western synthesis, contains a murder-mystery plot in a frontier setting where the protagonist functions as a detective. The intergeneric connection begins with the first shot: an overhead angle of a fatal poker game, which, unlike the card game in *Young Billy Young*, uses hard, high contrast and low-key expressionistic lighting. Noir style later represents death when a shot of a body swinging from a church bell emphasizes horror and suggests an askew world through dim lighting and a low angle. Such stylistic choices suggest that even the era's traditionalist Westerns had a certain formal freedom without necessarily evincing the progressive excesses associated with Peckinpah's or Leone's productions.

Dissolves are another optical effect and usually suggest a temporal ellipsis between scenes. The primal flashback in *Young Billy Young* provides a smooth transition into Sheriff Kane's memory and lets him seemingly watch over his own narration of a traumatic event. In contrast, dissolves are occasionally used "inappropriately" and become noticeable. For instance, the opening scene of Hawks's final production, *Rio Lobo*, depicts a Union train's sabotage and promiscuously employs this device (which canonically signals time passing) unhindered by narrative logic, since other shot transitions during the same sequence, which occurs without any significant temporal ellipses, use straight cuts. For instance, a dissolve is used from Union Colonel McNally (John Wayne) sending a telegraph to Confederate saboteurs intercepting his message. Following this, a straight cut reveals the communication's intended receiver. Another standard edit, back to the saboteurs, follows, and then a further seemingly random dissolve reveals a clicking telegraph machine. Hawks's technique seems even more random since the sequence also uses cross-cutting, which further suggests simultaneity, and involves a "real-time" relation between plot and story. Ultimately, straight cuts and dissolves are whimsically, unclassically employed rather than signifying temporal continuity or a narrative ellipsis.

In contrast, cross-cutting, a staple of classical style dating back to Griffith, functions conventionally in many traditionalist Westerns. For instance, a sequence of parallel actions in *The War Wagon* depicts both Jackson (John Wayne) and Lomax (Kirk Douglas) simultaneously checking their watches, and various others also preparing to rob the war wagon, itself shown unwittingly heading into danger. Cross-cutting often suggests similarities. For instance, the two protagonists in *The Undefeated* fought on opposing sides in the Civil War, but are both strong, determined personalities. Parallel editing reveals each man's group, albeit not simultaneously, crossing the Rio Grande into Mexico.

The traditionalist Western also employed point-of-view editing conventionally, as in *The Way West*, which placed the spectator in front of a covered wagon riding through a buffalo herd in hopes of increasing the audience's excitement. In contrast, aberrant use of this method eschews its linkage to a single character's subjectivity. In *Firecreek*, a teenage girl barely escapes attempted rape by an outlaw, yet traditional identification with her is denied since both victim and culprit receive point-of-view shots. Similarly, a villain's view is represented near the end of *Valdez Is Coming*, perhaps par for the course in the decade's later slasher films but unusual for a Western.

Finally, noting credit sequences again reveals the presence of putatively maverick traits within these traditionalist texts. For instance, *The*

Day of the Evil Gun directly copies Leone's titles through Morricone-inspired music and blending animation, moving images, color tinting, and freeze frames. An MGM Western imitates Italian productions based on American models, which makes sense when tarting up a star vehicle for the stalwart, aging Glenn Ford. Similarly, the film's violent moniker evokes a different mood than the conventional title—*The Last Challenge*—of the actor's prior Western. The blend of live action and freeze frames was also employed the next year by Peckinpah in *The Wild Bunch*.

Theme songs also characterize these opening sequences. "The Ballad of John Chisum," sung by Merle Haggard, literally valorizes tradition through lyrics such as "Chisum, John Chisum, weary, saddle worn . . . and he still keep goin' on." This sentiment conveys the typically weary, elegiac tone of the period's maverick and traditionalist Westerns and suggests the immutability of Chisum, Wayne, and the genre. More aberrant is this credit sequence's use of a documentary style, later exemplified by the PBS opuses of Ken Burns, involving zooming in on details of a painting and adding sound effects. For instance, a Remingtonesque depiction of cattle stampeding in a storm is accompanied by audible thunder and lighting, while a zoom in on an image of Indians attacking includes gunshots on the soundtrack.

∽

This image portrays a vital frontier lifestyle yet presents it through mediated images suggesting only representation can currently invoke the cowboy myth. It proves as fitting as any moment to close out this discussion of the last of four narrative modes characterized by a seeming "traditionalism" performing the same dialectical synthesis of form and content as other maverick texts. Similarly, the presence of older ideologies and formal practices coexists with progressive viewpoints and innovations of narrative structure and style and helps characterize a neglected corpus of rich films within a frequently discussed historical period. Brief consideration of the era's culmination, and the fate of the four genres, rounds out this study.

Conclusion

1972: Lost Horizons

When *Lost Horizon* was released in early 1973, many agreed it was an anachronism. Pauline Kael aptly notes, in a highly negative and mocking review, that all its producer Ross Hunter's films (such as his previous smash hit, *Airport*, from 1970) were "lost horizons" because they appealed to "people nostalgic for a simpler pop culture" (Kael, *Reeling* 194). David Cook calls it a "certified, late-sixties style disaster" since it lost $8 million of its $12 million investment (Cook 212). As with many films discussed above, *Lost Horizon* actually contains potentially progressive dimensions, but these aspects of similarly traditionalist texts are usually critically elided. I hope to have shown that this construction never sufficiently fit the movies included under the heading since they are far too divergent in their formal and ideological tendencies for such classification. Cook's description, though, also suggests that *Lost Horizon* is not just generically old-fashioned, per Kael's critical savaging, but that it belongs in another era—the late 1960s, which suggests the need for a few comments on periodizing the end of the era I've studied.

During the previous year, Francis Ford Coppola's *The Godfather* replaced *The Sound of Music* as all-time box-office champ and was the first of many financial triumphs for the film-school-educated "movie brat" generation of its creator and his cohort, most notably George Lucas and Steven Spielberg ("All-Time Boxoffice Champs"). Its juxtaposition with *The Sound of Music* speaks volumes about the era they bookend. The latter inaugurated and personified the trend of studios sinking large sums into old-fashioned, expensive roadshow spectacles, such as the late-appearing *Lost Horizon*, which, if successful, literally forestalled financial ruin, but typically lost money. Ironically, *The Godfather* was directed by Coppola, then best known for the financially unsuccessful (although not ruinously so, like *Star!* or *Hello, Dolly!*) traditionalist musical *Finian's Rainbow* (Cook 134–35). *The Godfather* also resembles maverick titles such as *Bonnie and Clyde*, though as a crime film featuring graphic violence and meticulous period detail by the same production designer, Dean Tavoularis. Glenn Man, in fact, treats it as a seminal example of the "radical visions" possessed by the small canon his study of the Hollywood Renaissance constructs.

Nevertheless, as with *Lost Horizon*, Coppola's instant classic may also be more complex and harder to pigeonhole than expected, except that it contains the diachronic remnants of earlier film practice, particularly the gangster genre, within a popular and critically valorized movie rather than the synchronic presence of progressive discourses within a seemingly traditionalist text. *The Godfather's* narrative structure, with exceptions such as a brief flash-forward, is mostly classical, just as Coppola, some Eisensteinian editing aside or starting the film without a typical establishing shot, mostly hews to stylistic transparency. The cast features a legendary star, yet many actors and many creative personnel were newcomers. Discussing creative personnel, and noting that a star of Altman's maverick *M*A*S*H* (Sally Kellerman) appears with venerable performers such as Charles Boyer, Peter Finch, and John Gielgud in *Lost Horizon*, begs the question: Does separating the two films make sense beyond making a seemingly obvious distinction between a tragic, violent text that creates a shadow version of American history and family drama through the Mafia and a wholesome family production set in a nonexistent fantasy kingdom? Can any description of the complete nature of these films truly construct coherent traditionalist and maverick categories despite the general opinion of historians who would easily place them in separate camps? *Lost Horizon*, though, is part of a trend that had ebbed enough by 1973 that David Cook suggests the film is dated, although there were still a few examples of unsuccessful mainstream musical adaptations such as *Mame* (Gene Saks, 1974) and *The Little Prince* (Stanley Donen, 1974) in years to come. *The Godfather* is a harbinger of future developments in the film industry.

Coppola's film ushered in a new style of blockbuster moviemaking based on studio promotion and opening a film in wider release. According to David Cook, "Strategic or 'scientific' marketing in the motion picture industry began in 1972 with Paramount's spectacular success in promoting Francis Ford Coppola's *The Godfather*, which by the time of its release had attained 'event' status through mass sales of the Mario Puzo novel (published during production) and intense publicity focused on both the shooting of the film and protests by Italian-American groups about its supposed prejudicial content" (Cook 14). Things never being so pat,

Figure C.1. New and old stars: Marlon Brando and Al Pacino in *The Godfather* (Francis Coppola, 1972).

Cook later discusses how both *Airport* (considered ultra-"traditionalist") and another Paramount/Bob Evans triumph, *Love Story*, had also become hits based on best-sellers, with the later film also being novelized, like *The Godfather*, after a script was written (Cook 30–33). *The Godfather* was also distributed differently and set a precedent for the mass release of smash hits later in the decade, such as *Jaws* (Steven Spielberg, 1975) and *Star Wars* (George Lucas, 1977), by opening in five first-run theaters in New York and nationwide in over 300 venues. This was antithetical to the limited, audience-building strategy of only one A-class theater per urban market, which might hold onto a film for up to a year (Biskind, *Easy Riders* 162–63). The film's significance is furthered as its financial success led to "almost single-handedly restoring confidence in the blockbuster formula" and earning almost 10 percent of the year's total gross receipts (Cook 14).

The year 1972 also serves as a sociopolitical border. By this point feminism, Chicano activism, and gay rights movements, which were nascent or nonexistent in 1967, had achieved gains. In contrast, the civil rights movement had already made significant strides and fragmented into its own traditionalist and maverick branches, the latter represented in the public imaginary by the Black Panthers. More specifically, Richard Nixon was reelected in 1972 while the war in Vietnam sputtered to a conclusion. These twin events beached the political and cultural

Left and rendered them temporarily weakened (after the liberal presidential candidate George McGovern was trounced) and causeless (once the Indochinese conflict petered out). A relatively quiet era dawned that continued the experimentation with drugs, sex, and alternative forms of spirituality begun by the counterculture yet spawned a generation who often viewed the developing Watergate scandal as further proof of the inherent corruption and nefariousness of government. Nevertheless, changes in the American public's basic attitudes toward imperialism, the American dream, minority rights, and environmentalism survived as a legacy of the era's turbulence. Hollywood, though, reflected the general trend toward apoliticality by veering away from overtly ideological productions and trying to mirror society through regrouping from, albeit indelibly marked by, the previous half-decade's tumult.

In terms of the genres discussed above, a brief description of their fate following the Hollywood Renaissance shows that their continuance of classical paradigms was no longer a hindrance, and perhaps was even a bonus, once a more putatively conservative era, as critically constructed, dawned by the late 1970s. After all, accounts such as Mast and Kawin speak of "a return of the myths," where genre films are reembraced, not questioned (Mast and Kawin 585). Could they also remain acceptable synchronic expressions as society and film practice continued to evolve? In most cases, the answer is a limited "yes."

The musical, despite attempts at relevance via sympathetic, progressive representations of women and minorities, questioning social organization, and indulging in the era's stylistic hyperbole, ultimately declined rapidly after 1972, yet it never completely disappears. The cost, and frequent and well-publicized, even notorious, financial fallout of such productions hastened their initial demise. In fact, the bloated musicals particularly characterize the discourse about the period that seeks to contrast maverick productions to these white elephants. When considering that they became extinct, their "failure" seems only more noteworthy and a perfect foil to more favored films. Therefore, it is also understandable that only a few economically and critically unsuccessful titles followed immediately, such as *Mame*, *The Little Prince*, *At Long Last Love* (Peter Bogdanovich, 1975), and *Funny Lady* (Herb Ross, 1975), a sequel to *Funny Girl*. After 1977, musicals of any type have been rare except for the occasional Broadway adaptation such as the Oscar-winning Best Picture *Chicago* (Rob Marshall, 2002) and *Les Misérables* (Tom Hooper, 2012). None of these, though, incurred ridiculous production costs or was expected to single-handedly turn a studio's fate around. The genre, therefore, exists as a sort of occasional, possibly profitable novelty no longer particularly associated diachronically with old Hollywood—yet still borrowing some of its vestigial glamour—or the Renaissance era's disasters. Interestingly, talented singers and dancers still flourish, while onstage the genre has maintained popularity, and many animated films are de facto musicals. Therefore, the presentational style where characters express themselves musically seems acceptable in less naturalistic media. Furthermore, the genre is not yoked to a particular setting, tone, or sociohistorical concerns, so its scarcity seems unattached to synchronic irrelevance. Perhaps the critically and financially acclaimed revival of MGM-era tradition (mixed with Jacques Demy) *La La Land* (Damien Chazelle, 2016) points to a renewal through telling a modern story of stardom with contemporary morals that also revives classical narrative patterns and story lines.

The World War II film also declined precipitously after 1972, but has proved hardier than the musical; combat narratives in general continue to excite, inspire, and disturb audiences. During the next five years, *Midway* (Jack Smight, 1976), *A Bridge Too Far* (Richard Attenborough, 1977), and *MacArthur* (Joseph Sargent, 1977), performed indifferently. Each of these productions featured an aging lead actor (e.g., Charlton Heston, Gregory Peck) and were directed by an undistinguished journeymen. This is understandable in an era typified by a battle-fatigued public's disenchantment with the Vietnam War and its aftermath and not indicative of wariness toward the combat spectacle itself. Nevertheless, neither had much appeal to younger viewers. Following the Reagan administration and two military engagements in Iraq, World War II narratives have reemerged as sheer bellicose epic entertainment for a mass audience. These productions feature young stars (Ben Affleck, Matt Damon) and are helmed by hot directors such as Steven Spielberg or Michael Bay and often enhanced with current computer-generated imagery, as with Michael Bay's *Pearl Harbor* (2001). Such films are historically removed enough to serve as vehicles for nationalistic reaffirmation both diachronically continuing World War II–era patriotism yet related to a then-current desire to valorize America's once impregnable world image. They also contain graphic violence unthinkable even in the Hollywood Renaissance's most iconoclastic combat movies. Steven Spielberg's *Saving Private Ryan* (1998), for instance, depicts gruesome death and palpable terror while sentimentalizing American heroism. In contrast, Terence Malick's philosophical, ambiguous *The Thin Red Line* (1998) signaled both the return, after a twenty-year absence, of an archetypical maverick director of the 1970s and the costly, studio-released art movie à la *2001: A Space Odyssey*.

Furthermore, Vietnam itself eventually became fit for (mostly) revisionist and negative accounts, such as *The Deer Hunter* (Michael Cimino, 1978), *Coming Home* (Hal Ashby, 1978), *Apocalypse Now* (Francis Coppola,

1979), *Platoon* (Oliver Stone, 1986), *Casualties of War* (Brian De Palma, 1989), and *Born on the Fourth of July* (Oliver Stone, 1989). Finally, as war inevitably recurs throughout the world and the United States battles terrorism after 9/11, films such as Kathryn Bigelow's *The Hurt Locker* (2008) and *Zero Dark Thirty* (2012) explored ambivalent attitudes toward military engagement.

These two modes had enough history and cultural significance to survive while remaining plastic enough in theme to synchronically reattune. The naughty sex comedy had neither virtue and was almost completely finished by 1972, since direct representation of eroticism was permitted and concerns about changing mores could be presented more explicitly. Television resuscitated the subgenre for a while since the medium was rigorously self-censored for longer than motion pictures and thus a perfect vehicle for "naughtiness." Most notably, the late 1970s sitcom *Three's Company* lucratively and sniggeringly represented two women and a man (platonically) cohabitating; it consistently included belabored mistaken-identity farce narratives and featured in its later years the erstwhile Love God—Don Knotts—as a cast member.

The Western's rapid decline after 1972 seems particularly inexplicable since this seemingly popular perennial mode had proven synchronically adaptable for varied allegorical purposes and able to incorporate formal innovations. John Wayne made four final forays into the genre he dominated: *The Train Robbers* (Burt Kennedy, 1973), *Cahill, U.S. Marshall* (Andrew V. McLaglen, 1973), *Rooster Cogburn* (Stuart Millar, 1975), a sequel to *True Grit* co-starring the equally legendary Katharine Hepburn, and *The Shootist* (Don Siegel, 1976). In the last-mentioned, the aging star's real-life illness—cancer—is presented, although his fictive avatar goes out with guns blazing and successfully slaughters three nemeses. A few other traditionalist titles were released, such as *Showdown* (George Seaton, 1973) with Dean Martin and Rock Hudson. When two Westerns emerged in 1985—*Silverado* (Lawrence Kasdan) and *Pale Rider* (Clint Eastwood)—their mere existence seemed noteworthy. In the early 1990s, two Best Picture Oscars were awarded to *Dances with Wolves* (Kevin Costner, 1990) and *Unforgiven* (Clint Eastwood, 1992) and a mild generic resurgence followed. Currently, an occasional Western appears theatrically. These include art films (*Meek's Cutoff*, Kelly Reichart, 2010), relatively meat-and-potatoes remakes updated with contemporary-style rapid cutting and quick-paced mayhem (*3:10 to Yuma*, James Mangold, 2007; *The Magnificent Seven*, Antoine Fuqua, 2016), and special-effects-laden comic-book-style productions set on the frontier (*Cowboys and Aliens*, Jon Favreau, 2011; *The Lone Ranger*, Gore Verbinski, 2013). Television is the fading tradition's refuge, with programs such as HBO's critically acclaimed and revisionist David Milch–helmed *Deadwood* (2004–2006) and the more recent AMC offering *Hell on Wheels* (2011–16). Interestingly, phrases such as "outlaw," "cowboy," and "sheriff" persistently color the American imaginary while Bruce Willis/John McClain in the *Die Hard* franchise (1988–??) famously shouts "Yipee-ki-yay" when dispatching villains. Nevertheless, despite its endlessly possible synchronic relevance to an era's formal and ideological contours, the genre is a shell of its former glory.

∾

Hopefully this study also suggests a necessary, ongoing project of discussing a wider cinematic corpus than a favored canon of classics and questioning the periodizing of American film history. Considering Hollywood's incredible range, and each individual text's complexities, a more particular, exhaustive attempt at sifting through and detailing a monumental filmography is required. Focusing on an alternative tradition within one supposedly iconoclastic era, albeit a type of traditionalist film practice that had actually dominated the American cinema prior to 1967, provides a more nuanced, less caricatured view of 1967–1972 as a period and I hope it encourages similar projects.

The era's traditionalist movies dialectically engaged with progressive societal and aesthetic developments. Hopefully, delineating their ambiguous, complex nature—and the divergences between individual films, genres, and the works of directors—may provide impetus for exploring neglected pathways and remaining open to complexity, nuance, and even incoherence. Trying to conclude with a more definitive statement than that would rob the traditionalist corpus of its perplexing, ambivalent nature.

Works Cited

Abramson, Leslie H. "1968: Movies and the Failure of Nostalgia." *American Cinema of the 1960s: Themes and Variations*, edited by Barry Keith Grant, Rutgers University Press, 2008, pp. 193–216.
Adler, Renata. "The Screen: *The Impossible Years* Opens: David Niven Stars in Joyless Comedy Many Circumlocutions in Music Hall Film." *New York Times*, 6 December 1968.
Agel, Jerome. *The Making of Kubrick's 2001*. Signet, 1970.
"All-Time Boxoffice Champs." *Variety*, 3 January 1973, p. 30.
Althusser, Louis. "Ideology and Ideological State Apparatuses (Notes Towards an Investigation)." *Lenin and Philosophy and Other Essays*. Translated by Ben Brewster, Monthly Review Press, 1971.
Altman, Rick. "Reusable Packaging: Generic Products and the Recycling Process." *Refiguring American Film Genres*, edited by Nick Browne, University of California Press, 1998, pp. 1–41.
———. "A Semantic/Syntactic Approach to Film Genre." *Film Theory and Criticism*, edited by Leo Braudy and Marshall Cohen, Oxford University Press, 2004. pp. 680–690.
Balio, Tino. "Retrenchment, Reappraisal and Reorganization, 1948–." *The American Film Industry*, edited by Tino Balio, University of Wisconsin Press, 1985, pp. 401–47.
Barthes, Roland. *Mythologies*. Noonday Press, 1972.
Bazin, Andre. "The Evolution of the Language of Cinema." *What Is Cinema?*, vol. 1, edited and translated by Hugh Gray, University of California Press, 1967, pp. 23–40.
Belgrad, Daniel. *The Culture of Spontaneity: Improvisation and the Arts in Postwar America*. University of Chicago Press, 1998.
Belton, John. *American Cinema/American Culture*. McGraw Hill, 2005.
Benjamin, Jessica. "Master and Slave: The Fantasy of Erotic Domination." *Powers of Desire: The Politics of Sexuality*, edited by A. Snitow, C. Stansell, and S. Thompson, Monthly Review Press, 1983, pp. 280–99.
Beuka, Robert. "'Just One Word . . . PLASTICS.'" *Journal of Popular Film & Television*, vol. 28, no. 1 (Spring 2000), pp. 12–21.

"Big Rental Pictures of 1962." *Variety*, 9 January 1963.
"Big Rental Pictures of 1965." *Variety*, 5 January 1966, p. 8.
"Big Rental Pictures of 1966." *Variety*, 4 January 1967, p. 8.
"Big Rental Films of 1967." *Variety*, 3 January 1968.
"Big Rental Films of 1968." *Variety*, 8 January 1969.
"Big Rental Films of 1969." *Variety*, 7 January 1970.
"Big Rental Films of 1970." *Variety*, 6 January 1971.
"Big Rental Films of 1971." *Variety*, 5 January 1972.
"Big Rental Films of 1972." *Variety*, 3 January 1973.
"Big Rental Films of 1973." *Variety*, 9 January 1974.
"Big Rental Films of 1974." *Variety* 8 January 1975.
Biskind, Peter. *Easy Riders, Raging Bulls: How the Sex-Drugs-and-Rock 'n' Roll Generation Saved Hollywood*. Simon & Schuster, 1998.
———. *Seeing is Believing: How Hollywood Taught Us to Stop Worrying and Love the Fifties*. Henry Holt and Company, 1983.
Bliss, Michael. "Martyred Slaves of Time: Age, Regret and Transcendence in *The Wild Bunch*." *Peckinpah Today: New Essays on the Films of Sam Peckinpah*, edited by Michael Bliss, Southern Illinois University Press, 2012, pp. 36–45.
Bogdanovich, Peter. *Who the Devil Made It?* Alfred A. Knopf, 1977.
Bordwell, David. "Classical Hollywood Cinema: Narrational Principles and Procedures." *Narrative, Apparatus, Ideology: A Film Theory Reader*, edited by Philip Rosen, Columbia University Press, 1986, pp. 17–34.
———. *Narration in the Fiction Film*. University of Wisconsin Press, 1985.
———. *The Way Hollywood Tells It: Story and Style in Modern Movies*. University of California Press, 2006.
Bordwell, Davis, Janet Staiger, and Kristin Thompson. *The Classical Hollywood Cinema: Film Style and Mode of Production to 1960*. Columbia University Press, 1985.
Bordwell, David, and Kristin Thompson. *Film Art: An Introduction*. McGraw-Hill, 2013.
Branigan, Edward. "The Point of View Shot." *Movies and Methods*, vol. II, edited by Bill Nichols, University of California Press, 1985.
"Broadway's Brightest Comedy Hit Blossoms on the Screen . . . *Cactus Flower*." Press release, *Cactus Flower* clippings file. Academy of Motion Picture Arts and Sciences, Margaret Herrick Research Library.
Brown, Norman O. *Life Against Death: The Psychoanalytical Meaning of History*. Wesleyan University Press, 1959.
Cameron, Allan. *Modular Narratives in Contemporary Cinema*. Palgrave Macmillan UK, 2008.
Canby, Vincent. "'Movie Review: *Man of La Mancha* Comes to Screen." *New York Times*, 12 December 1972.
———. "Movie Review: *True Grit*." *New York Times*, 4 July 1969.
———. "Screen: A Blow-Up of *Sweet Charity*." *New York Times*, 2 April 1969.
Casper, Drew. *Hollywood Film 1963–1976*. Wiley-Blackwell, 2011.
"Catch-22." http://www.the-numbers.com/movies/1970/0CT22.php.

Champlin, Charles. "*Anzio* Opens Citywide Run." *Los Angeles Times*, 17 July 1968.
———. "Can TV Save the Films?" *Saturday Review* 24 December 1966, pp. 11–13.
"Charles Evans Hughes." US Department of State, Office of the Historian. http://history.state.gov/departmenthistory/people/hughes-charles-evans.
Comolli, Jean-Louis, and Jean Narboni. "Cinema /Ideology/Criticism." *Film Theory and Criticism*, edited by Leo Braudy and Marshall Cohen, Oxford University Press, 2004, pp. 812–19.
Conant, Michael. "The Paramount Decree Reconsidered." Balio, pp. 537–73.
Cook, David A. *Lost Illusions: American Cinema in the Shadow of Vietnam and Watergate*. Charles Scribner's Sons, 2000.
"*Devil's Brigade* Gets Army Cooperation OK." *Hollywood Reporter*, 15 March 1967.
Display Ads. *Los Angeles Times*, 1 January 1967.
———. *Los Angeles Times*, 1 January 1970.
———. *Los Angeles Times*, 19 March 1971.
———. *Los Angeles Times*, 1 January 1973.
Dunne, John Gregory. *The Studio*. Simon & Schuster, 1969.
Dyer, Richard. "Entertainment and Utopia." *Genre: The Musical*, edited by Rick Altman. British Film Institute, 1981, pp. 175–89.
Ebert, Roger. "*Cactus Flower*." 29 December 1969. http://www.rogerebert.com/reviews/cactus-flower-1969.
———. "*Easy Rider*." 28 September 1969. http://www.rogerebert.com/reviews/easy-rider-1969.
———. "*Paint Your Wagon*." 31 October 1969. http://www.rogerebert.com/reviews/paint-your-wagon-1969.
———. "*Goodbye Mr. Chips*." 19 November 1969. http://www.rogerebert.com/reviews/goodbye-mr-chips-1969.
Fanon, Frantz. *The Wretched of the Earth*. Grove Press, 2007.
Farber, Stephen. "The End of the Road." *Film Quarterly*, vol. 23, no. 2, Winter 1969–1970, pp. 3–16.
"Film Review: *Anzio*." *Daily Variety*, 19 June 1968, pp. 3, 11.
"Film Review: *Bandolero!*" *Daily Variety*, 3 June 1968.
"Film Review: *The Devil's Brigade*." *Daily Variety*, 2 May 1968.
"Film Review: *How to Save a Marriage (and Ruin Your Life)*," *Daily Variety*, 18 January 1968.
"Film Review: *The Last Challenge*." *Daily Variety*, 4 October 1967.
"*Firecreek*: Conflict of Good and Evil in a little Frontier Town." *The Film Daily*, 24 January 1968.
Fleming, Anne Taylor. "Movies a Go-Go." *Los Angeles Magazine*, March 2012, pp. 94–96.
Foucault, Michel. *The Order of Things*. Vintage Books, 1970.
Friedan, Betty. *The Feminine Mystique*. Norton, 1963.
Gottfried, Martin. *All His Jazz: The Life and Death of Bob Fosse*. Da Capo Press, 2009.

Greenwood, Jeremy, and Nezih Guner. "Social Change: The Sexual Revolution." *The University of Pennsylvania Population Studies Center Working Papers Series*, 21 April 2009. http://repository.upenn.edu/cgi/viewcontent.cgi?article=1011&context=psc_working_papers.

Grubb, Kevin Boyd. *Razzle Dazzle: The Life and Work of Bob Fosse*. St. Martin's Press, 1989.

Grunenberg, Christoph, and Jonathan Harris. *Summer of Love: Psychedelic Art, Social Crisis and Counterculture in the 1960s*. Vol. 8. Liverpool University Press, 2005.

Guerrero, Ed. *Framing Blackness: The African American Image in Film*. Temple University Press, 1993.

Gustafson, Robert. "'What's Happening to Our Pix Biz?' From Warner Bros. to Warner Communications, Inc." Balio, 574–86.

Halliwell, Leslie. *Halliwell's Film Guide*, 4th ed. Charles Scribner's Sons, 1983.

Harris, Mark. *Pictures at a Revolution: Five Movies and the Birth of the New Hollywood*. Penguin Press, 2008.

"Harry Stradling." *Internet Movie Database*. http://www.imdb.com/name/nm0005889/bio.

Heath, Stephen. "Narrative Space." *Narrative/Apparatus/Ideology: A Film Theory Reader*, edited by Philip Rosen, Columbia University Press, 1986, 379–420.

Henderson, Brian. "*The Searchers*: An American Dilemma." *Film Quarterly*, vol. 34, no. 2 (1980–1981), pp. 10–23.

Historical Statistics of the United States: Colonial Times to 1970. Part I. United States Department of Commerce, Bureau of the Census, 1975.

Horkheimer, Max, and Theodor Adorno. "The Culture Industry: Enlightenment as Mass Deception." *Dialectic of Enlightenment*, Continuum, 1986.

"Housework in Late 19th Century America." *Digital History*. http://www.digitalhistory.uh.edu/topic_display.cfm?tcid=93.

Ingram, Bob. "Save Your Money." *Inter/View*, vol. 1, no. 4, 1969. Clippings file. Academy of Motion Picture Arts and Sciences, Margaret Herrick Research Library.

"Is God Dead?" *Time* Magazine cover. 8 April, 1966. http://www.time.com/time/covers/0,16641,19660408,00.html.

Jacobs, Diane. *Hollywood Renaissance: The New Generation of Filmmakers and Their Works*. Delta Books, 1977.

James, David. *Allegories of Cinema: American Film in the Sixties*. Princeton University Press, 1988.

Jameson, Fredric. *The Political Unconscious: Narrative as a Socially Symbolic Act*. Cornell University Press, 1981.

Kael, Pauline. *Deeper into Movies*. Warner Books, 1973.

———. *Going Steady*. Warner Books, 1979.

———. *Reeling*. Warner Books, 1976.

Karp, Alan. *The Films of Robert Altman*. The Scarecrow Press, 1981.

Kehr, Dave. "New DVDs." *New York Times*, 11 January 2005. http://www.nytimes.com/2005/01/11/movies/11dvd.html?_r=0.

Klein, Amanda Ann. *American Film Cycles: Reframing Genres, Screening Social Problems, and Defining Subcultures*. University of Texas Press, 2012.
Klein, Andy. "Blood Sport." *New Times Los Angeles*, vol. 3, no. 5, p. 13.
Kolker, Robert. *A Cinema of Loneliness: Penn, Stone, Kubrick, Scorsese, Spielberg, Altman*, 3rd ed. Oxford University Press, 2000.
Kracauer, Siegfried. "The Establishment of Physical Existence." *Movies and Methods*, vol. I, edited by Bill Nichols. University of California Press, 1976, pp. 303–13.
Leff, Leonard J., and Jerold L. Simmons. *The Dame in the Kimono*. Doubleday, 1990.
Lev, Peter. *The Fifties: Transforming the Screen 1950–1959*. University of California Press, 2003.
Lewis, Jon. *Hollywood v. Hard Core: How the Struggle over Censorship Saved the Modern Film Industry*. New York University Press, 2000.
Mahoney, John. "Frankovich *Cactus Flower* Smash Comedy Box Office Hit." *The Hollywood Reporter*, 3 September 1969.
———. "*How to Save a Marriage* Plus Picture, Consistently Funny." *The Hollywood Reporter*, 18 January 1968.
Man, Glenn. *Radical Visions: American Film Renaissance 1967–1976*. Greenwood Press, 1994.
Mast, Gerald, and Bruce Kawin. *A Short History of the Movies*, 11th ed. Longman, 2011.
McCarthy, Todd. *Howard Hawks: The Grey Fox of Hollywood*. Grove Press, 1997.
McQueen, Amanda. "*Sweet Charity*: The Musical Pulse of 1969." *University of Wisconsin Cinematheque program notes*, 28 January 2016. http://cinema.wisc.edu/blog/2016/01/28/sweet-charity-musical-pulse-1969.
Metz, Christian. *The Imaginary Signifier*. Indiana University Press, 1982.
Milliken, Christine. "1969: Movies and the Counterculture." *American Cinema of the 1960s: Themes and Variations*, edited by Barry Keith Grant. Rutgers University Press, 2008, pp. 217–38.
Monaco, Paul. *The Sixties: 1960–1969*. University of California Press, 2001.
"Mondays TV Programs," *Los Angeles Times*, 22 November 1971.
"Most Popular People with Date of Death in 1967." *The Internet Movie Database*. http://www.imdb.com/search/name?death_date=1967-01-01,1967-12-31.
"Movies Continuing." *Los Angeles Times*, 1 January 1967.
Mulvey, Laura. "Visual Pleasure and Narrative Cinema." *Narrative/Apparatus/Ideology: A Film Theory Reader*, edited by Philip Rosen, Columbia University Press, 1986, pp. 198–209.
———. *Visual and Other Pleasures*. Indiana University Press, 1989. "The New Films." *Film Daily*, 22 January 1968.
Nichols, Bill. *Introduction to Documentary*, 2nd ed. Indiana University Press, 2010.
"The 1967 Arab-Israeli War." *U.S. Department of State: Office of the Historian*. http://history.state.gov/milestones/1961-1968/arab-israeli-war-1967.
"*The Owl and the Pussycat*: Trivia." Internet Movie Database. http://www.imdb.com/title/tt0066195/trivia?ref_=tt_trv_trv.

"The Pistolero of Red River." *Films and Filming,* September 1967, p. 24.
Pomerance, Murray. "1967: Movies and the Specter of Rebellion." *American Cinema of the 1960s: Themes and Variations,* edited by Barry Keith Grant, Rutgers University Press, 2008, pp. 172–92.
Parish, James Robert. *Fiasco: A History of Hollywood's Iconic Flops.* Wiley, 2006.
Pratley, Gerald. *The Cinema of John Frankenheimer.* A. Zwimmer Ltd. and A. S. Barnes & Co., 1969.
Ryan, Michael, and Douglas Kellner. *Camera Politica: The Politics and Ideologies of Contemporary Hollywood Film.* University of Indiana Press, 1988.
Salt, Barry. *Film Style and Technology.* Starword, 1983.
Sarris, Andrew. *The American Cinema: Directors and Directions 1929–1968.* E. P. Dutton, 1968.
Schatz, Thomas. *Boom and Bust: American Cinema in the 1940s.* University of California Press, 1997.
———. *Hollywood Genres: Formulas, Filmmaking, and the Studio System.* Temple University Press, 1981.
———. "The New Hollywood." *Film Theory Goes to the Movies,* edited by Jim Collins, Hilary Radner, and Ava Preacher Collins, Routledge, 1993, pp. 8–25.
Schlesinger, Jr., Arthur. "*Cactus Flower.* 'Prodigy of Miscasting.'" *Vogue,* 1 November 1969.
Seydor, Paul. *Peckinpah: The Western Films, A Reconsideration.* University of Illinois Press, 1997.
Singer, Ben. *Melodrama and Modernity: Early Sensational Cinema and Its Context.* Columbia University Press, 2001.
Sklar, Robert. *Movie Made America: A Cultural History of American Movies.* Vintage Books, 1994.
Slotkin, Richard. *Gunfighter Nation: The Myth of the Frontier in Twentieth-Century America.* Atheneum, 1992.
Smith, Murray. "Theses on the Philosophy of Hollywood History." *Contemporary Hollywood Cinema,* edited by Steve Neale and Murray Smith, Routledge, 1998.
"Statistics on Women in the World War II Era Work Force." *CUNY Center for Media and Learning: American Social History Project.* http://herb.ashp.cuny.edu/files/original/statistics-on-women-in-the-world-war-ii-era-workforce_47398d4f04.pdf.
Studlar, Gaylyn. "Masochism and the Perverse Pleasures of Cinema." *Movies and Methods.* Vol. II, edited by Bill Nichols, University of California Press, 1985, pp. 602–21.
Toossi, Mitra. "A Century of Change: The US Labor Force, 1950–2050." *Monthly Labor Review,* vol. 125, 2002, pp. 15–28.
"*Tora! Tora! Tora!* For the Crew. May 29, 1968." *Tora! Tora! Tora!* clippings file. Academy of Motion Picture Arts and Sciences, Margaret Herrick Research Library.
Turnock, Julie. "The Screen on the Set: The Problem of Classical-Studio Rear Projection." *Cinema Journal,* vol. 51, no. 2 (Winter 2012), pp. 157–62.
Untitled item. *The Hollywood Reporter,* 19 October 1967.

Untitled, undated review of *Bandolero! Playboy*. *Bandolero!* clippings file, Academy of Motion Picture Arts and Sciences, Margaret Herrick Research Library.

White, Mimi. "1970: Movies and the Movement." *American Cinema of the 1970s: Themes and Variations*, edited by Lester D. Friedman, Rutgers University Press, 2007, pp. 24–47.

Whyte, William. *The Organization Man*. Doubleday, 1957.

Woller, Megan. "The Lusty Court of Camelot (1967): Exploring Sexuality in the Hollywood Adaptation." *Music and the Moving Image*, vol. 8, no. 1, 2015, pp. 3–18.

Wood, Robin. *Hollywood from Vietnam to Reagan*. Columbia University Press, 1986.

Zimmerman, Paul D. "Connubial Clichés." *Newsweek* 29 January 1968.

Index of Films

Anzio (Edward Dmytryk and Duilio Coletti, 1968), 56–60, 58f
Avanti! (Billy Wilder, 1972), 98–100, 99f

Baby Doll (Elia Kazan, 1956), 2
Bandolero! (Andrew V. McLaglen, 1968), 127, 142, 147
Big Jake (George Sherman, 1971), 132–36, 134f
Birth of a Nation (D. W. Griffith, 1915), 27
Bob & Carol & Ted & Alice (Paul Mazursky, 1969), 89—90
Bonnie and Clyde (Arthur Penn, 1967), xiii–xv, 3–7, 5f, 46, 166
Bridge at Remagen, The (John Guillermin, 1969), 52, 56–58, 65
Bridge on the River Kwai, The (David Lean, 1957), 57

Cabaret (Bob Fosse, 1972), 13
Cactus Flower (Gene Saks, 1969), 77, 78, 87–89
Camelot (Joshua Logan, 1967), xv, 18–20, 34, 44–45, 47
Catch-22 (Mike Nichols, 1970), 66
Chase, The (Arthur Penn, 1966), 28
Chisum (Andrew V. McLaglen, 1970), 151
Cowboys, The (Mark Rydell, 1972), 130–32, 136, 153, 154f, 156

Day of the Evil Gun, The (Jerry Thorpe, 1968), 160, 163
Death Wish (Michael Winner, 1974), 141–42
Devil's Brigade, The (Andrew V. McLaglen, 1968), 64–65
Dirty Dozen, The (Robert Aldrich, 1967), 52, 63–66, 71
Dirty Harry (Don Siegel, 1971), 133–34
Doctor Dolittle (Richard Fleischer, 1967), 14, 25, 35–36

Earrings of Madame De . . . , The (Max Ophüls, 1953), 158
Easy Rider (Dennis Hopper, 1969), xiii, 29
El Dorado (Howard Hawks, 1967), 1, 129–30, 130f, 140, 158–59, 161

Feminine Mistake, The. See *Secret Life of an American Wife*
Fiddler on the Roof (Norman Jewison, 1971), 15–18, 17f, 27–28, 34–35, 44, 46, 48–49
Finian's Rainbow (Francis Ford Coppola, 1968), 26–29, 28f, 41–42, 47–48
Firecreek (Vincent McEveety, 1968), 144–46, 145f, 162
Fistful of Dollars, A (Sergio Leone, 1964), 8, 125

Index of Films

5 Card Stud (Henry Hathaway, 1968), 146, 153, 156, 161
For a Few Dollars More (Sergio Leone, 1965), 8, 125
Funny Girl (William Wyler, 1968), 22–24, 24f, 34, 43

Godfather, The (Francis Ford Coppola, 1972), 1, 165–66, 167f
Gone with the Wind (Victor Fleming, 1939), 27
Good, the Bad, and The Ugly, The (Sergio Leone, 1966), 8, 125
Goodbye, Mr. Chips (Herbert Ross, 1969), 21–22, 38
Graduate, The (Mike Nichols, 1967), xiii–xv, 7, 12, 74–75, 93, 95, 106
Great Train Robbery, The (Edwin S. Porter, 1903), 132–33
Great Waltz, The (Andrew L. Stone, 1972), 43
Green Berets, The (John Wayne and Ray Kellogg, 1968), 52, 71–72, 146, 148
Guide for the Married Man, A (Gene Kelly, 1967), 78, 80–82, 90

Hello, Dolly! (Gene Kelly, 1969), xvii, 12, 15, 43
How Sweet It Is! (Jerry Paris, 1968), 108–12
How to Commit Marriage (Norman Panama, 1969), 77–79, 104–8, 105f, 110
How to Save a Marriage (And Ruin Your Life) (Fielder Cook, 1968), xv, 76, 79, 82–84
How to Succeed in Business Without Really Trying (David Swift, 1967), 35
Hurt Locker, The (Kathryn Bigelow, 2008), 170

I Love My Wife (Mel Stuart, 1970), 90–93
Ice Station Zebra (John Sturges, 1968), 52, 69–71, 70f

Impossible Years, The (Michael Gordon, 1968), 101–4, 108–10, 116

Kiss Me, Stupid (Billy Wilder, 1964), 19, 74, 83, 98

La La Land (Damien Chazelle, 2016), 169
Last Challenge, The (Richard Thorpe, 1967), 127, 135, 137, 138, 140, 142, 151, 155–56
Last of the Red Hot Lovers, The (Gene Saks, 1972), 96–98
Little Big Man (Arthur Penn, 1971), xiv, 151
Lolita (Stanley Kubrick, 1962), 2
Longest Day, The (Ken Annakin, Andrew Marton, and Bernhard Wicki, 1962), 51, 54
Lost Horizon (Charles Jarrott, 1973), 30–32, 165–66
Love God?, The (Nat Hiken, 1969), 79f, 112–17, 114f, 123
Loved One, The (Tony Richardson, 1965), 6–7

Man of La Mancha (Arthur Hiller, 1972), 38
Manchurian Candidate, The (John Frankenheimer, 1962), 113, 114
Marriage of a Young Stockbroker, The (Lawrence Turman, 1971), 93–95, 121
M*A*S*H (Robert Altman, 1970), xiv, 8, 52–53, 55, 66
Mickey One (Arthur Penn, 1965), 6–7
Midnight Cowboy (John Schlesinger, 1969), 125

On a Clear Day, You Can See Forever (Vincente Minnelli, 1970), 37, 41, 45–46
Once Upon a Time in the West (Sergio Leone, 1968), 126, 142, 158
Owl and the Pussycat, The (Herb Ross, 1970), 97, 117–23, 119f

Index of Films

Paint Your Wagon (Joshua Logan, 1969), 20–21, 25, 32–33, 33f, 38–39, 42f, 47
Patton (Franklin J. Schaffner, 1970), 51–56, 55f
Pawnbroker, The (Sidney Lumet, 1965), 6–7
Pearl Harbor (Michael Bay, 2001), 169
Pillow Talk (Michael Gordon, 1959), xviii, 76
President's Analyst, The (Theodore J. Flicker, 1967), 8

Raid on Rommel (Henry Hathaway, 1971), 62–63
Rio Lobo (Howard Hawks, 1970), 159, 162

Saving Private Ryan (Steven Spielberg, 1998), 169
Scalphunters, The (Sydney Pollack, 1968), 151–53, 158, 160
Seconds (John Frankenheimer, 1966), 7, 7f
Secret Life of an American Wife, The (George Axelrod, 1968), 78, 86–87, 120
Seven Year Itch, The (Billy Wilder, 1955), xviii, 74, 86, 98
1776 (Peter H. Hunt, 1972), 29–30, 47
Shootist, The (Don Siegel, 1976), 170
Shootout (Henry Hathaway, 1971), 137–39, 156–59
Sound of Music, The (Robert Wise, 1965), 12, 165
Star! (Robert Wise, 1968), 22–24, 36–38
Straw Dogs (Sam Peckinpah, 1971), 145
Sweet Charity (Bob Fosse, 1969), 15–16, 35, 41, 43–44, 46–47

Thin Red Line, The (Terence Malick, 1998), 169
Thoroughly Modern Millie (George Roy Hill, 1967), 14–15
Tobruk (Arthur Hiller, 1967), 56, 58, 60–63
Too Late the Hero (Robert Aldrich, 1970), 67–68
Topaz (Alfred Hitchcock, 1969), 71
Tora! Tora! Tora! (Richard Fleischer, Toshio Masuda, and Kinji Fukasaku, 1970), 52–54, 56
True Grit (Henry Hathaway, 1969), xv, 126–27, 129, 137, 139–41, 141f
2001: A Space Odyssey (Stanley Kubrick, 1968), xiii–xv

Undefeated, The (Andrew V. McLaglen, 1969), 147–49, 160–62

Valdez Is Coming (Edwin Sherin, 1971), 140–42, 154, 162–63

War Wagon, The (Burt Kennedy, 1967), 136–37, 161, 162
Way West, The (Andrew V. McLaglen, 1967), 143, 149–50, 162
Where Eagles Dare (Brian G. Hutton, 1969), 65–66, 66f
Where Were You When the Lights Went Out? (Hy Averback, 1968), 84–86
Who's Afraid of Virginia Woolf? (Mike Nichols, 1966), 4, 7
Wild Bunch, The (Sam Peckinpah, 1969), 46, 126, 128, 135–36, 158
Will Success Spoil Rock Hunter? (Frank Tashlin, 1957), 76, 112

Young Billy Young (Burt Kennedy, 1969), 137, 142–43, 155, 159–62

Zero Dark Thirty (Kathryn Bigelow, 2012), 170

Index

Abramson, Leslie H., xiv
Adams, John, 29
Adler, Renata, 102–3
adultery/infidelity, 76, 80, 83–84, 87, 96–98. See also monogamy; naughty sex comedies
  in *Avanti!*, 98, 99f
  in *Bob & Carol & Ted & Alice*, 89
  Camelot and, 18–20, 34, 44–45
  endorsement of, 76, 82. See also therapeutic adultery
  A Guide for the Married Man and, 76, 78, 80–83
  in *I Love My Wife*, 91, 92
  as inevitable, 81, 82, 91
  in *The Last of the Red Hot Lovers*, 96, 97
  rationalizations for, 81, 91
  in *The Secret Life of an American Wife*, 86, 97, 98, 120
  therapeutic, 19, 81, 83, 86, 87, 98, 99f, 100
  in *Where Were You When the Lights Went Out?*, 84–87
African Americans, 25, 141, 153. See also slavery
  internal colonization and, 152
  stereotypes of, 27, 153
  vigilantism and lynchings of, 153, 154f
Aldrich, Robert, 63–68, 72
Altman, Rick, 76, 80, 160

Altman, Robert, 52, 160
American Indians. See Native Americans
anachronism, 78–79, 82, 165
Andrews, Julie, xvi, 14, 22, 36–37
animated credit sequences, 76–77
antiauthoritarian, 51, 64, 67–68
antiwar films, 56, 57, 63
antiwar protesters. See protests and demonstrations: antiwar
Arabs, 61. See also Israelis and Palestinians
Arthur, Maureen, 79f, 112
Arthur, Robert, 16
Astaire, Fred, 26, 27, 42
Axelrod, George, 86, 98

Barthes, Roland, 15, 81
Bay, Michael, 169
Beatty, Warren, 6, 21
Belton, John, xv
Benjamin, Richard, 93
Bergman, Ingmar, 59
Bigelow, Kathryn, 170
bigotry, 26, 152
Biskind, Peter, xiv, xix, 2, 10
black-and-white vs. color film, 9, 10, 44
blacks. See African Americans
body parts, 89, 119, 119f. See also specific body parts
  fetishism and fetishizing of, 39, 41, 47, 80, 103, 118–19

Bordwell, David, 33–36, 39–40, 133
Borgnine, Ernest, 70f
Bradley, Omar, 55
Brando, Marlon, 167f
breasts, 75, 80, 89, 103, 118, 119
   bare, 74–75, 89, 99
Browne, Roscoe Lee, 153, 154f
Buñuel, Luis, 86
Burns, Ken, 163
Burton, Richard, 62, 65
buttocks, 75, 80, 103, 119

Caan, James, 1
camera, hand-held, 160–61
camera angles, 161
Canby, Vincent, 38, 126–27
capitalism, 31, 99–101, 106, 116, 118
career vs. marriage, 14–15, 21–23
careerism, 91, 102. *See also under* dialectics; marriage/matrimony
Casper, Drew, xiii, xiv
causal gap, permanent, 34, 35
causality, 33–35, 158
celibacy, 24, 84, 115
Champlin, Charles, 10, 59
Chayefsky, Paddy, 20
"cinema of sensation," xviii, 126
cinematic techniques, 40. *See also specific techniques*
Civil Rights Movement, 49, 148, 150, 167
   in 1967, 9, 167
   law enforcement and, 25, 26, 28
   maverick films and, 25, 167
   race and, 25, 26, 150, 153
   and the South, 26, 29, 148
   utopia and, 27
   violence and, 9, 28
Civil War, American, 147, 148, 161, 162
Clark, Petula, 28f
classicism, 17, 35, 41
closure, 33, 34, 39–40
Cold War, 68–71, 146, 149, 150
colonialism, 25, 149
   European, 148

color(s), 78. *See also* black-and-white vs. color film
   psychedelic, 43
comedies. *See* naughty sex comedies
commitment and committed relationships, 92, 116. *See also* marriage/matrimony; monogamy
How to Commit Marriage, 77–79, 104–8, 105f, 110
communism and anticommunism, 28–32, 68, 70, 71
communities (and communes), 28–32, 144
   in *Fiddler on the Roof*, 16–19
Confederacy vs. Union, 29, 148, 162. *See also* Civil War
continuity, 140, 162
   intensified, 39–40
continuity editing, 6. *See also* continuity
Cook, David, 12–13, 126, 165–67
Coppola, Francis Ford, 26–27, 47–48, 165–66
Corman, Roger, 48
credit sequences, 43, 97, 163
   animated, 76–77
cross-cutting, 162

Daniels, William, 78
Darby, Kim, 141f
Davis, Ossie, 151
Day, Doris, xv, xviii, 15, 74, 82, 84, 102
Declaration of Independence, writing of, 29–30
Dern, Bruce, 154f
dialectical synthesis, 148
   of form and content, 163
   of values, 44, 74, 88, 100, 104, 110, 122
dialectics, 34–35, 37, 75, 88, 138, 139
   law/criminality, 126
   love/career, 23
   maverick/traditionalist, 52, 67, 75. *See also* maverick films: traditionalist films and

of opposing opinions, 29
past/present, 37, 42
traditional/progressive dimensions of films, 23–24, 42–43, 66–67, 100, 104, 139, 163, 171
of war narratives, 52, 59, 67, 72
wife/performer, 23
Diamond, I. A. L., 87, 98
Dickinson, Angie, 155–56
dissolve (filmmaking), 162
divorce, 83, 104
"Dollars" trilogy, 8
Douglas, Kirk, 130, 136, 143, 149, 162
Dunaway, Faye, 5f, 6
Dyer, Richard, 30, 39

Eastwood, Clint, 38, 42f, 65–66, 66f
Ebert, Roger, 20, 38–39, 87
editing, 8, 39
　associational, 13
　avant-garde, 58
　ecstatic, 95
　innovative, 126
　parallel, 162
　point-of-view, 41, 162
　time-fragmented, 8. *See also* time fragmentation
editing "rules," breaking, 47–48
editing techniques, 40, 45–48, 111. *See also* continuity editing; editing
employment. *See also* career vs. marriage; careerism
　women in labor force, 21
espionage, 71
Evans, Bob, 20, 167
existential questions and existential crises, 97–98

Fanon, Frantz, 25
Farber, Stephen, 12–13
fashion, 44
　fetishizing and, 118–19, 119f
fast cutting, 46, 47
female agency, 21
femininity, 15, 91–93, 121, 156, 157

feminism, 24, 25, 49, 83, 120, 137, 154, 167
　The Marriage of a Young Stockbroker, 93–94
　musicals and, xviii, 154
　psychiatry and, 94
　rise during 1960s, 154, 167
　Thoroughly Modern Millie and, 14–15
fetishes, 117, 119. *See also* perversion
fetishism and fetishizing, 39, 47, 78, 87, 118–19, 157
　body parts and, 39, 41, 47, 80, 103, 118–19
　fashion and, 118–19, 119f
fetishistic close-ups, 39, 47, 75. *See also* fetishism and fetishizing: body parts and; zooming: and fetishizing
film studios, 1, 9, 10, 12
　finances, vii, xiii, 2, 3
　independent ownership, 9
　technology and, 2
Fink, Harry, 133–34
Fink, Rita, 133–34
flashbacks, 23, 35–37, 39, 44, 80, 162
　in Westerns, 159–60
flat lighting, 79f
Fonda, Henry, 54, 67, 126, 130, 140, 144
Ford, Glenn, 127, 163
Ford, John, 140
foreign policy, xix, 61, 146–47. *See also specific topics*
Fosse, Bob, 12, 13, 16, 20, 41, 43–44, 46–47
Fraker, William, 8
Frankenheimer, John, 10
Franklin, Benjamin, 29
freeze frames, 42, 43, 47, 48, 90, 94, 103, 104, 117, 163
Friedan, Betty, 94

Garmes, Lee, 78
gay characters and homosexual tendencies, 13, 21, 76, 85, 119, 135

gender equality, 15, 27. *See also* feminism
gender roles, xviii, 21, 118–21, 154, 155. *See also* femininity; patriarchy
gender stereotypes, 91
Gitlin, Todd, xiv
Gleason, Jackie, viii, 104, 105f
Gordon, Michael, xviii, 74, 78
Grey, Joel, 13
Guthrie, Woody, 28

hallucinatory imagery, 42, 46
hand-held camera, 160–61
Harris, Jonathan, 40, 41
Harris, Mark, 74
Hathaway, Henry, ix, xv, xix, 62–63, 126, 137, 139, 141, 143
Hawks, Howard, 1, 129–31, 140, 158, 161, 162
Hecht, Harold, 149
Hefner, Hugh, 114–15
Hefti, Neal, 97
Henry, Buck, 117
Hepburn, Katharine, 170
Hispanics, 150, 152–54
history, allegorical use of, 49
Hollywood Renaissance, xiii, xiv, xxi, 140, 160, 166. *See also specific topics*
  formal devices employed in, 40, 41, 46, 128
  minorities and, 150, 153
  musicals and, xvii, 49
  scholarship on, xii–xiv
  sexuality and, 74
  traditionalist films and, xvii, xx, 46, 146
  viewed as revolutionary, xiv
  violence and, 135, 166, 169
  Westerns and, 135, 146, 163
homosexuality, 13, 21, 76, 85, 119, 135
Hope, Bob, viii, 104, 105f
Hopper, Dennis, 29
Howe, James Wong, 7

Hudson, Rock, viii, xv, xviii, 24, 60, 69, 70f, 82, 148, 170
Hughes, Howard, 69
Hunter, Ross, 16, 165
Hutton, Brian G., viii, 65, 66
hysteria, 62, 145, 145f

infidelity. *See* adultery/infidelity
Ingram, Bob, 75–76, 88
interracial comradeship, 152
interracial marriage, 25
interracial romance, 117–18
interreligious marriage, 17, 28
Israel, 60, 61
Israelis and Palestinians, 28, 61

Jackson, Anne, 83, 86
Jameson, Frederick, 27
Jefferson, Thomas, 29
Jewish martyrs, sacrifice of, 61
Jewish mother, 97
Jewison, Norman, 17, 45, 48
Jews, 61
  Fiddler on the Roof, 15–18, 17f, 27–28, 34–35, 44, 46, 48–49
  German, 60, 61
Jones, Jack, 59

Kael, Pauline, 38, 82, 165
Kawin, Bruce, xiv, 168
Kellogg, Ray, 71–72
Kelly, Gene, vii, xvii, 11, 45
Kennedy, Arthur, 58, 160
Kennedy, Burt, 126, 128, 136, 161, 170
Klein, Andy, 4
Knotts, Don, 112–15, 114f, 170
Kovács, László, 93
Kracauer, Siegfried, 44
Kubrick, Stanley, 43

Lancaster, Burt, 151, 154
Lang, Charles, 78
Laszlo, Andrew, 117
Latinos. *See* Hispanics

Lawrence, Gertrude, 36–37
Lemmon, Jack, viii, 98, 99f
Leone, Sergio, 8, 125–26, 142, 162, 163
libertinism, 113, 114, 116
  European, 108, 110
linearity, nonlinearity, and alinearity, 33, 35–37
Logan, Joshua, vii, xv, 33, 42
Lucas, George, 165
lynching, 144, 150, 153, 154f. *See also* vigilantism

MacLean, Alistair, 69
Mahoney, John, 82
Malick, Terence, 169
Man, Glenn, xiv
Marowitz, Charles, 3
marriage/matrimony, 14, 15, 18, 19, 21, 80, 92, 93, 106. *See also* monogamy; naughty sex comedies
  vs. career, 14–15, 21–23
  as inevitable, 77, 82, 86
  interreligious, 17, 28
  love and other motivations for, 18, 27
  matchmaker-arranged, 16–17, 19, 27
  in musicals, 14–25, 27, 43–45, 48
  musicals challenging, 15, 18–19, 25
  naughty sex comedies and, 80–90, 92, 94–96, 103–11, 116, 117, 123
    films defending matrimony, xx, 73–74, 76–77, 80–84, 86, 96, 101, 104, 117
    films questioning matrimony, 80–83
  nonromantic, 18
  problems with, 15, 18, 92, 106
  public opinion about, 18
  sexual revolution and, 73–74, 100
  societal impediments to, 15–16
  threats to, 73–74, 100–101, 117
    women in labor force, 21
  in Westerns, 143
  woman sacrificing career for, 21–22

marriage-minded female characters, films portraying, 14–15
Marshall, Garry, 109
Martin, Dean, xv, xviii, 76, 82–83, 126, 130, 140, 142, 146, 147, 170
Marvin, Lee, vii, 21, 24, 33f, 38, 63
Mast, Gerald, xiv, 168
Matthau, Walter, xvi, 15, 77–78, 80, 87–88
maverick films, xiv–xv, xviii, xx, 3, 7, 11, 26, 34, 52, 56, 160, 163, 166. *See also* naughty sex comedies: maverick; *specific films*
  allegorical use of history, 49
  Bonnie and Clyde and, 3–4, 6, 7, 70, 166
  Civil Rights Movement and, 25, 167
  Drew Casper and, xiii, xiv
  editing techniques used in, 46
  Godfather and, 166
  Hollywood Renaissance and, 3–4, 6, 46, 142, 146
  issues often ignored in, 49
  matrimony in, 15
  maximalist style in, 13
  musicals, 26, 31, 168
  naughty sex comedies and, 72, 73, 90
  traditionalist films and, xv–xvii, xx, 1, 3, 41, 163. *See also* dialectics: maverick/traditionalist
  visionary science fiction, 43
  Westerns and, 126. *See also* Westerns: maverick
maverick/traditionalist dialectic. *See* dialectics: maverick/traditionalist
maximalist style, 13
Mazursky, Paul, 89
McEveety, Vincent, ix, 130, 145
McLaglen, Andrew V., 64, 126, 129, 170
"melting pot" discourse, 98–99
method acting, 6
Mickey-Mousing, 77–78

Middle East. *See* Israelis and Palestinians
midlife crisis and adultery, 96, 97
Mills, Juliet, 99f
Minnelli, Vincente, 37, 41
Mitchum, Chris, 133, 134f
Mitchum, Robert, 58f, 129, 130f, 137
Monaco, Paul, 3, 10, 126
monochrome. *See* black-and-white vs. color film
monogamy, 122, 123. *See also* adultery/infidelity; marriage/matrimony
   films refraining from challenging, xvi
   musicals challenging ideologies of patriarchal, 33
   naughty sex comedies defending, xx, 73–74, 76–77, 82, 96, 117–18, 122, 123
   threats to, 100–101, 117
   sexual revolution, 73–74, 100
Morse, Robert, 35, 80, 84
Motion Picture Association of America (MPAA) film rating system, xvi, 20. *See also* motion picture content rating systems
motion picture content rating systems, xvi, 4–5, 14, 112–13
Motion Picture Production Code, 6–7, 66, 74, 81
   Bonnie and Clyde and, 3–5
   content forbidden by, 83, 155, 160
   demise, 3–4, 19
   A Guide for the Married Man and, 81
   nudity and, 4, 6–7, 14, 74, 115
   replacement by rating system, 4, 13, 14
   sex and, 19, 74, 81
Mulvey, Laura, 87
musical numbers, 37–40
   fast cutting destroying the rhythm of, 47
musicals, big-budget, 11–13
   feminism and, xviii, 154

   ideologies of form
      narrative structure, 33–40
      style, 40–49
   race and, 25–27
   romance in, 14–25
   super-musicals, xvii–xviii, 40, 53, 56, 57
   utopia in, 18, 19, 27–33, 44–45

nakedness, 5, 86, 89, 90, 99, 99f, 115, 155. *See also* breasts: bare; nudity
Native Americans, 143, 149–51, 160
   The Scalphunters, 151–53, 158, 160
naturalization, 81
"naughtiness," 81, 87, 108, 113, 116, 118
   concept of, 75
   nakedness and, 99, 99f
   television and, 170
naughty sex comedies, 73–76. *See also specific topics*
   aesthetics and, 75–80
   characteristics, 76–80
   family values and, 100–112
   love and marriage, 80–89
   maverick, 73–76, 78, 79, 82, 85, 90, 93, 116–17
   1960s and, xviii, 73–75, 80, 89, 95, 96, 98, 100, 112
Nazis, 13, 57, 60, 61, 63
Nichols, Bill, xv–xvi, 46–47
Nichols, Mike, 76
1960s, xiv, xv, 2. *See also* sexual revolution; *specific topics*
   1967 as "watershed" year, 3. *See also* Civil Rights Movement: in 1967; Summer of Love
   naughty sex comedies and, xviii, 73–75, 80, 89, 95, 96, 98, 100, 112
   periodizing 1967–1972, 2–10
Nixon, Richard M., 140, 167
North, Alex, 64
nuclear weapons and potential nuclear apocalypse, 70, 71

nudity, 8, 126. *See also* breasts: bare; nakedness
  Production Code and, 4, 6–7, 14, 74, 115

O'Brien, Edmond, 79f
O'Connor, Caroll, 64
Ophüls, Max, 158

Pacino, Al, 167f
Paramount, United States v., 2
Paris, Jerry, 108–9
Parrish, James Robert, 20, 39
patriarchal monogamy, ideology of, 33
patriarchs, 17, 104, 108, 115–16, 131, 138, 145
patriarchy, 15–17, 22, 92, 94, 121, 142, 155, 157
Patton, George S., 54–56
Peckinpah, Sam, 125–26, 128, 145, 160, 162, 163
Penn, Arthur, 5, 6, 151
perversion, 85, 97, 103–4, 117–19, 156, 157. *See also* fetishes
point-of-view editing, 41, 162
point-of-view shots, 36, 41, 48, 94–96, 160–62
Poitier, Sidney, 25–26
poker, 161
Polan, Dana, 126
Pollack, Sydney, 126
Pomerance, Murray, 5, 8, 75
Porter, Edwin S., 132–33
precredit sequence, 45, 94–95
Production Code. *See* Motion Picture Production Code
promiscuity, 13, 14, 90, 95, 96, 122. *See also* adultery/infidelity
prostitution, 6, 44, 186
  MPAA and, 20
  in naughty sex comedies, 86, 87, 118, 119, 122
  realistic portrayals of, 156
  veiled, 20
  in Westerns, 138, 139, 145, 156

protests and demonstrations, 101
  antiwar, 9, 27, 67, 99, 109
  civil rights, 9, 26–28
  in films, 28, 45, 99, 101, 109, 113
  against particular films, 166
  1960s, xiv, 9, 26
psychedelic aesthetic, xviii, 40, 41, 43, 45, 46
psychopaths, 63, 131, 146, 154f. *See also* sociopath

quick cuts. *See* fast cutting

race, 54. *See also specific racial groups*
  Civil Rights Movement and, 25, 26, 150, 153
racial integration, 28, 28f. *See also* interracial romance
racial stereotyping, 27, 151, 153
racism, 25–29, 54, 61, 71, 99, 127, 148, 152, 153. *See also* lynching; slavery
rape, 62, 142
  attempted, 143, 144, 147, 162
Richardson, Tony, 6–7
Roberts, Marguerite, 139
rock 'n' roll, 77, 107
romance. *See under* musicals; *specific topics*
  in musicals, 14–25
Ross, Herb, 38, 97, 119, 168

sadomasochism, 97, 157. *See also* perversion
Saks, Gene, 96, 166
Sarris, Andrew, 158
Schatz, Thomas, 8
Schlesinger, Arthur, Jr., 87
scopophilia, 94–95
Scott, George C., 55f
Seberg, Jean, 38–39
"seven-year itch," 86, 97
sex comedies. *See* naughty sex comedies
sexual liberation, 14, 80, 101, 114, 122
sexual revolution, xv, 14, 100
  marriage and, 73–74, 100

sexual revolution *(continued)*
  satires and spoofs of, 112
  as threat to monogamy, 73–74, 100
Shamroy, Leon, 78
Shapiro, Stanley, 76, 82–83
Sharif, Omar, 24
Simon, Neil, 96–97
Sklar, Robert, xiv
slavery, 29, 148, 151, 152
Slotkin, Richard, 126, 146–47
slow motion, 42, 44, 62, 126
sociopath, 106. *See also* psychopaths
sociopolitical changes, 8–9. *See also specific topics*
South, American. *See also* Civil War; Confederacy vs. Union
  Civil Rights Movement and, 26, 29, 148
special effects. *See* visual tricks
Spielberg, Steven, 165, 169
split screen, 45, 46, 48, 78
spy narratives, 71
stewardesses, 87, 88, 93, 100
Stewart, James, ix, xv, 10, 115, 126, 128, 130, 142, 144, 145f, 147
Stradling, Harry, 117
Streisand, Barbra, 6, 22–24, 37, 43–45, 119
  musicals, 117
  personality, 117
  photos, 24f, 119f
studio set, 78–79
Summer of Love, 8, 31
super-musicals, xvii–xviii, 40, 53, 56, 57
superimposition, 45–46, 114f, 159
Surtees, Robert, 46–47
swingers, 88, 93, 96, 115, 117
synchronization
  of character movements with music, 77
  of lips and singing, 39
synchronized lip movements, 39
synchronized singing and dancing, 37
synchrony, xx, 1, 14, 20, 38, 88, 91, 101, 123, 125, 127, 139, 166, 168–71

synchronic relations with period's progressive dimension, 16, 57, 63, 73, 150, 166

Tashlin, Frank, xviii, 74
Taurog, Norman, 10
telephoto lens, 13, 41–42, 42f, 57
television, 2, 9–10, 88, 170–71
television industry's purchase of films, 9
theme songs, 163
therapeutic adultery/infidelity, 19, 81, 83, 86, 87, 98, 99f, 100
therapeutic value in casual sex, 100
time fragmentation, 8, 37
time-lapse photography, 45
Topol, Chaim, 17f
tradition, 26, 163
  vs. change, 34–35
  in *Fiddler on the Roof*, 16–18, 17f, 27, 31, 34, 46
  replaced with modernity, 16
traditional values and progressivism, synthesis between, 104
traditionalist films. *See also specific topics*
  characteristics and nature of, xv–xvi
  Hollywood Renaissance and, xvii, xx, 46, 146
  maverick films and, xv–xvii, xx, 1, 3, 41, 163. *See also* dialectics: maverick/traditionalist
  as part of historical continuum, xx
  reasons for studying, xvi–xvii
  viewed as progressive, xx
traditionalist musicals, xvii–xviii. *See also* musicals
traditionalist narrative structure, xvi
Truscott, John, 32
Tucker, Larry, 89
Turman, Lawrence, 93

Union vs. Confederacy, 29, 148, 162. *See also* Civil War
United States, founding of, 29–30

utopia, 54–55, 55f, 150
  lost, 18, 19, 44–45
  in musicals, 18, 19, 27–33, 44–45

Valenti, Jack, 4
Viet Cong, 60, 63, 72
Vietnam War, 58, 68, 149
  ending of, 168–69
  movies functioning as metaphors for, 51, 126, 128
  opposition to U.S. involvement in, xviii, xix, 9, 27, 68, 99, 101, 109, 169
  U.S. troop behavior in, 57, 147, 148
Vietnam War era, 68, 71, 146
Vietnam War films, 169–70
  The Green Berets, 52, 71–72, 146, 148
  M*A*S*H, xiv, 8, 52, 53
  World War II films and, 71–72, 146
vigilantism, 138–39, 141, 142, 144, 153. *See also* lynching
violence, xiv, 8, 9, 115, 126, 157, 166, 169. *See also specific topics*
  Bandolero! and, 127
  Bonnie and Clyde and, xiv, 5
  civil rights and, 9, 28
  in war films, 66, 169. *See also* war films
  in Westerns, 8
virgins and virginity, 101, 102, 112–16
visual tricks, 78
voice-over, 35, 39, 65, 133, 158
voyeurism, 81, 93–95, 119f, 119–21

Walker, Alexander, 3
Walker, Robert Jr., 137
war films, 51–52. *See also* antiwar films; Vietnam War films; World War II films
  maverick, 52, 53, 64, 66–67, 70
Warner, Jack, 18
Waugh, Evelyn, 7
Wayne, John, 57–58
  dying onscreen, 130–31
  in *The Green Berets*, 71–72

  photos, 130f, 141f
  refused to work on pro-Indian *Cheyenne Autumn*, 151
  in Westerns, 129–33, 130f, 135–37, 140–41, 141f, 153, 157, 163
  final Western films, 170
Wayne, Patrick, 133
Webb, Charles, 93
Westerns, 125–28
  decline after 1972, 170–71
  foreign policy and, xix, 146–47
  law and order, 139–46
  matters of form, 158–63
  maverick, 34, 125–28, 134, 137, 142, 145, 146, 149, 151, 157, 158, 160, 163
  as metaphors for Vietnam War, 51, 126, 128
  struggles by the internally colonized, 128, 150–58
wide-angle lens, 7, 7f, 42
Wilde, Cornel, 58
Wilder, Billy, xviii, 74, 96, 98–100
Wise, Robert, 12, 36–37, 65
Woller, Megan, 19
women. *See also* femininity; feminism
  in labor force, as threat to matrimony, 21
  liberation of, 25. *See also* feminism
work vs. love. *See* career vs. marriage
World War II, 109. *See also* Nazis
  aftermath, 125
World War II era, 21, 90
World War II films, 51–53, 55, 63, 65–66, 69, 72, 90
  after 1972, 62, 169
  Anzio, 56–60, 58f
  The Bridge at Remagen, 52, 56–58, 65
  Cold War and, 68–69, 146
  compared with super-musicals, xviii
  The Devil's Brigade, 64–65
  The Dirty Dozen, 52, 56, 59, 63–66, 71, 72
  military cruelty in, 57

World War II films *(continued)*
  Patton, 51–56, 55f
  Raid on Rommel, 62–63
  subgenres, 51–52, 65–67
  Tobruk, 56, 58, 60–63
  Too Late the Hero), 67–68
  Tora! Tora! Tora!, 52–54, 56
  Vietnam War films and, 71–72, 146
  Westerns and, 72, 146
  Where Eagles Dare, 65–66, 66f
Wyler, William, vii, 2, 10, 24

Zimmerman, Paul D., 79, 82
Zionism, 61
zooming (and the zoom lens), 6, 40, 46, 80
  excessive use of, 41
  and fetishizing, 41, 75, 80, 119f. *See also* fetishistic close-ups
  functions of, 40–41, 160, 161
  instances of, 41, 47, 52, 57, 81, 119f, 126, 160, 163
  overview of, 40–41

THE SUNY SERIES

HORIZONS OF CINEMA

MURRAY POMERANCE | EDITOR

Also in the series

William Rothman, editor, *Cavell on Film*

J. David Slocum, editor, *Rebel Without a Cause*

Joe McElhaney, *The Death of Classical Cinema*

Kirsten Moana Thompson, *Apocalyptic Dread*

Frances Gateward, editor, *Seoul Searching*

Michael Atkinson, editor, *Exile Cinema*

Paul S. Moore, *Now Playing*

Robin L. Murray and Joseph K. Heumann, *Ecology and Popular Film*

William Rothman, editor, *Three Documentary Filmmakers*

Sean Griffin, editor, *Hetero*

Jean-Michel Frodon, editor, *Cinema and the Shoah*

Carolyn Jess-Cooke and Constantine Verevis, editors, *Second Takes*

Matthew Solomon, editor, *Fantastic Voyages of the Cinematic Imagination*

R. Barton Palmer and David Boyd, editors, *Hitchcock at the Source*

William Rothman, *Hitchcock: The Murderous Gaze, Second Edition*

Joanna Hearne, *Native Recognition*

Marc Raymond, *Hollywood's New Yorker*

Steven Rybin and Will Scheibel, editors, *Lonely Places, Dangerous Ground*

Claire Perkins and Constantine Verevis, editors, *B Is for Bad Cinema*

Dominic Lennard, *Bad Seeds and Holy Terrors*

Rosie Thomas, *Bombay before Bollywood*

Scott M. MacDonald, *Binghamton Babylon*

Sudhir Mahadevan, *A Very Old Machine*

David Greven, *Ghost Faces*

James S. Williams, *Encounters with Godard*

William H. Epstein and R. Barton Palmer, editors, *Invented Lives, Imagined Communities*

Lee Carruthers, *Doing Time*

Rebecca Meyers, William Rothman, and Charles Warren, editors, *Looking with Robert Gardner*

Belinda Smaill, *Regarding Life*

Douglas McFarland and Wesley King, editors, *John Huston as Adaptor*
R. Barton Palmer, Homer B. Pettey, and Steven M. Sanders, editors, *Hitchcock's Moral Gaze*
Nenad Jovanovic, *Brechtian Cinemas*
Will Scheibel, *American Stranger*
Amy Rust, *Passionate Detachments*
Steven Rybin, *Gestures of Love*
Seth Friedman, *Are You Watching Closely?*
Roger Rawlings, *Ripping England!*
Michael DeAngelis, *Rx Hollywood*
Ricardo E. Zulueta, *Queer Art Camp Superstar*
John Caruana and Mark Cauchi, editors, *Immanent Frames*
Nathan Holmes, *Welcome to Fear City*
Homer B. Pettey and R. Barton Palmer, editors, *Rule, Britannia!*
Milo Sweedler, *Rumble and Crash*
Matthew Lau, *Sounds Like Helicopters*

www.ingramcontent.com/pod-product-compliance
Lightning Source LLC
Chambersburg PA
CBHW030652230426
43665CB00011B/1052